An Extraordinary Journey

Journey

The Memoirs of a Physical Medium

by

Stewart Alexander

Published by
Saturday Night Press Publications
Beaconsfield, England.

snppbooks@gmail.com

ISBN 978-0-9557050-6-9

Printed by
Lightning Source
www.lightningsource.com

'People sometimes complain that the facts on which we base our conclusions are undignified and trifling! Who is to say what significance may not attach to trifles when properly studied and understood? A finger print is a trifle – a dirty smudge not worthy of notice – but it is no trifle to the criminal when submitted to expert scrutiny. . . . . .

'Basing my conclusions on experience I am convinced not only of survival but of demonstrated survival, demonstrated by occasional interaction with matter in such a way as to produce physical results. These effects may be accomplished through the loan of other organisms, submitted to the control of an alien intelligence; that is the commonest way.'

Sir Oliver Lodge, *The Reality of a Spiritual World'*

Dedicated to

My 'Little Sis'
who sat loyally at my side in the
home circle for over twenty years

Gaynor Singleton

1952 - 2009

Acknowledgements

I would like to offer my thanks to Dr Annette Childs and to Dr Alan Gauld for the invaluable help, advice and encouragement that they unfailingly gave to me as I wrote this book. Also I wish to state that the opinions, views and arguments expressed within these pages are solely my own. Whilst Dr Childs and Dr Gauld may not always have agreed with them, at least they 'understood' and for that I am grateful.

My appreciation must also go to Ann Harrison of Saturday Night Press for her support and expertise as she edited the book and as its publisher, drew its many elements together. For all of that I can only say thank you.

And finally my gratitude goes to Sue Farrow for her guidance at the start of the project; to Margaret Wood who did the laborious and essential job of proof reading and Hilde Aga Brun for her invaluable input in the design of the cover.

Contents

Author's Letter to his Readers

In writing this book I have been ever conscious of the fact that to write about oneself could so very easily be interpreted by the reader as an exercise in egocentricity.

Therefore, whenever possible, I have made use of the previously published accounts and reports of others concerning my mediumship although I have recognised that this may also lead to the presumption that I have merely indulged in self-aggrandisement.

However, that was unavoidable, since to tell my story in full, it was necessary to provide a faithful account of all that has befallen me throughout my long journey of discovery.

Contained within is the literal truth and I would ask the reader to accept that my sole motive and intention has been, from the start, to share with all who read this chronicle, the wondrous reality of human survival beyond the grave.

To have witnessed reunions, on a countless number of occasions, between the living and the dead, within the séance room, has not only been profoundly moving, but also the greatest possible privilege that one can experience.

I sincerely hope that what now follows will be accepted as a creditable and sincere record of my deep involvement in Spiritualism, and that it will offer comfort and reassurance that death is not the end but a passage into that other world into which, one day, we shall all pass.

Stewart Alexander

(2010)

Foreword

The literature on most aspects of mediumship is extensive and informative, but there is nevertheless a shortage of good first-hand accounts by physical mediums of their experiences in the séance room, and of the development of their gifts. The result is that we have insufficient knowledge of what it is actually like to be a physical medium. There are two obvious reasons for this shortage. Firstly, physical mediums are usually deeply entranced when phenomena are produced, and therefore often know less of what takes place than do those attending the séance. And secondly, there have been all too few good physical mediums. Thus I warmly welcome Stewart Alexander's book. Stewart is not only an outstanding physical medium, with a deep and extensive knowledge of his own gift, he also has a scholarly interest in physical mediumship in general, and is a mine of information on the subject.

I have been involved in psychical research for more than 30 years, and have been fortunate to have had sittings with Stewart both as a member of public circles and as a guest at his private home circle, and I can therefore speak of his mediumship from personal experience. Moreover, having known Stewart as a personal friend for many years, I can bear witness to his integrity and to the unswerving dedication that he has brought to his mediumship. A man of great modesty and humility, he regards his mediumistic gift as a trust to be used in the service of others, and as a channel for demonstrating the reality of survival of physical death, and thus for illuminating some of the deeper mysteries of the human spirit.

Readers of this book will be left in no doubt of the long and demanding journey that Stewart has undertaken in the development of his mediumship. Those who question why good physical mediums are so few and far between – particularly in this materialistic age – will find the answer here. Those who read the book with an open mind will readily understand the hard and self-demanding path that the good physical medium has to tread, and why, on the rare occasions when good physical mediums do appear, they need our support and encouragement. Equally important, they need to be protected when phenomena are being produced for, as history shows, physical mediumship of the kind associated with Stewart makes excessive demands upon the medium's health and vitality. Furthermore, any attempt by misguided individuals suddenly to grasp hold of the medium, turn on the lights, or interrupt the séance in other ways in a vain attempt to 'expose fraud' poses a grave additional risk to his or her well-being. As Stewart makes abundantly clear in the book, he has been very fortunate in having a close-knit and dedicated home circle, the members of which have stayed together over many years, devoting themselves to providing him with this essential support and protection, and long may this happy situation continue.

All mediumship is of potential value to those interested in exploring the possibility of life after physical death and the existence of paranormal abilities in general, but physical mediumship is unique among mediumship in that it provides us with objective visual evidence of the interaction between different dimensions. All attentive observers at a séance see the same thing, and can afterwards discuss their impressions and their conclusions as to its meaning. Nevertheless, despite these benefits, physical mediumship has always been a particular target for criticism by sceptics. Above all, sceptics demand to know why, if everything is above board, the phenomena produced at physical séances occur primarily in darkness. If the phenomena require darkness then, so the argument goes, this must be because the phenomena are fraudulent. We are told that all sorts of nefarious things can take place once the lights are extinguished. Accomplices can creep into the room to provide ghostly voices, wires can be attached to trumpets in order to 'levitate' them, and to sources of light such as LEDs in order to swing them above the heads of sitters to resemble spirit lights. The medium can slip unseen out of the cabinet or from wherever he is sitting and can touch sitters with supposed spirit hands, can don luminous masks and simulate materialisations and so on. The list of charges is endless, most of them increasingly fanciful, and owing more to over-vivid imagination than to actual experience in the séance room.

The fact is that darkness is usually required because light inhibits phenomena. This is not as surprising or as suspicious as critics would have us believe. Many natural phenomena, such as the germination of seeds, gestation in the womb, and the development of images on photographic plates, take place in the absence of light or in the presence only of a dim red light (a light which is in fact sometimes used in physical séances, including those of Stewart Alexander). It is true that some poltergeist phenomena, which are also physical, can take place in daylight (I can vouch for this from personal experience), but the physical phenomena of the séance room are very much more sophisticated than poltergeist disturbances, and demand in addition the presence of a medium who is particularly vulnerable to the presence of light while deeply entranced. Even the very few physical mediums in history who could sometimes work in natural (albeit subdued) light, such as D.D. Home, Eusapia Palladino, George Spriggs and Alec Harris, worked best in darkness. Even infra-red viewers, despite the fact that they actually add no light of their own to the room, appear to interfere with some phenomena. No, it seems that we simply have to accept darkness if we wish to observe physical phenomena. The extraordinary thing is not that it happens in darkness, but that it happens at all. Darkness is simply the condition under which it best occurs. Scientists have no difficulty in accepting that many scientific experiments only work in the presence of certain specified conditions, and there need be no mystery about the fact that this appears to be also true for physical phenomena. If we wish to study these phenomena, then we have to accept, whether we like it or not, that darkness is one of the conditions under which they occur.

Another claim frequently made by sceptics is that all phenomena seen in physical séances could easily be duplicated, in light or darkness, by any good professional conjuror. The answer to this claim is that any good professional conjuror is welcome to try, provided he or she does so under the same controls as those imposed for example on Stewart Alexander. These include no unsupervised access to the room before the séance in order to hide conjuring equipment; submission to bodily searches as a precaution against concealing such equipment on the person; and agreement to be securely bound by foolproof restraints in order to prevent movement during the séance. In addition, the room must be available for searches by experienced observers to ensure there are no hidden entrances or exits (including trap doors), that the furniture is restricted to a table and a circle of chairs placed close together so that movement anywhere in the room can be easily detected, and that each chair together with the table and any other potential hiding places in the room are available for thorough examination by the observers. Finally, the sitters must all be experienced in séance room phenomena (not naïve subjects who can be easily duped) and above suspicion, and there must be no money or promise of money involved, and the conjuror must agree to have the results of the session made public. I do not know that many professional conjurors are queuing up to produce convincing physical phenomena under such conditions. Even the great Houdini, in his investigations into mediumship, much preferred to duplicate what he considered to be séance room fraud under his own conditions. But even if we discount the ill-informed charges of fraud advanced by sceptics – most of whom are conspicuously lacking in direct experience of physical phenomena – can we ever be convinced that the possibility of fraud can be satisfactorily ruled out? The presence of conditions such as those detailed in the last paragraph, together with the known integrity of the medium, are an obvious starting point. We can then apply the so-called bundle of sticks principle. One stick can easily be broken, but put a large bundle of sticks together and they can defy human strength. Applying this principle, it becomes clear that even if the most sceptical observer could advance explanations, no matter how unlikely, of how each individual phenomenon occurring in the course of a séance could just possibly have been produced by subterfuge, when all are put together the explanation becomes untenable. Put another way, even if one occurrence could in theory have been performed fraudulently, the belief that a range of disparate phenomena – many of which follow each other in rapid succession, or occur simultaneously or in parts of the room difficult of immediate access – could be produced by sleight of hand becomes nonsensical.

Apart from the very few and unconvincing accusations made against him by ill-informed individuals which he details in the book, Stewart's long career has been free from attempts to cast doubt on the genuine nature of the phenomena associated with his mediumship. This in itself is a tribute to his work, as is the fact that Stewart decided in the fullness of time to allow his mediumship to be generally known. He could very easily have confined himself to sitting privately with his home circle, with the sole purpose of researching physical mediumship and channelling communications relevant to circle members. His decision to let others know of his mediumship was taken for the benefit of mediumship and not for himself. He has never sought either fame or money. As a businessman by profession he has in fact taken risks with his career by being associated with something as suspect in the eyes of many people as mediumship. His courage in this respect speaks volumes for his dedication to what he holds to be one of the greatest of all truths, man's survival of physical death. As for any reservations that readers may have about the genuine nature of physical mediumship, I can say that I have observed Stewart's work under conditions in his home circle that more than satisfy the bundle of sticks principle. The circle meets in a small room in the home of Ray, the circle leader. The room has only one door, no hidden trapdoors or entrances, and no hiding places. When the circle is seated there is no possibility of movement without detection, no possibility of accomplices entering the room, and no chance of Stewart freeing his hands or feet, which are strapped to his chair and have to be cut free at the end of the séance. Yet over the course of the séance the phenomena, as described by Stewart in the book, continue unabated.

Those who have researched physical phenomena in the years since members of the Society for Psychical Research commenced investigations under controlled conditions in 1882 have been interested above all in four things. Firstly, are the phenomena genuine? Secondly, if they are genuine, by what means unknown to science are they produced? Thirdly do they add to the evidence for survival of physical death? And fourthly, what makes a good physical medium? Stewart's book significantly advances our knowledge on each of these questions, and does so from the perspective of one who is, after all, in the best position to address them, namely the person without whom the phenomena would be unable to occur. The many eye-witness accounts of the phenomena apparent while Stewart is deeply entranced included in the book compensate for the fact that for much of his mediumship he has been unaware of what takes place, but an added bonus is that recently the phenomena have sometimes occurred while he has been fully conscious, thus enabling him to give us some of his own descriptions of events. I am delighted at this new development. Throughout his mediumship Stewart has been oblivious of the remarkable events taking place around him. Now at last he has the just reward of seeing at least some of these events, and recognising for himself the reason why others have marvelled at them so consistently over the years.

Those of us who know and admire Stewart and his mediumship, and all those who have been fortunate enough to have had sittings with him, will be delighted to see this book in print. It provides us with an exceptionally clear, well-written and convincing account of what it is to be a physical medium, and of what it means to act as a channel between one level of reality and another. It is thus a must for everyone with an interest in this extraordinary and baffling field of psychical research. Stewart has been urged for years by his very many friends to write it, and it richly deserves to be acclaimed and widely read. It is a lasting testament to the life and work of a rare and much loved man and medium. I wish it every success. It serves as a landmark in the literature on mediumship, and will be warmly welcomed by all those interested in what must surely be the most important question facing us all, namely the question directed by the Sadducee to Jesus Christ, 'If a man die, shall he live again?'

Professor David Fontana
Former President, Society for Psychical Research

An Appreciation

With this book, Stewart Alexander contributes much to what has been written about the topic of physical mediumship. Reading his book is like taking hold of a gentle hand at the start of an unknown journey, and we are guided both by what he says and what he does not say.

The topic of physical mediumship is a highly debated one and often people fall staunchly on one side of the proverbial fence or the other. As Stewart tackles difficult terrain on topics such as the provability of physical phenomena and the history of fraud among physical mediums, he does a skillful job of giving a refreshingly grounded voice to the argument – no small task when one takes into account that he is considered by many eminent researchers to be an untainted and genuine possessor of the rare gift of physical mediumship. Stewart allows the reader a new vantage point on how physical mediumship has become the powder keg of controversy that it has by thoroughly discussing the good, the bad and the ugly of its history. He does not shy away from any of it, nor does he attempt to beat sceptics down with harsh words. He is a true gentleman in every conceivable sense of the word and by using eloquence, sincerity and stark honesty, he does an excellent job of exposing both the powers and the vulnerabilities of this subject.

Stewart himself possesses a sensational gift for physical mediumship, yet there is nothing at all sensational about Stewart Alexander. His voice on this subject is one that arrives so softly, you must become quiet within yourself and reach up beyond the ruckus of both the staunch believers and the staunch sceptics in order to receive it. Readers

20

may be surprised to find that this book provides none of the bells and whistles that might work well to attract people to modern physical mediumship. What Stewart does provide is a humble, balanced and respectful voice that comes to us from a very high vantage point, the vantage point of a physical medium himself. As readers, we must take his information and lay it before us, like pieces of a puzzle.

In essence, Stewart does not try to manufacture truth for his readers. Instead, he lays before us all the raw material he has collected in his forty years of physical mediumship; he wisely leaves to us the task of putting it all together in a way that is meaningful.

Annette Childs Ph.D.

USA

(Clinician – Psychologist – Author)

Introduction

My decision to write this book was born out of a strong desire to chronicle and leave on record my extraordinary journey within the Movement of Spiritualism. Additionally, to present my observations and the deductions I have made along the way in respect of relevant historic and contemporary affairs.

In the first part of the book I outline how it was that I came to discover that I was the possessor of a rare, almost extinct form of mediumship, usually referred to as 'physical'. I also tell of its gradual unfoldment and much of what has befallen me since. In doing so, I firmly believe that on many levels I can offer the reader an unparalleled and unique insight into my world of physical interaction between the living and the so-called dead.

In the second part of the book I discuss such matters as Spiritualism as a Religion and also the Movement's sad decline these past fifty years. I have also formulated a reply to the sceptics and present my defence of physical mediumship which throughout history has suffered such a bad press. Other relevant matters are also addressed.

Within these pages I will introduce readers to some of the people I have met and known these past forty-two years, and from whom I have learned such a great deal. Although I may not always have agreed with their views and their arguments about spiritual matters, I have, in recognising the reasoning and sincerity behind them, respected and valued their opinions. Sadly such people have been counterbalanced by the many others who crossed my path whom I regarded as the *'unknowledgeable knowledgeables'*. Predictably, these were never short of a thousand words. In my judgement such people performed a disservice to Spiritualism, and perhaps unknowingly and innocently, they manipulated and distorted its very essence so that realism was replaced by what I felt was their own misleading and inconsequential reality. The rational and the irrational often existed side by side. So often I found myself disappointed when I encountered rank ignorance, both written and spoken (from the top to the bottom), concerning so many aspects of the Movement but particularly with regard to physical mediumship.

Down the years I have, on rare occasions witnessed wonderful demonstrations of mediumship at the Spiritualist churches and other venues, although most I found to be embarrassingly poor. I have known both the highs and the lows – the best of Spiritualism and the worst of Spiritualism. I have been exhilarated by events that I have experienced within the genuine séance room and I have been vexed, astonished, mystified and occasionally amused at séances which, beyond doubt, were highly questionable. All these things and a great deal more I shall reveal in this book but before I invite you – the reader – to embark with me upon my journey, I would first like to outline in brief my views on Spiritualism as it exists today, since they will inevitably have a direct bearing upon all that you will discover herein and which I explore more fully in Part Two.

The glorious revelation of survival beyond death, around which so-called modern Spiritualism was created, was born into our world over 150 years ago. Like a forest fire it quickly spread across America, throughout Europe and then into England. For over a century, it fearlessly and unwaveringly proclaimed its beliefs to a disbelieving world and remained unbending before the derision and onslaught of its many critics.

Millions of converts from every walk of life – from Royalty to statesmen, and from the scientist to the man in the street succumbed to its astounding new philosophy which promised to counter materialism and replace hope with certainty. Back then it must have seemed that it would only be a matter of time before survival and communication would be conclusively proved and widely accepted. For over a century Spiritualism looked up at the stars imbued with the pride which was woven throughout its very fabric. And yet by degrees all its early vigour, potential and promise has been frittered away in recent years and in its place jealousy, egotism, backbiting and infighting has emerged like a deadly cancer which has steadily consumed its fibre and its core. Today

– a shadow of its former self – it is afloat upon a spiritual sea polluted by falsehood, fantasy and commercial enterprise. In its determination to achieve respectability and shy away from controversy, it has – perhaps inadvertently – betrayed the hopes and aspirations of its brave pioneers and also those of the Spirit World. Like Nero it has fiddled while Rome burned.

A former editor of the creditable Spiritualist newspaper *Psychic News* wrote a few years ago that the Movement ' ... *is like a ship without a rudder with no sense of direction and has been cast afloat upon a sea of indifference becalmed and stupefied by apathy'.*

Those poignant and obviously heartfelt words could have been written today, for they are just as relevant – perhaps even more so?

Shakespeare wrote:

'There is a tide in the affairs of men

Which, taken at the flood, leads on to fortune;

Omitted, all the voyage of their life

Is bound in shallows and in miseries'.

I would suggest that once, until around half a century ago, there was a tide in the affairs of Spiritualism which had developed gradually over a period of a hundred years but which Spiritualists failed utterly to take at the flood. As a direct consequence, the Movement lost impetus and without protest watched as its very purity slowly gave way to absurdity and general mediumistic mediocrity – perhaps forever. Those beliefs have accompanied me upon my fascinating voyage of discovery and understandably will be evident throughout this book.

In what now follows you will find a faithful account of my spiritual journey, warts and all, and become familiar with my observations along the way. That which I relate may often leave readers incredulous, particularly if they have no previous knowledge of the so-called physical phenomena of the Spiritualist séance room. Such a reaction I totally understand because much that I shall reveal may be beyond your experience whereas I have been singularly fortunate over the past forty years to witness, or be a part of, the manifestation of physical phenomena within the séance room, of which most of the human race has no conception. However, I would insist that because such phenomena are little known or understood, it must not be assumed that they are the product of over active imaginations nor that they owe anything whatsoever to fantasy.

What I have written about took place exactly as I have recorded it and it has not been embellished in any way.

In the case of second-hand accounts, I am satisfied that the experiences included in this book were exactly as my contacts claimed, and I have duly retold them as they were first told to me.

And so I invite you, the reader, to join me now as I set foot once again upon that remarkable path which was to change my life forever.

Stewart Alexander

As this book was being prepared for the second print-run David Fontana and Tom Harrison took their transition to the Spirit World within 5 days of each other, on the 18th and 23rd October 2010, respectively.
Both men, who were good friends, will be sorely missed by many people.
We honour their memory here.

Stewart Alexander and SNPP

Part One

My Journey

Chapter One

The Journey Begins

I discover Spiritualism and begin my research ~ I am invited to join a circle ~ One year later it ends in farce ~ I form my own circle with family and neighbours ~ Two years on I am entranced by a 'spiritual guide'.

Forty-two years ago, when I first read Arthur Findlay's classic book, 'On the Edge of the Etheric', I did not suspect that my life was about to be changed forever. As I turned its first page I did so knowing nothing of Spiritualism, nothing of mediumship and having given little thought as to the possibility of a life after death. Perhaps, in common with most people who are in abject ignorance about such matters, I had always imagined that Spiritualism attracted elderly ladies who sat around tables asking, 'Is there anybody there?'

However, like many before me, that book was to introduce me to the Movement and presented most intelligible and compelling evidence in support of the author's astounding arguments in respect of survival beyond the grave and of two-world communication.

In short it had a profound effect upon the way that I had previously viewed such matters by making the implausible plausible. First published in 1932, it was to go into over sixty impressions, be translated into nineteen languages and produced in Braille; in 1971 Corgi Books released it as a paperback. With the subtitle 'Survival after Death Scientifically Explained' – and indeed, that is precisely what its author sought to do – Arthur Findlay (a one-time Scottish stockbroker) introduces his readers to the exceptional Glasgow physical medium, John Campbell Sloan, in whose séance room the voices of the dead were heard to speak quite independently of and at a distance from him.

Unlike most mediums who produce subjective survival evidence (mental mediums) the manifesting phenomena to which Findlay forcefully testified had been tangible and objective. Whilst this is not the place to detail the extraordinary evidence presented by the author in support of his claims, suffice it to say that this most informative book excited my interest and dynamically appealed to my reason. Indeed it launched me upon a serious investigation and a personal journey both within and outside the séance room, which has now extended for over forty years and which has finally culminated in my determination to write this book. At the time, however, little did I realise just how frustrating, exciting, vexing, exhilarating, disheartening and rewarding that long twisting path of discovery would prove to be. Along the way I encountered wonderful characters who enriched my life and at whose feet I learnt such a great deal. Others (and there were many), in posing as experts in all things spiritual, so often disappointed, angered and saddened me that I judged them to be either fools or woefully naïve. In those early days I had no idea of the people and the events that would enter my life and profoundly influence its future direction in a variety of ways.

When I had finished the book, indeed when I had read it for a second time, my brother and I discussed it at some length, for it was he who had discovered it in the first place, in a second-hand shop in the city of York. Because we both had an insatiable appetite to learn more, much more, we began to read everything that we could about Spiritualism and physical mediumship. Soon we were to reason that if what we were reading was only partly true then this was surely something which the whole world should know about. The more we read – the more we wished to know. The more we knew – the more we realised we simply did not know.

Eventually we began to visit our local Spiritualist churches, and quickly discovered that they were largely a great disappointment. The generally disenchanting proceedings could best be summed up as semi-religious services with a demonstration of mental mediumship tagged on and a cup of tea to follow.

One is bound to wonder how many potential Spiritualists have been lost to the Movement over the years after entering such establishments in a spirit of genuine enquiry, only to witness the kind of service that we regularly experienced. Of course, there were occasions when my brother and I heard philosophical addresses and witnessed demonstrations which were truly impressive, inspirational and invigorating, but these were rare events.

Then, about six months after we had first started to visit the churches regularly, a lady approached us one evening following a service, and introduced herself as the wife of one of our city's most noted private trance mediums. Telling us that she had seen us regularly at that particular church, she asked if we would be interested in joining their home circle which was held every Monday evening. At that time neither of us had ever witnessed trance mediumship outside the churches, and this, of course, seemed too good an opportunity to miss. We immediately accepted the invitation and the following Monday evening we arrived, filled with anticipation, at the semi-detached Victorian home of our hosts. Once admitted we were shown into a large lounge where we joined about twenty other people – the regular members – all sitting in a circle configuration. We were made to feel most welcome.

Evenings of Bewilderment and Embarrassment

We were soon to discover that their home circle night always followed the same format.

We all arrived about thirty minutes prior to the sittings and engaged in general conversation. The medium entered, took his seat, and the single red bulb which hung in the centre of the room would be dimmed. He would then exchange a few pleasantries before opening the circle with what could only be described as a form of incantation.

Shortly afterwards his head would fall upon his chest and a few grunts and groans later we would be joined by 'the scientist' or 'the priest' or some other exalted visitor from the Spirit World. Then, for the next sixty minutes, or thereabouts, we would sit listening to an 'address' delivered through the apparently unconscious medium which, to my brother and me, (and perhaps to everyone else) was totally incomprehensible and seemed to have nothing whatsoever to do with Spiritualism. When finally the medium returned to consciousness, his wife would ask every sitter, in clockwise rotation, if, apart from the address which had come through her husband, anyone had seen, heard, sensed or experienced anything of a spiritual nature. We were soon to discover that surprisingly, every single person had done so with the exception of ourselves – we saw nothing, we felt nothing, heard nothing and sensed nothing at all. In short, after attending for some weeks, we started to feel bewildered by the fact that the various discourses by the alleged visiting Spirit people were lost on us and we also suffered a sense of embarrassment by our evident lack of any psychic ability. However, we were certainly willing to 'stick with it'; if for no other reason than that we assumed that our inability to understand the communications was possibly due to our own ignorance. And so, the weeks turned into months and we never missed a circle. Then, one most memorable night, things took a turn for the worse. The medium walked into the room, but instead of taking his seat and joining in with the usual friendly chit-chat, he walked directly into the centre of the room, lifted a gleaming dagger into the air and called upon archangels, Michael, Gabriel, Raphael and Uriel to come to the circle's aid in the unification of the two worlds.

It was time to leave.

We never returned.

As a footnote, we did hear some time later that Humphrey Bogart had started to put in an appearance at the circle, as well as several other deceased personages from the acting profession.

Sadly, it was all to end in tears. One night the medium and his wife had attended his company's Christmas function and he had, apparently, had rather too much to drink.

In a moment of intoxicated madness, and no doubt much to his wife's astonishment, he suddenly began to entertain everyone at the bar with his impressions of the Hollywood greats, including the late, great Humphrey Bogart.

Whether the circle collapsed as a result I have no idea but I did hear that a few months later he had visited and demonstrated his mediumship at the headquarters of one of Spiritualism's most respected, noted and credible organisations!

Our first Home Circle

Almost two years had passed since I had first read Findlay's 'On the Edge of the Etheric' and I was still reading – and still visiting the local churches: the word 'tenacious' springs to mind! Then, one day, I decided that I would form a home circle, and because my introduction to Spiritualism and my intense interest had always been in respect of physical mediumship, it would of course have to be a physical circle.

Since I was by then well aware of the necessary obligatory conditions required for just such a circle, I would arrive home from work every Monday evening and then spend two hours achieving a total blackout in our front lounge with its large bay window. Anyone who has ever attempted to eliminate all light from a room will readily understand what a difficult task I was faced with. Two hours to achieve it and thirty minutes afterwards to put everything back as it was.

Darkness, we fully understood, was an absolute essential, since we hoped to develop contact with the Spiritual Realms on a physical level. Such manifestations are believed to be inhibited by the presence of any form or degree of light. Understandably, this often leads to suspicion within the sceptical mind. However, irrespective of how it may appear to some, the fact is that there are sound reasons for such conditions. In assuming that all such séance rooms harbour fraud, one would be guilty of making a monumental error. One might as well argue that the darkroom was unnecessary for early photographic development. No one today would question the absolute fact that light is fatal to particular micro-organisms, and to the germination of seeds. Nor would anyone question the fact that the development of an embryo in the darkness of the womb is essential for the creation of life itself.

Is it therefore logical to dismiss and reject utterly the dark conditions of the séance room, based upon little more than ignorance of the delicate mechanics involved or merely upon unreasoned suspicion? We knew, from all that we had read, that for any physical manifestation to occur then mediums must possess within them an abundance of the elusive living energy known as 'ectoplasm'[1] and although it exists to a greater or lesser degree in all life forms such mediums are believed to possess a surfeit. In character it is neither physical nor spiritual. It is unique to neither world but it is common to both.

The Spirit people are believed to extract it through the nose, mouth ears or the solar plexus of the medium. At that stage it is said to have the consistency of smoke or liquid but in an instant, can be converted to something with a molecular structure as substantial as steel. In ways that we largely do not understand, it is the basis upon which all physical manifestations are created and upon which they rest and depend.

That was the theory and back then the circle was willing to accept it on a *prima facie* basis. It was all so exciting, and from the beginning we had a true family circle, with the addition of our next-door neighbours who were themselves extremely interested.

Since this was to be a physical circle then we also understood that we must introduce a séance room trumpet. Such a device should not to be confused with the musical instrument. It is a tapered cone (funnel) that rather resembles a simple megaphone. Constructed from aluminium it weighs about 100 gm. It is usually about 0.5m long, and 100 mm in diameter at the large end tapering to an approximate diameter of 20 mm

---

(1) *Ectoplasm (from the Greek ekteneie and plasma: exteriorised substance).*

at the small end. The theory as we understood it was that by means of the energy ectoplasm, the trumpet would levitate without any physical contact from any of the sitters. As in the case of John Sloan, the medium whom Arthur Findlay immortalised in his book 'On the Edge of the Etheric', a trumpet would – like goldfish in a bowl – float around the room without making contact with anyone or anything. Then, it may stop in front of a sitter's face and out of it would issue the voice of a deceased loved one or another spirit person. As improbable and as unbelievable as this may appear, the evidence in support of the reality of this extraordinary yet rare phenomenon is voluminous and extends back 150 years. So – at each meeting of our new circle we duly placed our home-made trumpet in the centre of the circle standing upright on the carpet. I am sure that everyone present observed it as keenly as I myself did. Of course nothing ever happened – nothing whatsoever.

We would sit for about sixty minutes and as the hour drew to a close our thoughts would invariably turn to the tea and cakes that would shortly follow. Gradually, those nights became almost social events and we all looked forward tremendously to being together, sitting in the dark, listening to music and sharing each other's company.

I have often thought since, that there are innumerable circles today (many of whom have in recent years complained to me about their lack, or absence, of progress) who, in their anxiety to achieve results are quite unable to see that in reality they are so very fortunate.

Where else, in our hectic troubled world, can people meet together as friends with the same hopes and aspirations and in total harmony, close the door to the outside world and be together as one, in fellowship, and *simply enjoy the moment*?

To be a part of that is marvellous, and even should a breakthrough constantly elude them, they still gain individually and collectively. Surely, that aspect of circle work is sadly so often overlooked today simply because many circles fail to appreciate what they already have. If results are finally achieved and a breakthrough is made, then that will be the cherry on top of the proverbial cake, although, back then, I doubt that these things would have occurred to us either. However, we always sat with optimism in spite of our constant lack of any apparent progress, and from time to time we would invite a local medium to sit with us. These would be marvellously eventful evenings, as the mediums would describe their impressions, etc and certainly they were always most encouraging. The months passed and still we met and still we sat and still we achieved no discernible results. It seemed then that mediumistic potential amongst us all was absolutely absent. Then one night it all changed.

The Breakthrough

'Sue (his wife at that time) and I are thinking of having a sitting – do you fancy coming?' asked my brother on the phone to me one evening.

Being particularly tired that night I declined his invitation but as soon as I put down the receiver I began to have misgivings that if I did not sit, he would ring me the next morning with the exciting news that at last the Spirit World had been able to communicate – that the long awaited breakthrough had been made.

No doubt they would have a full form materialisation[2] and, after all the many months of patience, I was about to miss the great occasion.

I picked up the phone – rang him back and told him that I would be there.

For fifty-eight minutes we sat around a table in dim red light – hands lightly resting upon its top, and as always, no results whatsoever. Not a creak, not a movement (slight or otherwise), not a feeling or sense of being joined by a presence, no sudden or even a gradual drop in temperature – in fact, nothing but music quietly playing in the background.

My thoughts had just started to turn to the fact that shortly we would be enjoying a cup of tea when quite suddenly, and without any warning whatsoever, I heard a voice in my left ear, saying: 'Turn out the light – continue to sit'. This, to say the very least, startled me, but I said nothing, in spite of the fact that without variation those precise words were repeated again and again just as if they were on a loop on a magnetic audio tape.

Strange as this may sound, it never occurred to me at the time that I was actually experiencing clairaudience[3]. I could hear the voice clearly and incessantly, but that was all, and I never even attempted to analyse what was taking place, nor to speak about it.

Then, my brother said, 'Shall we close the circle and put the kettle on?' I immediately replied, 'No – switch the light out and let's continue to sit for a while.'

---

(2) *Materialisation: The tangible manifestation of a spirit person in temporary solid physical form.*

(3) *Clairaudience: The ability to hear, mentally, the voices of the dead.*

Without questioning this he reached up, switched off the light and instantly I was aware that 'something', a presence – outside of myself, was rapidly approaching me. But here I have a considerable difficulty, for how does one attempt to describe that which is indescribable?

I can only say that as it forced itself to merge with my very being, every nerve and every muscle in my entire body began to react violently, and it set in motion uncontrollable spasms and tremors. At the same time my consciousness seemed quickly to locate itself outside, behind and to the left of my body and from that position I observed my mouth fall open and with a rush the following words issued forth: 'I come speak, brother, sister', – every word of which I heard very clearly. To say this was unnerving, for us all, would be to understate everyone's feelings at the time, although as the final word was spoken, so everything quickly returned to normal. The uninvited reptilian feeling I had experienced quickly left me and shortly afterwards we were enjoying tea and cakes. So unexpected had that event been, we ate and drank in relative silence. However, the following morning as I arrived in my office, my telephone was ringing and when I answered it I heard my brother eagerly enquiring: 'Do you fancy coming to our house for another sitting tonight?' To which my reply was, 'Not bloody likely.'

The whole painful experience had frightened me, although it would prove to be the first and the last occasion that I would ever feel fear within the séance room.

Those words, 'I come speak, brother, sister', spoken by my principal spiritual guide were to be the first of many, and today, all these many years later, he is still manifesting through me. Was he a secondary personality – a figment of an over-active imagination that manifested to meet expectation?

Of course, at that time, I was to suffer constant nagging doubts.

Had he been and was he merely a product of my own self that unconsciously, and in some mysterious manner, I had conjured up after all those years of hoping for a breakthrough?

That precise dilemma, I fervently believe, is one which confronts most developing trance mediums. To be of good conscience, no one wants to be guilty of fooling themselves and, even worse, fooling other people.

I was filled with self doubt but we, nevertheless, continued to sit every Monday evening in our home circle, although things had now, understandably, taken on much more interest.

If my guide – who subsequently identified himself as White Feather – manifested through me, then it would always be within a few minutes of the commencement of our sittings, otherwise they would be blank.

But when in those very early days he did come, I would quickly become aware of his presence because of the uncomfortable physical effects I would begin to experience.

It was always as if my conscious self became submerged and dissociated from my body and I would feel totally subdued, as though I were on the verge of sleep.

When he spoke I would hear his words, seemingly from a distance, but I was quite unable to interfere with their flow and I could exert no influence in any way upon what was taking place. His words were clear but his vocabulary and grasp of the English language was, at that time, extremely limited. As he approached me (I can think of no other description) my left hand would immediately begin to curl in upon itself as if grossly deformed, and then the remainder of the entrancement process would quickly and forcefully follow. That precise physical effect was, in the future, to provide irrefutable evidence that in reality he was exactly who he claimed to be – an independent intelligence.

I doubt that back then he ever uttered anything which could be considered profound, because he was evidently working towards perfecting the process of control and yet I still tortured myself with innumerable doubts, so that my feelings concerning the whole matter would fluctuate wildly. One day I would accept and believe that he was who he claimed to be. The next I would be dubious – surely he had to be an aspect of myself, surely that had to be the true explanation. So – one evening just before my wife left home to attend her weekly night school – I asked her if she would write something on a piece of paper and then seal it in an envelope without telling me what she had written.

I reasoned to myself that if this supposed guide from the next world could reveal to me her words, then I would never doubt him again.

And so she left for her night school and I posed the question in my mind, 'Look – if you are who you claim to be – tell me what is on the paper and if you can do that then I shall never doubt you again.' After a while I clearly saw in my mind's eye a river bank with a dog barking whilst busily running up and down and the whole scene was bathed in sunlight. Of course, it had to be my imagination – or so I thought. When my wife returned home, I asked what she had written and she suggested I should look. Opening the envelope, these were the words that I read: Sun shining – dog running up and down river bank barking. Well – that was it then. He was who he claimed to be. A great weight lifted off my shoulders. I was a medium in the early stages of development. How surprising, yet how exciting that was.

My journey had truly begun.

Sadly, those euphoric feelings of absolute certainty only lasted for about five days, after which my mind rationalised that the result had to be telepathy between my wife and myself and so I was back to square one. However, in spite of such doubts we continued to sit, and did so for a further two years, either in my home or that of my brother during which time my supposed mediumship (or whatever it was) continued to develop and reveal itself.

Then, we got the opportunity on several occasions to sit with the direct voice[4] medium, Leslie Flint, and everything changed.

---

(4) *In the presence of a direct voice medium the voices of the dead are heard by everyone to speak in their own voices, quite independent of, and at a distance from the medium. This is a form of advanced physical mediumship. Trumpets are not used.*

Chapter Two

The Wonderful & the Bizarre

The circle sits with celebrated 'direct voice' medium Leslie Flint in London ~
I receive evidence my 'spiritual guide' is not a figment of my imagination ~
Some bizarre séance room events experienced in my early development.

On 10th November 1973 at 2.30pm, we were sitting in Leslie Flint's blacked-out lounge, which doubled as his séance room, in Westbourne Terrace, London. It was an occasion that I doubt any one of us would ever forget.

Flint knew nothing about us, other than the fact that we had travelled down from Yorkshire, that we were all seriously interested in Spiritualism and that we had our own home circle.

My brother and I, together with our wives, were part of the small group of people who had travelled from diverse parts of the country to be there. I recall very clearly my feelings as the lights were turned off and we sat together chatting amiably amongst ourselves.

Having read six years earlier of Arthur Findlay's experiences with the Scottish trumpet medium John Campbell Sloan, it occurred to me that here, in this room, we were about to experience what he had written about forty years before and which had so profoundly excited our interest. Here at last we were about to hear the voices of the living dead – readers may imagine our feelings as we eagerly anticipated what, we hoped, was about to take place.

I believe that we waited for over thirty minutes until quite suddenly our conversation was interrupted by Flint's cockney guide, Mickey, who spoke from a point in space on a level with the medium's left shoulder, but approximately twelve inches away from it.

Mickey, it has to be said, was a jaunty, funny, wonderful character.

Instinctively, and no doubt in consequence of many years' practice, he knew what to say and when to say it, in order to lighten the inevitable nervous tension that understandably resulted when people were sitting for the first time. Laughing and joking, he proclaimed that there was a proper crowd of us but even more of them 'over there' all hoping to 'get through' – and so it proved. Whilst I shall refrain from detailing here all that occurred, I must record the fact that for over two hours we heard and held sustained conversations with loved ones who had passed through the gates of death and returned to speak to us in their own individual voices. These included a relation of my wife.

What I can also say is that, later, as we walked back to our car, I felt as if I was literally walking several inches above the pavement. How marvellous it would have been to share such an extraordinary and unique experience with the strangers who passed by. If only they had known what I had witnessed over the past two hours – if only I could have told them how privileged and truly fortunate I felt.

Several months later we returned to sit again with Flint, but this time we took with us the remainder of our circle.

Throughout my personal spiritual journey I have, from time to time, encountered what I consider to be milestones – occasions and events which for various reasons have proven to be most significant in respect of my own mediumistic development.

Such was the case on that particular day, in that particular room, with a medium who justifiably now belongs within Spiritualism's 'Hall of Fame'. We had been sitting for over an hour when suddenly I heard the voice of my grandmother. She had been a mother figure to me and had taken a central role in raising me following the collapse of my parents' marriage. On the day she passed over, just two weeks before our sitting – a fact entirely unknown to Flint – I had sat at her hospital bedside – just the two of us. She had been unconscious but I sat holding her hand and something had passed between us, which was known to only two people – myself being one and she the other. Suddenly, there with Flint, of her own volition, she mentioned this to me and thereby proved beyond any conceivable doubt that she had survived death and that the voice I was listening to belonged to her and her alone.

As her words faded away, I was left with a feeling of intense gratitude, not only to her for making the supreme effort to return to me, but also to everyone at both sides of death who made that wonderful communication possible. Then as I was reflecting on the conversation, suddenly, out of the darkness, another voice began to speak and it was one that I knew only too well. It was that of my principal guide, White

Feather – the same guide who for some years had endeavoured to develop me and who, at times, I regarded as a genuine independent personality, and yet, at others, as a figment of my imagination.

In all good conscience I cannot tell readers what he actually said because I was in a state of shock, although at some point whilst he was speaking, it suddenly occurred to me that here was my golden opportunity. A chance to establish, once and for all, if he was who he had long claimed to be – an autonomous individual. The problem was how to accomplish it.

Then, the solution popped into my head and interrupting him I enquired if, during his earthly life, he had had a physical deformity. Instantly he replied – 'Do you mean my left hand?' To understand and appreciate my feelings as he uttered those words would be impossible to convey. Readers may recall that I wrote in the previous chapter of how, during my early development, whenever he sought to entrance me, my left hand would curl in upon itself as if grossly deformed. Now – in that room – in the presence of Leslie Flint, who was a virtual stranger and knew nothing of my guide, or indeed of my personal mediumistic development, he had uttered six words, *'Do you mean my left hand?'* The effect on me was profound.

Some days after our return home I received through the post a recording of the séance, together with a letter written by Leslie Flint's companion Bram Rogers.

This is what it said '... herewith a copy of the tape... whilst making the copy I listened to some of it and it seems that you really have got a wonderful thing going with your circle. Keep at it, as it may be that you will be able to carry on with the direct voice when it is time for Leslie to ease off ...'

After such a wonderful experience and as a result of those words of encouragement my development commenced in earnest – I would never doubt again. From that moment I dedicated myself to the 'great work'.

Simply Bizarre

Eight years after the commencement of 'my journey', with a young family to support, and the time-consuming responsibilities known to every parent, I was to find that I had precious little free time, although I always ensured that every week I would sit in the circle. Continuity, I firmly believed, was of such vital importance. However, with young children about the house, we were eventually forced to recognise, with regret, that the environment was no longer conducive to the work of the circle.

With few exceptions other members of the circle were in the same situation, with young families and the ensuing parental demands. It literally became impossible for us to continue to meet.

And to further complicate matters, the business which I had launched, together with my wife, some years earlier, was by then demanding evening cover every night of the week. Fortunately, my wife graciously volunteered to look after the children and man the office (which we ran from our home) in my absence, should I find another circle in which to continue with my development.

At that time, I had been sitting and developing my mediumship for over seven years. Although I was always aware of all that took place during my entrancement and of the words spoken by my guide, I was unable to interfere with or influence the flow of his words as I was always in a condition which could best be described as dissociation. However, I was happy to leave my development in his hands, although I have to admit that I would have much preferred to enter the deep trance state and therefore be unaware of everything that transpired. This, I know, would be welcomed by most trance mediums.

Whilst many invariably claim that they are in a totally unconscious state during trance, (commonly referred to as deep trance) I am convinced that such a situation is extremely rare indeed. The common belief is, of course, that if the medium's conscious mind is rendered inoperative, then whatever is transmitted must have an independent source and therefore be beyond their direct responsibility and control; in short, that they are omitted entirely from the equation. Whilst during my early development I am sure that I subscribed to that understandable belief I now feel that the depth and nature of trance is of little consequence. The acid test must always lie with the content of the communication and if that should prove to be outside the medium's knowledge, then we have gone a long way towards establishing the independent source of the transmission.

After we had taken the decision to disband our home circle, in the uncanny way that these things are inclined to happen an opportunity to continue my development was to present itself. Following a Sunday evening service at one of our local churches, I was approached by an elderly couple whom I shall call Jim and Ethel Hood, who, knowing of my trance development and of my present predicament, very graciously invited me to join their home circle. I was, of course, more than delighted to do so. I had known this couple for some time, having seen them often at the church, and I knew them to be very sincere, very amiable and what I considered to be 'old-time Spiritualists'. What had always struck me about them was that Jim occasionally had considerable problems walking and was often helped by his wife, who acted as a crutch as they struggled together up the church stairs.

Apparently he suffered from gout which, as is well known, can be very painful and debilitating, but they refused to allow this to interfere with their circle or with their regular church attendance. I only mention this because of its relevance to the narrative which follows.

The following Wednesday evening I arrived at their home and was introduced to the circle members including a lady called Cynthia who, like myself, had been invited to join and was also attending for the very first time. We were both made to feel most welcome.

What I had not realised until just before that first sitting was that Jim had acted as the trance medium to the circle for many years but, for whatever reason, had lost the ability some months earlier to enter the trance state. His exact words to me were: 'I just can't get away any more but one day I know it will return to me.'

Contact with the Spirit World had most disappointingly been lost and it seemed to me that my attendance at the circle was a kind of 'stop gap' – a tentative arrangement. Nevertheless, I was genuinely happy with that and considered that for however long it lasted this could be of mutual benefit - my development would continue and their contact would hopefully be restored. And so every Wednesday evening, for about six months, in an atmosphere of friendly unison and sincerity, I sat with the circle and my guide was able to communicate.

The circle was pleased, I was pleased and all was well.

And then, unavoidably, I was unable to attend one particular night.

I have long believed that in addition to the pure essence of Spiritualism, exist aspects, running in parallel, which defy comprehension.

'Hi Stewart', said Cynthia to me the following morning on the telephone, 'How are you?'

From the tone of her voice I knew immediately that, regardless of how I was, all was not well with her.

'What's wrong?' I asked.

There was a silence on the line for several seconds before she replied, 'Jim went into trance last night.'

'Brilliant,' I responded.

'Well, not really.'

'What do you mean? What's wrong?' I asked, thinking to myself that perhaps he had been taken ill during or after the sitting.

'Well,' she continued, 'as always we sat around the dining table and I found myself on his right hand side. We'd been sitting for about ten minutes when suddenly he started breathing heavily. Then his Indian guide began to speak and proceeded to deliver philosophy in full flow for about twenty minutes.'

'That must have been marvellous,' I interjected.

She laughed nervously and continued:

'It was, until I happened to shift in my chair and quite accidentally found my left foot pressing against, or on top of his right – I cannot recall which.'

'Oh dear,' I said, 'Well, what happened next?'

'You won't believe this,' she continued, 'The guide stopped talking instantly, and Jim, with a painful note and a rise in pitch, gasped out of the corner of his mouth: 'You're standing on my foot.' I quickly moved it and then the guide continued speaking as if absolutely nothing had happened.'

It is difficult to imagine just how shocked, bewildered and embarrassed she and the other sitters must have been, and, yes, how terribly disappointed they must have felt. Whether conscious or unconscious fraud I cannot possibly say but as a psychological conundrum it defied and continues to defy my understanding.

In the years that have since passed, I have often reflected upon that night, and wondered how I might have reacted had I been present to witness such a bizarre incident.

Needless to say, I took the decision not to sit again with the circle, as too did Cynthia, but the two of us, together with her husband and friends, went on to form our own circle, and sat together for about a year before that to came to an end, as circles are inclined to do after a period of time. Whilst all start with resolve and commitment, sadly many tend to have a short life span – perhaps a few months or a few years at most. When progress fails to match early expectations or tangible results constantly elude them, most become downhearted and all the early enthusiasm drains away. Then they collapse, leaving the individuals involved looking to join other circles or form new ones.

In my own case – following the collapse of that circle, I quickly found myself sitting in another and when that one eventually disbanded I moved on to yet another – a process which continued to repeat itself over the next two and a half years.

Throughout that period I was to occasionally witness aspects of human nature which I am convinced I would not have encountered in any other circumstance.

These occurred within circles which, although undoubtedly sincere in their motives, dedication and aspiration, afforded me an insight into how wishful thinking could so very easily lead to the total abandonment of rational judgement. People, who at all other times were, no doubt, sensible and responsible, appeared to leave their critical faculty outside the door when entering the séance room. Then, for a time, they freely engaged in a shared world of delusion. Crossing the threshold from the outside world into the séance room appeared to be an invitation for all the circle members to engage in a jointly created world of fantasy, where sitters jostled to establish amongst the group their own mediumistic prowess. Without the slightest intimation, many genuinely believed that they were mediums or they clung to the hope that following a few weeks of development, their supposed innate mediumship would reveal itself. Of course, this was not always the case, but often it was and I was always surprised why so many sitters had a compulsion and determination to become mediums. In some cases, no doubt because of a genuine desire to be of service, but in others, perhaps it was a matter of perceived enhanced status amongst their peers!

The leaders of two of the circles I sat with during that time, although obviously nice people, exemplified how ignorance can stifle the potential successful development of a circle. It was a matter of the blind leading the blind and where lip service alone was paid to the Spirit World. In other words the leaders dictated the conduct and practice of the circles, with little thought that lack of progress may just have been a consequence of failure to allow the Spirit World to play a significant part.

Of course, this was not always the case. Some circles were well run and did not suffer from over-active imaginations, coupled with the will to believe. A few were very promising and in them I was to witness the steady positive mediumistic development of several sitters. But that was a rarity and most certainly was not the norm.

Most people who have sat in Spiritualist circles would, if honest, admit to having experienced within them, an occasional absurd incident. One of the most amusing was related to me by the late Alan Crossley (more about Alan in Chapter 4). He was a man who, throughout his life, had a vast amount of séance room experience and he was one of the most knowledgeable and credible Spiritualists that I have ever met.

Apparently, at one of the circles he sat in, the entranced lady medium believing that she was controlled (possessed) by a pet dog suddenly got down on all fours and ran around the room barking. After a few moments of this 'jaw-dropping' idiocy a few of the sitters had muttered, 'God bless, you friend'. Although unquestionably funny it is also very sad.

My own experience during those years was mainly of being in circles where everyone else could sense, feel and/or see the presence of 'Spirit' although I was personally convinced that none was present.

I also listened to discourses delivered through people who were said to be in a trance.

Frankly, it has to be said that often they were an absolute insult to intelligence and to the Spirit World that they were supposed to represent. In fact, channelled gobbledegook in abundance! Mediumship in my view stands or falls according to the evidence it produces to substantiate the argument that the human soul survives death. Communication from a deceased loved one must surely be the ultimate in two-world communication. And yet, my personal experience within several so-called 'home circles' at that time was notable for the absence of anything which even remotely suggested the presence of the Spirit World. Carefully I listened to deceased scientists, priests, philosophers and exotic personages as they delivered their articulate (and not quite so articulate) messages.

Invariably I was left bemused and incredulous and I had sympathy for the position of the sceptic and the cynic. Such performances always left me baffled as to what had actually 'gone on' – and what it was that I had actually sat through! Was it a matter of unconscious or deliberate premeditated fraud? Although there was no way of knowing which, I knew these 'mediums' to be nice people and I considered that a psychologist witnessing such performances would have much to study. If these were bizarre then demonstrations of transfiguration that occasionally accompanied the entrancement process were even more so. This is where there is a change in the appearance of the medium's face as a dim red light illuminates it. In the case of genuine transfiguration, which is an aspect of physical mediumship, it is believed that the Spirit people extract ectoplasm from the medium which is then concentrated in front of and quite separate from the medium's face. The communicating spirit person seeking to create a likeness of their own facial features then impresses and moulds the ectoplasm into a mask – a facsimile of their own face. Throughout the history of Spiritualism several notable mediums have specialised in producing such phenomena and many people went on record claiming to have recognised their loved ones at such séances. Unfortunately, my own experience was somewhat different. What I invariably witnessed was a great deal of face pulling – a contortion of features – indeed performances which would have been envied by those people who are able to gurney. On such occasions I often found myself wondering why the spirit people were always 'so ugly'!

gurn

Never did I see an attractive or even a semi-attractive one. Surely, at least one transfiguration should have rivalled George Clooney or Marilyn Monroe in appearance.

Sadly – No.

However, in sitting with those circles, what was of real importance to me was that my development should continue, and now as I look back to those years, I am certain that the path that I resolutely followed was necessary for all that lay ahead of me – just beyond the horizon.

Chapter 3

I meet my first Mentor

I meet a lady medium very important to my mediumistic development ~ She forms a circle around me ~ Physical phenomena which defy any normal explanation finally manifest.

Twelve years had passed since I first read Arthur Findlay's 'On the Edge of the Etheric'. For eleven of those years I had sat weekly (occasionally twice a week) in various circles and for several of those years my principal guide had continued to work with me upon the long road of development. I was still aware of his words whenever he spoke through me, but pleasingly, he had for some years presented evidential survival communication to sitters. This confirmed to me that development was being maintained and, of course, evidence of survival is, or should be, intrinsic to Spiritualism.

Even more interesting was the fact that for some time he had been speaking of the possibility that, providing I remained patient and continued to sit for development every week, they in the Spirit World were confident that one day they would be able to communicate on a physical level. In other words, that physical phenomena would be introduced. Such a prospect was most exciting.

As I look back now to those early years of my journey I can clearly see a logical pattern of experience – significant episodes which played a major role in the scheme of things.

The formation and eventual collapse of my home circle. The sittings with Leslie Flint and the various circles that I had sat in were all of importance upon the path that I steadfastly trod.

My confidence in the Spirit World was absolute and I never doubted that my mediumship would continue to progress. However, for every eventful séance there would be at least two blanks where seemingly nothing or very little happened. One certainly required patience in bucket loads. And then, on one particular Sunday evening, my path was to change once again when I witnessed, at a local Spiritualist church, one of the finest demonstrations of clairvoyance[1] that I had ever experienced. The medium, who had been born and bred in Kingston Upon Hull (my home town) had, I was later to discover, lived for some years in London. She had just returned to live in Hull and that night she was giving her very first demonstration in her home town. Her name was Kath Matthews.

After the service we were introduced and I congratulated her on the outstanding demonstration that she had just given. I quickly learned that she was self-effacing and had little confidence in the wonderful gift that she undoubtedly possessed, believing always that she could have done better. In every sense she was one of the unsung heroes of Spiritualism. She sought no fame and her name would never be known throughout the Movement – she was what I call a 'working medium' who, although excellent, considered herself to be very ordinary.

Our conversation quickly turned to physical mediumship, in which she had a particular interest, and soon we were talking together about it like old friends.

Little did I realise then that this remarkable woman, whom I later came to regard as my first mentor, would soon play a central and invaluable role, not only in respect of supporting my mediumship but in the realisation of my years of endeavour to finally achieve physical manifestations within my own séance room. Within a few months of our first meeting, Kath volunteered to totally black-out her lounge on a Monday evening and create a circle to sit with me. This would be for the express purpose of presenting to the Spirit people the exacting conditions so necessary for the generation of physical phenomena. And so every Monday night for the next two years we sat together in harmony and friendship – eight people, all sharing the same hopes and aspirations. Trance communication with the Spirit World continued to develop and towards the end of that period there were frequent occasions when we heard rapping and tapping sounds that seemed to come from the walls. It was around this time that I met Ray Lister, whom Kath had invited to join the circle and who would one day become my circle leader and manager, organising and arranging my public work. He has now led our home circle for over twenty-five years. Ray was also destined to become a reliable, dependable friend and in

(1) *Clairvoyance: The ability to see the dead*!

many ways the mainstay of my mediumship. However, as we sat together in Kath's circle in those first two years, I doubt that any of us could possibly have realised just what lay ahead.

Success was on the horizon. That which for so long had always seemed unattainable was now almost upon us, and we were about to witness things that few human beings had ever witnessed before.

The Breakthrough

Fourteen years after my discovery of Spiritualism – thirteen years after my first sitting in a circle and two years after Mrs Kath Matthews had specifically created a circle to sit for my development – the long awaited and eagerly anticipated breakthrough finally came.

That night began no differently from any other circle night.

We all arrived at Kath's – we chatted together as we always did – the circle was opened – the light switched off – my guide entranced and spoke through me and one hour later the circle was closed and the light switched back on. A few minutes later we were enjoying tea and biscuits, after which everyone drifted away leaving just Kath, another lady member of the circle and myself. We were sitting at the dining table and I clearly recall that the trumpet was standing between us on the table as we discussed the progress of the circle. Then quite unexpectedly – and this had never happened before – I became aware of my guide returning and then nothing else until I 'awoke' shortly afterwards. I was then excitedly informed that during my unconscious state (for that is what it had been) White Feather – my guide – had asked for the light to be switched off and a few moments later, and for the very first time, the trumpet had risen into the air and his voice had been heard to issue directly from it.

Just one short sentence, but our feelings at the implication behind those few words, that, at last, our dreams were about to reach fruition, cannot possibly be imagined. The excitement was palpable. Sittings after that memorable night were akin to the breaking of a dam – communication on an entirely new and different level burst forth. However, if we thought then that we would quickly progress to the manifestation of partial or full form materialisation in lighted conditions, (the crème de la crème of physical mediumship) we would soon come to realise that it was not to be. If it was ever to occur, then it would only do so many years in the future.

As might be imagined, the following week the circle sat in an atmosphere of elation and acute anticipation and this was rewarded when again the trumpet levitated and a few words were spoken through it. Whilst this was occurring I was in a deep state of trance which thereafter became the norm whenever phenomena on a physical level occurred.

Trumpet levitation was maintained in subsequent weeks and as time went by so the Spirit people were able to extend the time that it sailed around the séance room.

Although the words spoken through it were few at first, it would float gracefully, sometimes describing intricate patterns in the air and sometimes gyrating and weaving around sitters at considerable speed without ever colliding with anyone or with anything. As small pieces of luminous tape were attached to its wide end sitters were easily able to follow its manoeuvres in the total darkness. This spatial awareness certainly demonstrated that the trumpet was at all times under intelligent control and as time passed so communication became more sustained.

At that time the circle was composed of four women and four men all of whom attended faithfully each week. Then one evening, several months after our monumental breakthrough, we were joined by a friend of one of the sitters who, we were informed, had a great interest in Spiritualism and who could be implicitly trusted not to violate our usual séance room conditions. Kath herself had agreed to the young man's visit and believed, as we all did, that there was nothing to fear, but that night we were all to learn a most valuable lesson.

The séance had started in the usual way and soon the trumpet was sailing around the room in its normal fashion. Ray was sitting at the far side of the circle to one side of the stranger. As the trumpet approached them he became aware that the man had started to move about in his chair and Ray asked him what on earth he was doing.

The reply was that he was trying to take hold of the trumpet to find out who was actually controlling it. Horrified, Ray immediately admonished him as did Kath.

It was assumed that the man had no concept of the danger that he was placing me in and, in absolute ignorance of the possible consequences, wanted to satisfy himself that the phenomena was genuine. On the other hand, if he did know, and merely wished to satisfy his curiosity, then such arrogance would defy belief. However, a moment later he began to shout out alarmingly, his voice ascending in pitch by several octaves. At the same time with both hands he began frantically feeling around his chair. Apparently it had levitated high into the air with him on it. 'I can't believe this – no one is touching my chair,' he shouted. Since it had been placed with its back close to the wall – as had all the chairs – it would have been impossible for any human agency to have effected the levitation by normal means. Soon after the séance ended he left, shaken, never to return. Understandably, following that night our home circle became ultra cautious regarding possible future visitors.

For several more months communication on a physical level continued with White Feather playing the principal role but then, one night, we had a most unexpected visitor from the Spirit World, who decided to remain with us for over a year.

When Kath had lived in London, she had befriended and often accompanied a medium by the name of Lila Josephs to her demonstrations at the Spiritualist churches in and around the city. From all accounts, Lila – who was often featured in the Spiritualist weekly newspaper *Psychic News* – was a larger than life character. Sadly, just before Kath had decided to move back to the North, Lila had been hospitalised and unexpectedly passed into Spirit. One night – probably about three months following the start of trumpet communication – my guide had finished speaking and the trumpet had settled gently on the floor when almost immediately it rose again, hovered in front of Kath, and the well remembered voice of Lila Josephs issued forth. In the following weeks it gradually became clear that this had been the first of what were to become regular visits.

What was always particularly intriguing to the circle was that not only did she manifest with her rather colourful character, but that she and Kath were able to reminisce about the good old days – the laughs, the incidents and the happy times that they had enjoyed in each other's company. It seems though that it was never intended that Lila should become a permanent part of what we subsequently came to regard as our 'Spirit team'. Evidently, she was there to fulfil a specific purpose, and perhaps it was her very forceful personality that had singled her out as best suited to break through in the way that she consistently did, and to stabilise trumpet communication.

Towards the end of that year she began to talk about a little boy who stood behind her, and who would one day play an essential role in the presentation of my physical mediumship. When that day dawned it would be time for her to leave – her job would be done. And so it came to pass that, when eventually little Christopher finally arrived, Lila, whom we had come to like immensely, gradually withdrew.

But it was not long before Christopher also endeared himself to the circle with his childlike, impish, amusing and mischievous ways.

Of all the various Spirit personalities that have worked with me since then, it is Christopher that has intrigued me the most. Down the years he has not changed and remains today as the one who never fails to amuse me with his banter, his warmth and obvious love of the job with which he has been entrusted. When people sit with me for the first time they often do not really know what to expect. Even ardent Spiritualists can be nervous when sitting in total darkness and about to experience physical phenomena for the first time. On such occasions White Feather is always the first to communicate with his blessing and then he is quickly followed by little Christopher who, within seconds, eases any tension amongst sitters in his own distinctive manner. He impresses everyone with his normality and his irreverence, but more of Christopher later.

The Incident of the Pink Pig

Had Sir Arthur Conan Doyle still lived upon the earth twenty-five years ago, and heard the following story, then I rather imagine that he may well have chosen 'The Incident of the Pink Pig' as a title for one of his Sherlock Holmes novels. Certainly the events that I am about to relate are just as mystifying as anything that came from the great writer's pen and a story based upon them would surely have intrigued his readers.

We had been enjoying voices through the trumpet, trumpet movement and various minor forms of phenomena for several months when one night we sat in the dark without any discernible manifestations whatsoever. The trumpet remained resolutely still throughout, I remained fully conscious and we all sat and talked until we decided to close the circle. Imagine then our amazement when the light was switched on. There, on the carpet, in front of every single member of the circle was a little plastic animal, about two inches (5cms) in height – dogs, cats, sheep etc. – a gift, no doubt, in recognition of each sitter's patience and dedication.

It was, I suppose, a kind of mass demonstration of the so-called apport phenomenon (Items being transported into a locked and sealed séance room) the mechanics of which are unknown to us.

Whilst everyone was understandably delighted, in front of Kath there was nothing at all. For whatever reason, she was the only person who had been missed out and understandably she was most upset – with very good reason too. She, as the circle leader, and my mentor, had gone to the trouble of blacking out her lounge each week for over two years. She had hosted the circle and yet the Spirit World had apparently failed to recognise and reward her efforts and her good will.

When we left that evening, we all did so with heavy hearts and quite unable to understand such an apparent oversight. However, early next morning she telephoned me in great excitement and told me the following most extraordinary story:

Apparently, when she retired to bed each evening, she was in the habit of reading. Then, when she began to feel tired, she would place her book on the bedside table and settle down. This she had done as usual the night before.

When she awoke that morning the first thing she had seen, sitting on top of her book, was a pink plastic pig, about four inches(10cms) in height – the very book she had placed there only eight hours previously. Now, readers may think that such a story is wonderful in itself but it is not the end of the tale. The following week, on arrival at Kath's for the circle, one of our members immediately identified the pig as one which belonged to him and which had gone missing from his home, many miles away, the previous week. Graciously he allowed her to keep it and for months afterwards she kept the pig in her glass-fronted china cabinet and everyone who visited her would be told the story, and she would take it out and show it to them.

Then, one day she noticed with alarm that it had gone. A thorough search of the room and then all of her rooms, failed to unearth it. One can readily imagine how devastated she felt, for it seemed to her that this gift from the Spirit World was not permanent, as she, and indeed we all, had assumed.

The weeks passed, and then one day a carpet fitter came to lay a new carpet in her lounge. The trumpet that we had used the night before was standing on her mantelpiece, and when the fitter had finished he turned to Kath and asked her if she held séances there.

Some years earlier he had apparently been interested in Spiritualism and he knew what such a trumpet was used for. When he was told yes, he immediately told her the following story, although he rather imagined that she would not believe him, because no one else did.

A few weeks earlier he had gone to bed and upon waking the following morning had seen, on his bedside table, a pink plastic pig. Kath Matthews, intrigued and excited by his story, then told him her own.

Remarkably the two of them had never previously met or known of each other's existence, and, in fact, lived about eight miles apart. It just so happened that he, from amongst all his company's fitters, had been sent to lay the carpet. It was as if the whole episode had been planned in advance. Kath told him that her pink pig had a distinctive mark at its base, and added that she would know immediately if his pig was, in reality, her pig. The fitter then agreed to return the following day, assuring her that if the mark was there, then she, as its rightful owner, could have it back. Of course it was hers, and true to his word, he left it with her.

Unbelievably that is still not the end of the affair.

In 1991, about eight years after the events described above I received a phone call from Mrs Matthews during which she revealed to me a most extraordinary postscript to the story.

Apparently, the original owner of the Pink Pig had just contacted her that day to enquire if she had realised that it was no longer in her possession. It seems that he had just obtained some new kitchen cupboard units and following delivery to his home he had opened one of them to find there the much travelled plastic animal.

We may think what we wish but the fact is that the two lived many miles apart and that Mrs Matthews no longer had it in her possession and he did! Ever since, that precious plastic figure became known as 'The Travelling Pink Pig.'

Mrs Kath Matthews came into my life at a most appropriate time. There can be no doubt that her confidence in me, and her consistent support, advice and encouragement, helped in the realisation of the kind of mediumship that had so captivated and infused my interest those many years earlier. I always regarded her as my mentor and I still do. Until ill health recently intervened, she still occasionally sat with my present circle which has now been meeting weekly for over twenty years and which is basically composed of two families – my own and that of Ray Lister.

Chapter 4

Over the Pennines to Elton

I meet Alan E. Crossley – celebrated champion of Spiritualism who, throughout his life, had sat with legendary physical mediums ~ He tells us of the extraordinary experiences he enjoyed in their séance rooms ~ A circle is formed around me ~ Major advances in my mediumistic development occur.

In the early 1980s my family and I were on vacation in Wales and on our car radio heard a BBC Radio 4 interview with a gentleman called Alan E. Crossley concerning his book, 'The Story of Helen Duncan'. Mrs Duncan throughout her life, and indeed even today, is celebrated and revered by the Movement as one of the finest materialisation mediums in history.

I discovered that Alan Crossley had known her well, and when she had given her renowned materialisation séances in the Liverpool area, he often had the responsibility of arranging her séance room lighting. I found the broadcast very interesting indeed – Alan was a direct link to this outstanding medium and I knew that from him I could learn so much. Since the history of the Movement in general and, of course, physical mediumship in particular had always enthralled me, I had long recognised the fact that I could learn such a great deal from what had gone before. Within days of returning from Wales I had obtained Alan Crossley's address, written to him and received a reply inviting me down to his home in the village of Elton, near Chester. Although the journey was long and it involved travelling over the Pennines, a few weeks later Ray Lister and I were making the trip and, I have to say, looking forward immensely to meeting this man whom I instinctively knew represented another milestone upon my journey and whom I would soon come to regard as a friend and as yet another mentor.

Alan lived on a residential park and it was there that we were to spend some of the most intriguing, interesting, and wonderful days that one can imagine. We were fortunate to have known him. His home generated warmth and the man himself exuded gentleness, wisdom and kindness. He had a broad knowledge of the Spiritualist Movement and we quickly came to realise that not only was he a direct link with many of the outstanding physical mediums of the past, but his experiences within their séance rooms were without equal. From him we could, and we did, learn an enormous amount.

He was a true pioneer who never tired of recounting his experiences.

He had personally known celebrated physical mediums such as Alec Harris, William Olsen, Jack Webber, Mrs Gunning and a host of others, including his friend Mrs Duncan about whom he had written his book. Alan, as a regular witness, entertained no doubts that in Mrs Duncan's séance room the dead had indeed materialised in solid form and that often recognition had been instant. The book was his attempt to vindicate her from what he regarded as ignorant, slanderous accusations of fraud which had persisted since a police raid at a séance she gave in Portsmouth in 1944.

This had led to her infamous trial a few months later in the Central Criminal Court of the Old Bailey under the archaic Witchcraft Act of 1735.

This stated that '... any person who pretended to exercise or use any kind of witchcraft, sorcery, enchantment or conjuration, shall be liable on conviction to a year's imprisonment'.

In spite of the fact that many creditable witnesses had given compelling evidence in her defence she was to be found guilty and sentenced to nine months' detention in Holloway prison. To Alan and many others her conviction was seen as a miscarriage of justice.

It caused an outcry of indignation throughout the Spiritualist Movement and would eventually lead to the passing of the 'Fraudulent Mediums Act' of 1951[1] which thereafter gave genuine mediumship a degree of legal protection against false allegations of fraudulence.

That visit to Elton was to be the first of many until eventually, some years later, Alan decided to create a circle to sit with me to assist in my further development. Ray and I were therefore destined to make that long journey over the Pennines every month for several more years.

---

(1) *The Fraudulent Mediums Act was itself repealed in 2008 and replaced by general consumer protection legislation..*

Each member was carefully chosen by him and later in the life of the circle, by Alan's invitation, we were to be joined by a young man called Simon Forsyth. Some months earlier – he, just as we ourselves had done – had made contact with Alan to discuss his own great interest in physical mediumship. He was a welcome addition to the circle and with his astute mind would some years later go on to launch the *Psychic World* newspaper and eventually *The Psychic Times* website. All the members of the circle, from its inception, were friends, committed, as Alan always said, '*To go where no one has ever gone before*'. Within a few years that special circle would become commonly known as 'The Project' and we shared the hope that one day, in co-operation with the Spirit World, we could capture on infra-red video film a physical séance from beginning to end; but more about that later. Our visits to Elton and to the home of Alan Crossley were a joy indeed, and I unreservedly pay tribute to all the circle members for their friendship, their unselfish dedication and their invaluable contribution to the development of that special circle.

Those were truly magical days and they have left me with fond and lasting memories that I shall treasure for ever.

Ray and I – occasionally accompanied by my sister Gaynor and Ray's sister-in law – always timed our visits to arrive shortly after lunch. Alan would greet us warmly and would usher us through to his small lounge. Once seated, he would enquire if we would care for a nice strong cup of tea and then position himself on the threshold of his kitchen. From there, he would regale us with spellbinding stories of what, many years earlier; he had personally witnessed in the séance rooms of historic celebrated physical mediums. When, following periodic reminders from us, we finally got our tea, it would be at least one hour later, but it did not matter in the least. He would fascinate us with his memories, and he knew how to tell a tale. We always felt highly privileged to be in the presence of such a man, whose love for and confidence in the Spirit people was absolute. Throughout the years that we knew him, we were to hear his stories many times, and yet they never varied in detail. Sitting there in his lounge, listening intently to what he had to impart, we felt as close to living history as it was possible to be. One knew that his recollections of those séances of yesteryear were the literal truth and that there was no embellishment involved. We never ever tired of hearing them, no matter how many times he told them.

Spiritualists of today, who fail to appreciate the significance of physical phenomena to the Movement, fail utterly to understand their nature and their fundamental importance.

In so doing, they have no realisation or conception of the revelations of the séance room, where belief can instantly become certainty, and from which Spiritualism, just as in the past, may in the future once again threaten to replace materialism.

Such is my belief that this may eventually be realised that I have, over the past few years, spoken many times of Alan's experiences at seminars and conventions both here and abroad. Invariably, my retelling of his stories has proved to be a source of absolute fascination and has introduced many unsuspecting people to the wonders of the séance room.

These talks have conveyed to audiences – most of whom have had little knowledge about physical phenomena – that the Spirit World could, and still does, under certain circumstances, physically manifest with demonstrations that leave nothing to the imagination. Often, those accounts have so enthused listeners that they have been motivated to form their own physical development circles, and perhaps one day, out of those, may eventually emerge a whole new generation of such mediums. In my view, such a realisation would greatly benefit the Movement of Spiritualism which, these past fifty years, has been corrupted, fragmented and compromised by watered down and highly misleading 'teachings' that have led directly to its sad decline. However, following my talks, it has many times been suggested that such wonderful stories of past séance room events should be permanently recorded to ensure that they would not, eventually, be lost to future generations. Therefore, in essential detail, I now faithfully present just three of them and would ask the reader to accept that these are neither fairy stories nor mere flights of fantasy. I am satisfied that they occurred exactly as Alan Crossley maintained they did and I shall retell them as I repeatedly heard them from him, so many years ago. He believed that all the experiences he spoke of were witnessed with his rational senses but never did he expect the listener to fully accept them. After all they were his own personal experiences and not theirs. He also insisted that neither hallucination nor collective hypnosis could explain them away. To him, such dogmatic views were, in essence, the result of ignorance of such séances and of the dynamic forces involved.

With those sentiments I entirely agree.

Mrs Gunning's Ivy.

Alan Crossley's very first experience of séance room phenomena occurred in Southend-on-Sea when he was a young teenager. His mother belonged to the circle of a Mrs Maud Gunning who was a powerful physical medium. Apparently, opportunities to join the circle as a member were few and far between since no one would give up their seat. Only death itself would present such an opportunity and eventually this was to happen and Alan, on his mother's recommendation, duly filled the vacant place and his life time of intense involvement with physical phenomena commenced. The stories that Ray and I and others were to hear about this remarkable medium were literally mesmerising and his experiences within her séance room – where the Spirit World communicated on a physical level – could only be regarded as astounding. There was one particular night, however, that Alan had always felt exceeded all others and which he often recalled in considerable detail. Understandably, the event had left an indelible impression on his mind.

Mrs Gunning, we were told, lived in an old house with walls covered entirely in ivy. One night in the darkness of the séance room, the sitters had become aware of a rustling sound and Alan and his fellow sitters could feel something creeping up their legs. Suddenly Mrs Gunning's guide had called through the trumpet for the light to be switched on for just a few seconds and then to be turned off again. As the room flooded in light so the sight that met their eyes had begged belief. From wall to wall the entire floor area up to knee height was deep in ivy. This, they could only assume, must have been taken from the outside walls and then deposited within the locked séance room.

The light was switched off – the guide immediately called for it again and as it came back on it could be seen that the ivy had totally disappeared, although now, running around the floor, were a few creepy crawlies. These, they assumed, must have been transported within the room along with the ivy and yet had been left behind, when the ivy had disappeared. How, one may wonder, could such an inexplicable phenomenon have occurred? Certainly it had happened, but later it was observed that the ivy on the outside walls appeared to be undisturbed. According to Alan it was just one example of what the Spirit people could do when they had a suitable medium to work with.

My later personal experiences told me quite clearly that no doubt he had been correct.

The Remarkable - Alec Harris

The Welsh medium, Alec Harris, was, like Helen Duncan, an outstanding materialisation medium. Although he passed into spirit in 1974 there are still people alive today who had the privilege of witnessing his wonderful mediumship. Over the years, I have been privileged to interview several of them. As with Helen, the dead materialised in his séance room in solid form and did so for over thirty-five years. Unlike Helen, in the many years that he demonstrated his remarkable gift, no controversy ever attached itself to him.

No imputation of fraud – no allegations and no incriminations. In his séance room sitters in attendance were able to see, embrace and hold conversations with their loved ones all of whom had passed through the change called death. Alan told us that he first met Alec Harris shortly after he found himself, as a travelling salesman, in lodgings in the home of a Mr and Mrs Harris who he quickly discovered were the brother and sister-in-law of Alec. Through them he was introduced to the medium and finally received an invitation to participate in one of those legendary séances. Since people would travel from all over the world to sit, one can imagine Alan's delight. Many were the stories that we were to hear all of which exceeded the 'boggle threshold' but I shall, at this point, share just one of them with readers.

Following his presence at a number of séances over a period of several years, Alec and his wife had, of course, got to know Alan well. On a few occasions he had found himself seated in a privileged and trusted seat immediately to one side of the cabinet. The cabinet was simply two curtains across the corner of a room behind which the medium sat. These parted in the middle and would be drawn back to allow materialised forms to venture out into the room. The purpose of the cabinet was not to hide from view the kind of tomfoolery and chicanery suspected by cynics but in order to concentrate the vital energy from which the entire materialisation process was conducted. In Alan's opinion – as he told me many times – the curtains also hid from view an aspect of dematerialisation that some observers may well have found to be rather unsightly and perhaps upsetting. The gradual disintegration of materialised 'loved ones' he believed could well prove to be a traumatic experience. He had little doubt that to some people the procedure could be considered a disagreeable aspect of the phenomena. The following account describes an event which inclined him to draw that conclusion. On that occasion he was able to observe closely three materialised forms out in the circle at exactly the same time – not an unusual occurrence at an Alec Harris sitting. All were guides of the medium who between them were responsible for conducting the séances. One was a North American Indian wearing a magnificent headdress with feathers which extended to the floor – one was an Arab and the third was a little Chinese man dressed in silk robes, a black hat and sporting a pigtail. All three were in different parts of the séance room – all were individuals and could be clearly seen in good red light[2]. Alan observed that occasionally both the Indian and the Arab broke off their conversations to return to the cabinet only to re-emerge moments later and continue with their conversations.

He assumed that there had to be a reason for this and that they were probably – in some way – recharging the energy out of which they were temporarily composed. He also observed that the Chinese man failed to do so until 'Suddenly,' said Alan, 'it was as if he had remembered, turned away from the sitter he was speaking to and scurried back towards the cabinet.' As he approached, Alan, looking directly at him, saw how his facial features had begun to crumple as if melting like wax before a flame. 'His face,' said Alan, 'had begun to fall in upon itself and his very figure began to sink downwards.'

Within seconds, as everyone watched, his form had disappeared leaving a mound of snow-white pulsating energy on the floor immediately in front of the cabinet curtains. Then, it was whisked within the cabinet and out of sight. This experience alone had led Alan Crossley to conclude that to see a materialised love one disappearing in such a manner would be both upsetting and unpleasant.

On the other hand, Bradley Harris, the son of the medium, although understanding Alan's view, recently wrote to me expressing his own, slightly different opinion:

'I must say that I was surprised that Alan found the process of dematerialisation rather unsightly, because on numerous occasions, when witnessing forms slowly dematerialising by melting into the floor, I personally found it to be an amazing experience. Also, to see a white piece of ectoplasm on the floor, just outside the cabinet, rise up to form a head shape which in a matter of seconds, rose in a fountain of ectoplasm to form a fully materialised spirit form which steps forward into the room, an

(2) *Whilst ectoplasmic energy is extremely light sensitive and the sudden introduction of any form of illumination can inhibit physical phenomena and seriously damage a medium's health, a well developed materialisation medium can generally tolerate the presence of red light of varying intensity but only ever as directed by the Spirit World.*

experience one never forgets and it was beautiful to behold. However I can understand that a person could feel distressed when a loved one that they had been embracing would start to dematerialise outside the cabinet before stepping into it. Sometimes the spirit would hold on to the loved one's hands, not wanting to go but in being unable to hold the power they would melt into the floor. However, people would react differently, which is only natural'.

❖ ❖ ❖

Mrs Duncan

Alex Harris was, as previously stated, amongst the very few materialisation mediums in history who, throughout his long career, remained untouched by defamatory insinuation and rumours and whose reputation remains to this day untarnished by controversy. On the other hand, Mrs Duncan's career was, from time to time, accompanied by allegations of fraud. Although there were countless credible witnesses to her séance room wonders willing to speak in her defence (who claimed that through her mediumship they had seen, spoken to, and sometimes embraced their deceased loved ones) there were others who spoke only of cheese-cloth masquerading as ectoplasm. The arguments during her lifetime and ever since her death have been endless and fact and fiction have become so inseparably intertwined that an impartial review of the entire case is probably no longer possible. The sceptics are largely dismissive of Mrs Duncan whilst believers passionately defend her. My own position rests largely upon the weight of historical human testimony, for and against. Perhaps I have something of an advantage over the cynics because of my singular good fortune to have met and spoken to people who attended her séances and who I judged to be sincere creditable witnesses. They had been there and they had formed their opinions based not upon hearsay but upon personal experience.

Amongst those was of course Alan Crossley, and although his recollections of Helen Duncan (always referred to respectfully as Mrs Duncan) were many, I shall recount here the details of just one, since it was typical of them all. This took place during a period of his life when, again as a travelling salesman, he travelled to many parts of the country.

When visiting a particular town in the North West he always stayed at a 'Guest House' run by a man who at one time had been his boss. He was assisted by his wife and the couple had a young son about twelve years of age. On several occasions Alan just happened to be in the town when Helen Duncan had been demonstrating in the area and he always took the opportunity to attend her séances. Sadly, on one of his visits he had arrived at the Guest House to be greeted with the news that his former boss had tragically died and that it was no longer being run as a business. However, because Alan was not merely an old customer but was regarded as a friend, the man's widow had graciously offered to accommodate him whilst he was working in the area. On that occasion, during dinner she asked him about Spiritualism and the séances he had attended in the past when staying there.

Alan explained about Helen Duncan and told her that he was due to attend a meeting with her a few days later. He offered to take her with him and she had agreed to accompany him but had asked if it would be acceptable for her to take her young son along. When the night arrived Helen had raised no objection to the boy sitting and so Alan, his landlady and her young son sat together in a circle with about fifteen other people. The sitters had a clear view of the cabinet which was illuminated by a red bulb located immediately above and in front of it.

Alan told us that neither the mother nor the boy appeared to be particularly nervous and that they seemed to take the proceedings in their stride. Shortly following the commencement of the séance, the medium had fallen into a deep trance as she sat in her usual position within the cabinet in full view of the audience. The curtains were then closed and moments later Albert, Mrs Duncan's principal guide, announced his arrival by asking: 'Is anyone going to say 'How do you do'?' The sitters immediately responded 'Good evening, Albert' and Albert, opening the cabinet curtains had displayed the medium in an unconscious state. Then he declared that he would stand Mrs Duncan up and move her forward and asked again if everyone could see her.

With the unanimous assurance that they could, there they had stood, medium and guide together – Albert dressed in a brilliant snowy-white garment. Then, he guided Mrs Duncan back into the cabinet and closed the curtains. Shortly after he announced that a gentleman was present who had come for the lady and the boy, sitting at the side of Alan and asked: 'Will the lady call the gentleman out?' As she did so the curtains slowly parted to reveal a figure, smiling broadly. In Alan's words:

'I recognised him immediately. Looking directly towards his wife he gasped excitedly: 'Hello Darling'. His son jumped up from his seat and recognising him, shouted: 'Skipper', the name by which he always addressed his father. The moment was dramatic and electrifying. His wife tried to speak but was so overcome with emotion that she found it impossible. 'My dearest,' said her husband, 'I want you to carry on from where I left off'. Then, with a wink in my direction, he said: Thank you, Alan, for making this possible'. He moved back a little, threw a kiss to his wife and son, and then dematerialised, seemingly through the floor!'[3]

❖ ❖ ❖

To most Spiritualists, she has, since her death, become a martyr who eventually gave her life in service to the great cause. In 1956, in Nottingham, another of her séances was interrupted when it was raided by the police causing electrical type burns to her breasts and stomach. These were believed to have been caused as a result of the shock sustained by the rapid return of the ectoplasmic energy to her body. Less than six weeks later she was dead, with the Spiritualist Movement firmly believing that she had been murdered as a result of rank ignorance.

Whatever the true nature of her mediumship, it is as stated earlier, a fact that throughout her mediumistic career, and ever since her death, there have been endless arguments surrounding it. Books and articles in profusion and acres of newsprint have repeatedly analysed it, and fact and fiction have long since become welded into one.

To most researchers however, Helen Duncan was an unmitigated humbug who demonstrated that in a dimly lit room, highly charged with expectancy, it is possible to deceive most of the people most of the time.

---

(3) *'The Enigma of Psychic Phenomena' - 1974 (Alan E. Crossley)*

Chapter 5

The Project

Tangible physical phenomena occur in the circle at the home of Alan Crossley
~ Highly evidential verbal communication is received from the Spirit World ~
I address the contentious matter of infra-red video equipment in the physical
séance room ~ Disagreement over its introduction destroys the circle.

In the late 1980s Ray and I decided that we could not reasonably expect Mrs Mathews to continue indefinitely to host the circle. We therefore took the decision to reform it and we relocated to a spare room of an apartment above a motor cycle shop where the owners lived. Since they too were interested in Spiritualism, they often sat with us as did Kath Matthews.

It was there that I took the decision to invite to the circle, representatives of the Society for Psychical Research – the SPR. I had been a member for some years and since we had been witnessing elementary physical manifestations for some time, I felt it a duty to proceed down that path.

Soon arrangements were made for two of their most respected investigators to visit and, it has to be said, that although I had been solely responsible for inviting them, as the day approached I became quite apprehensive at the thought of their presence.

In those early days, I imagined that researchers representing such an august body as the world renowned SPR would approach any investigation in a professional, scientific and fair manner. With that thought, and in spite of my unease, I finally approached that initial sitting believing that perhaps I could end up with a better understanding of my own mediumship.

When the night arrived, and we met, they proved to be very friendly and pleasant and immediately relaxed us all by making it clear that they were present simply as observers. As a result, I no longer felt quite so apprehensive and I began to relax. Thoughts that I had entered into some kind of self-imposed trial began to disappear.

Unfortunately, although they attended a number of circle sittings they never ever experienced what we regarded as a first class one. Understandably, I would have loved them to have been witness to the best of my mediumship as it then existed, but all these years later I believe that I now have an understanding of why it was not to be.

Mediumship, in many ways, functions in my view, largely on a psychological level. We are dealing with extreme sensitivity and not with cold, unthinking, unfeeling automata. This may provide the answer as to why demonstrations of any form of mediumship invariably reach a higher standard before a sympathetic Spiritualist audience than they generally do before analytical investigators.

No matter how kind and considerate a researcher may be, mediums know that they are being judged and evaluated and unfortunately that in itself can limit or close down entirely the psychic function.

Although it is fact that some past mediums successfully co-operated with the research world it is an equal fact that many more utterly failed. In my own case, I believe that the two researchers found little of real consequence to investigate and after attending the circle occasionally over a period of several months their visits were discontinued. However, all these years later, and in spite of what I assumed at the time to be an agreement of confidentiality, it would seem that one of them was of the opinion that what he witnessed could have been fraudulently produced.

Some years ago in his book, and no doubt to present an entertaining story, he told of those sittings and thinly disguised my identity. No doubt in doing so his conscience was satisfied and his honour preserved. Such nonsense and such an abandonment of ethical principle for reasons that can easily be guessed at can only be abhorred.

Thankfully, the other researcher did not share his views and has remained in contact with me. Today, and for some years past, he has attended our circle several times each year and not simply as a researcher but also as a friend. Together we share a great interest in historic and contemporary mediumship – in Spiritualism and in psychic matters. To discuss these topics freely is, to me, a great joy.

Our tenure of the room above the bike shop was to be short lived after which we moved to the home of Ray Lister and his wife, June. This also coincided with the commencement of our memorable sittings in Elton. From the beginning of the Project Circle Alan Crossley maintained that the séance room was not only the 'holy of holies' but was also akin to a laboratory –the place where the Spirit World is able to experiment and explore possibilities which may eventually lead to the development of varying forms and levels of mediumship.

I have always shared that belief.

Indeed, in that special place – in that special room in Elton – my mediumship was to accelerate in its development and the trumpet phenomena would be further refined and stabilised. Perhaps therefore, at this point in my story, it would be appropriate to recount a thought-provoking experiment which commenced in Alan's séance room about eighteen months after the circle was formed, together with details of two quite remarkable and interesting events that occurred a few months later. The experiment occurred wholly within the séance room.

One event commenced outside and ended up inside the room whilst the other began inside and ended outside it.

The Experiment

One night towards the end of a sitting, little Christopher, who was by then (as long ago predicted by Lila Josephs) a most active and essential part of our Spirit team, began to deliver a so-called book test. This was to be the first of several, spanning a period of many months, conducted within Alan's circle and also our own home circle in Hull. Over half a century earlier, 'book tests' had been synonymous with the celebrated trance medium Gladys Osborne Leonard (1882 – 1968). She was commonly regarded as Sir Oliver Lodge's medium[1], since it was through her that his son Raymond, killed on a First World War battlefield, communicated. These communications resulted in his total conviction in the existence of an afterlife and led, eventually, to the publication of his book 'Raymond'. Mrs Leonard was widely regarded to be the 'Queen of English Mediums', and also 'The Scientists' Psychic'. Over a period of many years she co-operated in a series of sittings organised by the Society for Psychical Research. During that time, the society sent a number of so-called 'proxy' sitters for private sittings with her. These were individuals who attended on behalf of someone else.

Mrs Leonard would frequently have no advance knowledge of the sitter's identity, and the sitter often had no knowledge of the person on whose behalf they were to sit. Therefore, telepathy would hardly be

(1) *Sir Oliver Lodge, F.R.S., D.Sc.,LL.D., M.A. – world famous physicist.*

tenable as an explanation to account for the evidential communications that were transmitted by the medium's guide, Feda, whilst throughout the sitting Mrs Leonard was in a deep state of trance.

A careful record of the sitting would be made, and any information thus conveyed would be passed on by the society to the target recipient for analysis. As the reader will appreciate, information which proved correct under such difficult circumstances would strongly suggest that its source had to be independent of the medium herself.

These experiments often included the presentation of a book test by her guide, Feda. The target sitter would be directed to a bookshelf in their home and told to count a stated number of books in from the left or right hand side. The book would be described – its colour etc. – and they would be told to turn to a particular page number. Counting from the top, the guide would specify a particular line upon which particular words, or a meaningful reference, would be discovered. Often, the particular book would be located and the words would be found to be as stated, or the text would prove to be highly significant to the target recipient. Of course it must be appreciated by the reader that Mrs Leonard had no prior knowledge of, nor access to, the locations of the volumes in question. A very strong case was thereby presented for the reality of her paranormal faculty. It takes no great intelligence to appreciate the enormous implications of successful book tests produced under the demanding conditions outlined above – with or without a proxy. Indeed, I would speculate that the odds of achieving such successful results must have been billions to one against – irrespective of what the world of magic may otherwise claim today[2].

By that time, my interest in these remarkable tests had extended back several years and I had researched and analysed them fairly extensively. Then, that night within Alan Crossley's séance room, little Christopher,

---

(2) *The magic fraternity always seeks to explain aspects of mediumship in terms of legerdemain, cold reading etc. Such a mindset is so deeply embedded within the profession that its members are singularly incapable of seriously considering any mediumistic/psychic production in any other way irrespective of their oft repeated counter claims made throughout history. In 2005, at one of my own public séances, the well respected and most creditable Scottish medium, Mary Armour, was given a book test which, upon her return home, she found to be correct. This was duly reported in the Psychic Press and shortly afterwards on a sceptic's internet site it was authoritatively stated that the explanation to account for the reported Stewart Alexander book test was well known to all magicians. The writer then went on to state glibly that in any event, readers only had the recipient's word for its accuracy.*

quite unexpectedly and much to my delight, successfully introduced such tests. Some proved accurate, some partly accurate and some totally wrong, mirroring exactly the outcome of those presented through the mediumship of Mrs Leonard. Interestingly, in the case of my own mediumship, the initial time span during which they were routinely produced was short, although many years later, in 2005, they were reintroduced on a regular basis and proved to be even more successful.

However, the full magnitude and significance of that very first book test only came to light almost twenty years after it was delivered. Firstly, it directed a sitter to a particular book in their home, and to a particular passage, which proved to be completely accurate. Secondly, the final word of the sentence was *'Freda'*.

It would be another ten years before Freda Johnson[3] would begin to manifest at my séances and subsequently be entirely responsible for presenting survival evidence, organising and helping spirit loved ones to personally communicate with sitters. And, it is she who, since 2005, has been wholly responsible for presenting these unique book tests. It would seem therefore that, although unknown to us at the time of that first test, she was destined to take on this role, years later. Astonishing indeed!

Although out of our present chronological order, I would like to give two examples of book tests which readers may find to be of some interest. The first was given at our home circle in March 2006 to Susan Farrow[4] (the future editor of *Psychic News*).

She was directed by Freda to the second or third shelf of her bookcase and told to take out the third or fourth book from the left. She would find that it was a red book and she was instructed to turn to page eighty-four which, she was informed, would be a left hand page. Near

---

(3) *It was in January 1996, and on only the second occasion that Freda had spoken through me and some months before she identified herself by name, that Christopher delivered his final book test – it was given to Tom Harrison. Remarkably, the individual marks on the cover of the book selected and the passage indicated were completely accurate and appropriate and are described in full in his book – 'Life After Death: Living Proof': published by Saturday Night Press 2008.*

(4) *Readers interested to learn more about the book tests, as presented through my mediumship, will find a brief account in 'New Wonders in Yorkshire' (Parts 1 & 2) by Susan Farrow published by Zerdin Phenomenal in their journal – No. 13, April 2007.*

the bottom she would find a reference to either fish or the sea. In her own words this is what Susan Farrow found:

'......... walked along the jetty towards the shore. Some man was standing on the jetty, smoking and spitting into the sea'.

'The test,' she wrote, 'proved correct in all respects; shelf, book number, page number and text. The cover was multi-coloured, predominantly red.'

Although many similar tests with Freda could be described, I shall include just one additional example and do so because it demonstrates clearly that language is no barrier to the Spirit World.

The séance took place in Basle, Switzerland in June 2006 and a few weeks after my return to England I received a letter from the lady recipient who wrote:

'Freda conducted a very interesting experiment with me. She told me that I should go to my bookshelves and take out the seventh or eighth book from the third shelf and open it to page 89 or 102 and then read the fifteenth line. I would find something about a crocodile or, at any rate, definitely something about an animal with fangs (snappers). Freda wanted to bring us proof that our loved ones from the world of Spirit are amongst us and also follow what is happening in our lives. The following day I went to my bookshelves with great expectation and I wondered, because I have three, which one she meant me to look in. In the first – I took from the third shelf the eighth book and turned to page 89. I found a picture of a sleeping tiger.

In the second of the bookshelves, third shelf, seventh book, same page I found a further picture of a sleeping tiger. Oddly, the first and second books are identical and are the only books that I have ever purchased in duplicate.

In the third set of bookshelves, third shelf, eighth book, page 102 I found a picture of a crocodile with his mouth stretched wide open. Freda was therefore correct on all accounts. I was deeply impressed and touched by this.'

Kathrin Walliser

Basle – Switzerland

19th July 2006

❖   ❖   ❖

The First Event

Approximately two years following the formation of the 'Elton Project Experimental Circle' we experienced the most extraordinary event which actually began outside the séance room and ended within it.

On what I clearly recall was a most beautiful, cloudless day, Ray, my sister Gaynor and I arrived in Elton as usual at about one o'clock. The sun was shining and there was a strong summer breeze.

As always, Alan greeted us warmly and within minutes we were sitting listening as he chatted away to us, standing as he always did, with one foot in his lounge and the other in his kitchen. By two o'clock the elusive cups of tea had still failed to arrive but, again as always, it did not seem to matter.

I was sitting immediately opposite one of the windows which was partly open and which had its blind lowered to keep out the sun. On a small table immediately in front of it stood a large vase filled with flowers, and I noticed that every few moments, the blind, caught by the breeze, would rattle against it. Alan was in the middle of relating one of his stories when, suddenly, the blind shot out and smashed into the vase, which tipped forward and fell towards the carpet. All four of us watched in horror at its descent, which seemed to be played out in slow motion. Before it ended its journey, we observed the flowers, together with what must have been a pint of water, parting company with the vase.

Alan ran into his kitchen and returned almost immediately carrying a floor cloth in order to mop up the water. Getting down on his hands and knees and feeling the carpet, he stopped after a while, rested back on his haunches and began to laugh. 'Come and see,' he said, 'Come and feel the carpet!'

Unbelievably, when we did so we realised that it was completely dry, and yet we had all clearly seen a large amount of water gush out of the vase moments earlier. It seemed inexplicable, and we spoke about little else for the rest of the day.

That evening, six hours after that mysterious event, we were sitting in the circle in Alan's small séance room when little Christopher, our Spirit communicator calmly announced that he had something for us. There followed a whooshing sound and in seconds we were all soaked to the skin by falling water. Understandably we were initially shocked and incredulous, but after a few moments we were highly amused.

Somehow, six hours previously, the Spirit people had dematerialised the water from the vase in an instant, held it in suspension somewhere, and then, hours later, returned it to us.

Such is the power of the Spirit World.

The Second Event

This directly involved a single member of the circle whose extraordinary experience began (unbeknown to her at the time) within and ended outside the séance room. Later she felt moved to write an account of the incident and this was published in November 1992 in the Newsletter of the now disbanded Noah's Ark Society for Physical Mediumship.

Under the heading *A Bracelet Too Far* this, is what she wrote:

I have known Alan Crossley for 9 years now, and have been to many sittings (séances) which have amazed me totally. Of these, few can match the sitting held in April 1992.

As always Stewart Alexander was the medium.

White Feather spoke and then little Christopher, his child guide, gave me a wonderful message from my brother, Donald, who died in 1972. Following this emotional message, and a superb sitting for all present, we closed the circle and went into the other room.

At this point I noticed that my bracelet was missing. I couldn't for the life of me figure out how it had come off, as it had a twisted trigger clasp which had jammed – making it impossible to take off, so I had to keep it on all the time. As it is a gold chain with a Figaro pattern, I was a little taken aback when I discovered it missing.

After a fruitless search, Alan assured me he would look for it later, and I felt that it would probably turn up there as I knew that I had been wearing it when I arrived at Alan's.

I went home to bed, still worrying, but woke up in the middle of the night when my husband, who had a chest infection, was sitting up because he was not able to breathe properly. Since we were both awake, we talked for a while, and then he got up to make some tea. Whilst he was downstairs, I laid there reading for some time, and at this point, there was definitely nothing on the bed as this was covered by a cream duvet, and anything on it would have stood out against it, and would instantly have been seen.

Then, as I was a little concerned about my husband, I went downstairs to check that he was O.K. However, after sharing a cup of tea together he told me that he was going to watch a little T.V. and I went back to bed.

Walking into the bedroom I immediately noticed my bracelet, right on top of the bed. It was opened out, but with the trigger clasp still bent, and there was no way that I could have put it back on in that condition as the clasp just could not be opened.

Needless to say, that bracelet will be even more precious to me now. Today, the chain has a new trigger clasp but despite that I cannot get the bracelet off by myself – it is simply impossible that it could just have fallen off my wrist.

❖ ❖ ❖

These and many other phenomenal occurrences took place during our association with Alan and 'The Elton Project Experimental Circle'. Nothing should have surprised us but it always did.

Elton was such a special place although eventually, to my everlasting regret, we were to have a dispute which sadly would never be resolved and would end for all time our special relationship. And all because throughout the circle's existence we had, as I mentioned earlier, entertained a common aspiration which involved filming on infra-red video a physical séance from start to finish so that the entire process could finally be captured on film. It was a dream that we all shared and everything appeared to be on course and moving in the correct direction.

The Spirit World had indicated that they themselves were willing to consider such a prospect and Alan began more and more to speak to us about '*going where no one had ever gone before*' – borrowing the phrase from the popular TV series of the time – '*Star Trek*'.

Of course, such footage would unquestionably have been without price and the possessor would, no doubt, have been considered as a kind of new Galileo.

Then, just when it was within our grasp, I attended a Seminar on Physical Mediumship which was to drastically change everything and lead to the collapse of the circle, lost friendships, recriminations and a parting of the ways.

The Beginning of the End

In 1992 my sister Gaynor, Ray and I attended a weekend residential seminar which had been organised by the Noah's Ark Society for

Physical Mediumship of which I had, in 1990, been appointed the Archives Officer. One of the lectures that weekend, delivered by a respected creditable psychical researcher, just happened to be in respect of infra-red in the séance room.

Following the talk I found myself standing in the hotel bar with a gentleman who was a member of the Society and a retired scientist. What branch of science he had been involved in I now have no recollection, but it quickly became very clear to me that he spoke as an academic with authority.

This is basically what he said to me: 'Stewart, listen to what I have to say and then accept or reject it – it's up to you. According to the speaker that we have just listened to, infra-red in the séance room is perfectly safe. I would put this to you: how does he know – how does he know exactly what the nature of ectoplasmic energy is and how it may react to infra-red and what the consequences may be to the medium? Quite simply – no one truly knows.' He then went on to explain why he believed that it could be far from safe and how he thought such a medium would pay a heavy price should they risk allowing infra-red cameras into their séance rooms. His words to me, which I have never forgotten, were: 'You, my friend, could literally be fried.' Sadly, since I do not possess a scientific mind, his argument was entirely lost on me but common sense told me that I would be a fool not to pay heed and err on the side of caution. In the years since then, I have, understandably, never forgotten his stark warning – after all he had absolutely nothing to gain by cautioning me other than to perhaps save me from entering into a situation that could be highly dangerous to my health. Of course, since the development of infra-red/night vision equipment many people – researchers, sceptics and Spiritualists – have called for its introduction into the physical séance room. The sceptics no doubt firmly believing that it would reveal fraud thereby justifying their suspicions. The genuine psychical researcher wishing to confirm the reality of such phenomena and then to understand the mechanics which lay behind it. To bring out of the darkness into the light the mysteries of the séance room which have existed since the birth of Spiritualism. And the Movement itself, after a wait of over 150 years, finally being able to demonstrate to the world that physical communication with the dead was a reality. In that event its case would, at long last, be proved.

Nevertheless, whilst trying to appreciate all points of view, this man's forceful authoritative arguments shook me and introduced concern and doubt into my mind. The key question that I dwelt upon was how those who insisted that it would be perfectly safe actually knew that with certainty? And – if I were to allow such equipment to be present and those who advocated its introduction were ultimately to be proved incorrect, and as a result I was to suffer drastic detrimental consequences to my health, who exactly would pay the price for their error?

Who, I wondered, would contact my family afterwards to deliver the bad news and apologise that they had quite simply *got it wrong*.

It seemed to me that the only people who could hold all of the answers and could be implicitly trusted would be our team of Spirit workers and finally I decided that I must be guided by them. After all, their vision would be far more complete than our own and to believe otherwise would be foolhardy and would be to display arrogance. I have always considered that Spiritualism as a Movement lost its way when it largely stopped listening to the Spirit World. During its first 150 years it grew and expanded remarkably. At its root, charting its course, working hand in hand with the Movement was the Spirit World.

Sadly, when Spiritualism largely became deaf to it then its decline inevitably commenced. My own view has always been that when working *with* those in the Spirit World who are close to us anything is possible; whereas working in isolation would make no sense at all. I, therefore, duly took the decision that I felt compelled to take.

I decided that I would defer to our Spirit friends since it was a matter which had literally thrown into monumental turmoil all that the Project Experimental Circle had long worked towards and upon which, in many ways, the entire edifice had been constructed.

However, before I was able to consult with them, further doubts began to arise. My mind was to turn upon issues that had not previously occurred to me and those did not directly involve the Spirit people. For example, would such a film be taken seriously? Would it be assumed that some kind of Hollywood wizardry, some kind of modern-day computer/photographic technology had been employed in its making? In that event then anyone entertaining hopes that it would lead to a revolution in man's thought and nature would be grossly mistaken.

Additionally, I was forced to ask myself whether I would be prepared to enter the glaring public spotlight.

The fact was that throughout my life as a developing physical medium I had never ever sought any form of notoriety because I was, and I still am, a very private man. In the event that a video which captured séance room physical phenomena was realised, and accepted as genuine, it was not at all difficult to imagine that it would overnight become global news. Doubtless, the world's press would have quickly descended since it would literally be the biggest story of all time!

I therefore reasoned that, very quickly, lives would be destroyed and that my circle, which had sat for so many years in quiet development would disintegrate. For me, such a prospect was, and still is, not only daunting but unthinkable. That was my belief then, and today my views remain unchanged. However, my decision not to proceed with the project followed considerable hesitation and soul searching because it was never a matter of simply saying 'no'. Without any doubt I knew that this would be a major disappointment for all concerned and would possibly involve me in protracted disagreement and no doubt in entrenched argument.

And so it proved to be. For some months following the announcement of my decision, we were to be locked in bitter dispute with letters passing constantly between Alan and myself and with Simon Forsyth entering the fray and arguing from Alan's corner. Arguments went back and forth and any thought of compromise seemed impossible. In the meantime the Project Experimental Circle was in a state of 'hold' and our visits to Elton had stopped. Eventually, and no doubt with a final throw of the dice Alan wrote to me suggesting that if we were to proceed with the project and successfully film the phenomena then he would ensure that it would forever remain in his possession and would never see the light of day. Sadly, by then so much acrimony had passed between us that there could be no turning back.

What was done could not be undone, and of course, it was simply not possible to believe that a virtual gold mine would remain forever unknown to the world. No doubt that Alan's intentions were sincere and honourable, but he had waited a lifetime to obtain such a permanent visual record and he was only human. This event marked the end of a most wonderful period of my life and we were never to see Alan nor visit Elton again. It would be a further sixteen years before Simon and I would at last heal our rift and cordially communicate, although sadly, this did not occur until after Alan had passed into Spirit. The filming issue remains to this very day a matter of disagreement between us but now, pleasingly, we have a greater understanding and tolerance of each other's views.

As I look back now to those far off magical days and to that decision which was to change the course and shape of my life yet again, I have often wondered if it had been the correct one to make.

My answer has always been 'yes'. However, to sceptics – to researchers and to Spiritualists, who cannot accept the views that I have outlined here, and would still wish to install cameras in the physical séance room, I have this to say; Form your own circles – develop contact with the Spirit World on a physical level and then you can do exactly as you would wish.

And finally, I end this chapter by recording, without any reservation or hesitation, that Alan E.Crossley was the most gentle of men. He was also infinitely knowledgeable in matters of Spiritualism and he wore his patent honesty upon his sleeve. It was wholly my great fortune to have met him and for a while to have walked at his side upon my long journey of rich experience and discovery. Thank you Alan.

Chapter 6

The Noah's Ark Society

A Society is formed to encourage the re-emergence of physical mediumship ~ International membership expands ~ I become its Archives Officer and later its President ~ Elderly Spiritualists tell of their memories of the great physical mediums of the past ~ I give physical séances for its members ~ My resignation.

So far in this book, I have endeavoured to provide the reader with an overview of my first twenty years within Spiritualism, whilst being mindful of the fact that I must, of necessity, merely touch upon the people, places and events that have influenced and shaped my spiritual life during that period. There was so much more that I could have told, but that has not been my purpose or my intention. I have outlined merely what I regard to be essential and interesting information from which I hope to have established my own credibility and gained the reader's confidence.

If I have achieved that, then perhaps I may additionally hope to elicit the reader's careful and fair consideration of my views concerning, what I believe to be the appalling state of the Spiritualist Movement of today. And since my overriding interest has long been with physical mediumship, which for over 150 years was central to, and which invigorated the Movement, it will come as no surprise that later in this book I intend to construct my arguments and my defence against its past and present denigrators. Additionally I shall briefly touch upon related matters.

In the past, it was the worlds of magic and psychical research that mainly engaged in the examination and invariable defamation of physical mediumship. Today, astonishingly, it is ostracised by whole sections of the Spiritualist Movement although once it was regarded as 'the goose that laid the golden eggs'. Such matters I shall address later but first I must introduce readers to an organisation whose views about such matters so closely matched my own.

In May 1990, an advertisement appeared in the *Psychic News* (the world's oldest and most respected weekly Spiritualist newspaper) from an organisation, recently launched, named *The Noah's Ark Society for Physical Mediumship*[1]. It invited people with an interest in such mediumship to apply for membership and my application was sent immediately. I duly became member number one; a fact that I was always proud of.

Within days, the chairman and motivating force behind the society, Robin Foy, contacted me by telephone. Upon hearing of my long research into, and my extensive library on physical mediumship, I was offered a place on the committee as the Society's 'Archives Officer'. Of course, I was delighted to take on the position and a few weeks later I attended my first committee meeting.

I was quickly to realise that we all shared a concern for the evident dearth of what we regarded to be a vital form of mediumship, which, by then, was literally on the verge of extinction. It was the Society's determination to arrest this alarming situation and restore it to centre stage. Through publicity meetings and residential weekend seminars – which were specifically designed to educate and inform – it was hoped that like-minded people would form their own development circles, and from them a whole new generation of physical mediums might emerge.

There can be no doubt that the Noah's Ark Society (NAS) or 'the Ark' as it became known, met with instant success, and within a couple of years it had an extensive international membership, and over a hundred circles all sitting under its umbrella and guidance – it was, quite literally, like a very large family, and one felt privileged to be a part of it.

Alan Crossley was to become its first permanent President, and when he unexpectedly retired from the position in August 1992, due to ill health, I was highly honoured to take his place until I relinquished it in June 1996 to concentrate singularly on its archives. These, I had always considered to be of crucial importance. From the day I was appointed as the Society's Archives Officer I endeavoured to seek out and interview (whilst there was yet time) elderly Spiritualists who, in

(1) *The Society was named after Noah Zerdin who, in 1931, founded 'The Link', which through its 'Newsletter' sought to unite and help Spiritualist home circles around the country. In early 1990 he allegedly communicated by independent direct voice at a circle in the Midlands calling for the launch of an organisation to promote physical mediumship which, at that time, was in danger of dying away. In the Bible 'Noah's Ark' was said to have saved animals from extinction and so to incorporate the word 'Ark' in the Society's title seemed highly appropriate.*

past years, had sat with celebrated physical mediums whom today one can only read about. I realised that those who had done so were a dying breed with ever decreasing numbers and so through advertising features in Spiritualist journals and the Ark's own monthly *Newsletter* I appealed to them to come forward. Thankfully several did and gradually I was able to assemble a small library of cassette tapes of these Spiritualists telling of their personal experiences. What always impressed me as I listened to them was the fact that invariably they were told with considerable emotion and enthusiasm. In every case it was almost as if they were describing events that had occurred the evening before as against the many years that had subsequently elapsed. The impression made upon them by those séances had been such that they had remained vivid within their memories and they had forgotten nothing.

Of all those I was to hear a few stood out very clearly – not because they were unusual but because they were recounted in such great detail. One experience came to me from a gentleman by the name of Norman Stacey, whom Ray and I were privileged to interview in the summer of 1990 at his home in Tyne and Wear in the North East of England. For some years he had personally known the late, and now legendary physical medium Hunter Selkirk.

Another came from an American gentleman called Gene Woods, who had been born into a Spiritualist family and had been a fighter pilot in the American air force during the Second World War. He had seen one of my published appeals in 1990 and he duly made contact with me after which we shared a friendly correspondence by means of cassette tape over a period of several years.

Yet another came to the archives through a Mr. William (Bill) Cookson, one of our elderly Scottish members whom I got to know very well indeed. Until his passing into Spirit we kept in close contact for a number of years by telephone and cassette tape. Bill was one of nature's larger than life characters and I liked him immensely. Eventually we were to meet when Ray and I, accompanied by two ladies from the Elton Circle, visited him in Blackpool where he and his wife Margaret were on holiday. His single experience of materialisation phenomena, which he had witnessed at a Helen Duncan séance as a young man, he never tired of recalling. Indeed, he had carried it in his mind throughout his life. Eventually he was to write an account of that most wonderful event and this was published in the society's *Newsletter*. It is typical of the experiences enjoyed by a great many people who had the good fortune to sit with the extraordinary medium Helen Duncan.

All three gentlemen are now in the Spirit World but their stories deserve to be preserved for ever because, if for no other reason, they perfectly illustrate the wonder of physical mediumship at its very best. In the next chapter I have included each event exactly as they were told to me and as they subsequently appeared in the Ark's monthly *Newsletter*.

Additionally, although I knew its author by name only, I include an article from an early *Newsletter* which concerned William Olsen – a little remembered trumpet medium. Hopefully, by including such astounding experiences in this book, they may live on to be enjoyed by future generations of Spiritualists and other interested parties.

Going Public

For the first few months of my involvement with the Ark neither its committee nor membership knew of my mediumship, simply because I had never entertained thoughts of demonstrating outside the safety of my home circle, and, frankly, I had always considered my mediumship to be a private matter.

However, the Ark believed that if members attending its residential seminars were given the opportunity to observe physical phenomena for themselves, this would greatly encourage them in their own circles.

They would witness what could be achieved and what might be possible. So, as time passed, a feeling grew within me that perhaps I was being selfish in keeping my mediumship exclusively within our home circle, and finally, on the occasion of the Society's first residential seminar, I revealed to a surprised Robin Foy, that I had, over a period of many years, developed such mediumship myself. Some months later, I was to give my very first public séance for the Society, supported mainly by the Elton circle.

For me to do that was a huge undertaking and it followed a day-long Publicity Seminar where Alan Crossley, Robin Foy, myself and other Ark Committee members delivered informative talks about the history and safe practice of physical mediumship.

That night was to mark the beginning of my demonstrations before the public and between then and my semi-retirement from such work in 2008 I have given almost one hundred further large public séances within the United Kingdom and abroad.

On that first occasion, and at my own request, I was firmly secured to my chair by means of ropes and strong plastic cable ties. This was a practice that I would insist on for all my public work over the next few years. I judged that since I would be a virtual stranger to the sitters it would be of critical importance that they should have the assurance that from the beginning to the end of every séance I was immobilised in my seat. And – just for good measure – I had small pieces of luminous tape stuck to my knees and luminous laces in my shoes so that, in the darkness, sitters would be able to see that I was exactly where I was supposed to be – in my chair throughout. Whilst this may appear to readers to have been a little extreme, one must never forget that throughout the history of physical mediumship fraud has always existed and as a result suspicion and doubt were only to be expected. The names of the infamous charlatans who have traded upon human emotion in the past and whose abhorrent practices have cast a stain and dark shadow upon Spiritualism are many.

Therefore, in taking the decision to emerge from my home circle and into the public arena, I considered that such measures must be imposed and believed that they would go some way toward satisfying the most critical of sceptics. However, in my innocence, I failed at that time to realise that such a prospect could never be realised.

Scepticism is a complex matter and exists on many levels. I shall return to this in a later chapter. For now I shall only say that today it is generally recognised that people are inclined to unconsciously block from their minds events and matters which their belief system simply cannot accept.

My First Public Séance

In March 1992 the Ark published a report in its monthly *Newsletter* about that Publicity Seminar which included details of my very first public séance. Since it was such a salient event in the story of my mediumship I reproduce a shortened account of it below.

It appeared under the heading:

Mischievous Spirit Boy Destroys Noah's Trumpet

'The Noah's Ark Society recently held a remarkably successful seminar and experimental séance at Faverdale Hall in County Durham. Hylton Thompson, a Chartered Engineer and Publicity Officer for the SNU (Spiritualists' National Union) Northern District

Council, was astonished at the sheer amount of precisely controlled physical energy released during the séance. He gives the following report;

The event began on the Friday evening when those lucky enough to be staying overnight were treated to a trance sitting with physical medium Stewart Alexander. One of Stewart's guides, White Feather, gave an introductory talk and then introduced the young child Christopher who held everyone spellbound with his quick wit and humour coupled with accurate evidence of survival for several of the sitters. Just before concluding, and with Stewart deeply entranced, Christopher invited us to switch on the lights and asked for a set of tweezers which one of the sitters promptly provided.

Alan Millichamp MSNU was then invited to test the depth of Stewart's trance by nipping his forearm with the tweezers. The medium did not respond but the mischievous Christopher was not satisfied and called upon George Cranley to 'have a go'. With the skill of a master butcher, George set about his allotted task – much to the horror of those nearby as he nipped, sliced and screwed the implement into the medium's flesh but to no avail. On returning from trance there was not a mark on Stewart's arm and he was not aware of what had happened until told later in the bar.

The daytime session on Saturday was taken up with seven excellent lectures by Officers of the Noah's Ark Society and an enthusiastic concluding 'question and answer' session and there were some fairly tough questions aimed at the panel by the 68 people who were all looking forward with excitement to the evening séance – they were not to be disappointed.

The medium was again Stewart Alexander and he was bound securely (checked by Judith Seaman MSNU and Hylton Thompson) into a strong armchair. The sitters were arranged in two concentric circles of twenty-four and forty-four, Stewart being a part of the inner one. White Feather commenced with an introduction explaining that this was the first séance in over twenty years which was outside the love and security of his home circle – there were a large number of sitters and the conditions were very different. Much depended upon harmony and the Spirit World would do its best to achieve success. He ended his eloquent address by saying that while the young boy Christopher endeavoured to reunite the two worlds, they would endeavour to gather energies both from the medium and from the circles for use in the experiment to create physical phenomena. Christopher – affectionately known to his circle as 'shuffle bottom' (and he did) – brought remarkably accurate evidence to several sitters interspersed with humorous banter. One of the most interesting was when Christopher approached a lady with a yellow jumper and silver hair (remember it was absolutely dark). There was no response until a lady in the outer circle admitted to having a yellow jumper. Asked what colour her hair was the lady said she liked to think of it as blonde. Amid the inevitable laughter, Christopher insisted that it was silver and asked us to put on the light which we did.

I think it safe to say that the majority took the same view as Christopher. A personal message then ensued and later the lady confirmed that it had been most evidential. Christopher then asked for music[2] to be played and eventually for everyone to sing. The drumsticks then began to beat loudly upon the small table in front of the medium and a hand bell rang loudly at such a rate of vibration that it would have been virtually impossible for a human hand to shake it fast enough – it sounded like an electric bell – and then it happened. One of the metal trumpets (identified by luminous rings on their bases) began moving slowly across the floor and almost appeared to investigate one of the microphones. It then took off and made several revolutions of the room just clearing the heads of the sitters. It then began to swing in time with the singing, almost as if conducting a choir. Then, increasing its speed, it began to describe a perfect circle in the vertical plane at such speed that it looked like a continuous luminous ring some 6 feet in diameter. The other trumpet then joined in and two luminous vertical circles were thus formed. The movements would periodically change into arcs; the trumpets then swinging independently rather like pendulums in time to the singing. The sophisticated form of levitation phenomena is often referred to as telekinesis which infers control by the mind. In this case the control was so precise and the energy expenditure so substantial that it could only be attributed to direct spirit control. Perhaps psychokinesis or dynamic levitation would be a more appropriate name. At one time Spirit simultaneously had the drumsticks beating, the bell ringing and both trumpets flying like two enormous Catherine-wheels.

---

(2) *Sound appears to be fundamental to the production of physical phenomena hence the sitters joining together in song at the appropriate time.*

This continued for a while until – and most of us assumed that Christopher was responsible – one of the trumpets came out of orbit and was beaten mercilessly and continuously against what we assumed and hoped was the floor. The overall noise at this time reached a crescendo and had to be heard to be believed. The experience of the séance, the harmonious atmosphere and indeed the humour therein will leave an indelible impression on all of our minds. This coupled with the knowledge gained from the most interesting lectures, leaves us all truly grateful to the NAS and to Stewart Alexander in particular for their efforts on our behalf.'

❖   ❖   ❖

This then completes the report of an early Noah's Ark Society seminar and my very first public séance. At that time my physical mediumship was still in an embryonic state and, as the reader will have noted, the phenomena were to some degree – disorganised although they were a clear demonstration of how the Spirit World can manipulate physical matter. However, as time passed, the phenomena were to be refined and developed as additional Spirit people became involved in their production and presentation.

Later reports will illustrate clearly that this was so.

Following that seminar séance event I continued to insist upon the application of restraints whenever I sat for the Society; ropes and ties securing my ankles, legs, chest and arms to the chair in which I sat and luminous knee tape and shoe laces. Such precautions enabled sitters to see that I remained secure in my seat throughout the course of the séances. As I pointed out earlier, these measures I firmly believed were very important if participants were to feel confident that the Spirit World alone was responsible for all that transpired and that I played no part other than in a passive sense. And so, for some years, that well established procedure was followed until, one night, two researchers attended an Ark séance. My wife, as always, was sitting outside the entrance door of the room in which it was held. This was to ensure that no one from outside could inadvertently enter once the séance was under way.

However, after it had finished and people were leaving the room, and as the two researchers passed by her she overheard one of them say to the other: 'Well, it was very interesting but did you notice that the ropes binding his chest were evenly spaced before the lights went out but were bunched together at the end when they came back on?'

Naturally she reported it to me.

My first reaction, apart from a sense of gross disappointment, was to instruct Ray Lister, our home circle leader, to have two metal plates made with a series of evenly spaced rings through which the ropes could pass. They would be screwed one at each side of the chair back rest and therefore the ropes slotted through the rings would then remain in their original position and separate from each other. This would immediately eliminate the possibility of any future doubt as a result of bunched chest ropes. Of course, Ray, understandably, objected. Rightly he pointed out that the researchers had merely betrayed their own jaundiced position in respect of physical mediumship. The ropes bunched because there was nothing to stop them doing so. Of course he was correct but I insisted and soon the plates were in place to be used at all sittings thereafter. Over time, I came to realise that irrespective of our efforts, it would never be possible to remove doubt from the minds of those whose psychological makeup was such that they would never be able to accept that fraud played no part.

Eventually, I took the decision to abandon most of the restraints. The luminous knee tape and shoe laces were both retained, as too were the plastic cable ties on the wrists and those because, by then, Walter, our Spirit communicator, largely responsible for the production and presentation of the physical manifestations, had developed the phenomenon of passing living matter-through-matter; freeing my arms by passing my wrists through the ties whilst often my hands were firmly held by the sitters on my left and right. I believed then, as I believe now, that the phenomena at my séances coupled with the survival evidence would surely speak for themselves! Having said that, floating trumpets and ringing bells in the dark séance room I have always accepted do not prove survival. However, if the medium is perfectly restrained so that he or she cannot possibly be physically responsible for such a demonstration, then one can safely postulate that some form of intelligence must be responsible. And when the physical phenomena are coupled with clear survival evidence, then the most logical conclusion must be that those who claim to be responsible are who they claim to be – visitors from the world of eternity!

On the Crest of a Wave – On the Horns of a Dilemma

During the Ark's early years, it looked very much as if it would go on to make a huge and far-reaching contribution to Spiritualism. It was filled with new ideas and had such aspirations, such hopes, such energy and vitality. Anything seemed possible then, and there was no question that it was working under the direction and guidance of the Spirit World. It had a wonderful committee of dedicated people all driven by the common belief that truly the Society was Spirit inspired. Seminar followed seminar at venues throughout the country and always with an experimental séance with Colin Fry (known then as Lincoln) or myself acting as the medium.

Then, in January 1993 the Ark conducted a full week seminar on Physical Mediumship at the headquarters of the Spiritualists' National Union (SNU) – the Arthur Findlay College at Stansted Hall, England. Once the home of Arthur Findlay, bequeathed to the Union on his death, it has long been regarded as the very Mecca of English Spiritualism.

Such was the interest in the Seminar that within forty-eight hours of the dates being announced publicly, it was fully subscribed with as many people again wishing to attend but unable to secure places.

I mention that event only because I was to give two physical séances during that week and shortly afterwards an article was published in the *Psychic News* in respect of them. Written by *Psychic Press* Chairman Roy Stemman, he commented that after witnessing trumpet aerobatics:

'A sceptical sitter may wonder why it was necessary to tie a medium so effectively when there were no controls over the other people present'.

The inference being of course that to the sceptical mind the medium could conceivably have had an accomplice responsible for manipulating the trumpets.

In response, and shortly afterwards, the following comment, written by Alf Winchester, appeared in the Ark's monthly *Newsletter*. At the time Alf was one of its committee members but would, a few years later, be appointed its President. As long valued supporters of my mediumship, he and his wife June were soon after that to be responsible for organising my seminars and occasionally my public séances at home and abroad.

'On Saturday February 27th 1993, at Scole[3] the spirit team of Stewart Alexander decided to demonstrate conclusively that there was no collusion by any incarnate individuals present at his séances whilst trumpet levitation was in progress. The demonstration was in response to a comment made in the psychic press concerning séances recently held by the Ark at Stansted Hall. Walter Stinson, the Spirit operative who fronts the Spirit team that produces the phenomena, instructed the sitters in the inner of the two concentric circles, to hold hands. The ladies who sat at either side of the medium were requested to place their free hands on the medium's knees so that both were controlled. The lady sitting to his left then placed her right foot on top of his left and the lady on his right placed her left foot on his right foot. Sitters in the outer circle were instructed to place their hands on the shoulders of the person sitting in front including the person sitting directly behind the medium. I was that person and as requested I immediately did as I was asked. Then whilst all participants were thus controlled, the two trumpets levitated and were said by some sitters to have reached up to 15 feet (4 metres) away from the medium. Whilst this phenomenon occurred all the sitters were satisfied that they had control of the adjacent sitters. The ladies seated at either side of Stewart Alexander reported the movement of ribbon-like trails across their arms as the trumpets flew and hovered round the room. Although some participants in the centre circle were the medium's circle members, the outer circle consisted of Ark members seated randomly around the circle'.

❖ ❖ ❖

At that time I naively believed that my mediumship could meet any objections and/or uncertainty expressed by possible denigrators and therefore quell adverse sceptical comment. But then of course, I failed utterly to appreciate that to have achieved that would have spectacularly surpassed the phenomena manifested in my own séance room.

Today I understand that the position of the hardened sceptic is immovable. However, the society continued its remarkable growth in membership both home and abroad. As it did so its monthly *Newsletter* was to be gradually converted from a piecemeal publication to a highly

---

(3) *During the early years of its existence the headquarters of the Noah's Ark Society was at Scole in Norfolk*

professional one. Excellent articles were published covering a whole variety of topics in respect of contemporary and historic physical mediumship. We were all on a roller coaster that promised to halt and reverse Spiritualism's decline. But then slowly and by degrees it all started to go wrong and in 1999, I was driven to make one of the most difficult decisions that I had ever had to make in my life.

For some time I had been uneasy in respect of the direction in which the society was proceeding. In addition, there were other important internal committee matters with which I emphatically disagreed. Although there is no necessity for me to expand upon them here, my conviction at the time was that the Society was no longer upon the same spiritual pathway as myself. It was time to go and I duly tendered my membership resignation.

Although I have hesitated considerably over revealing the following details, I believe that they are of such fundamental importance to, and have such a direct bearing upon My Journey that I am left with no choice but to do so.

At that time I had a great many friends amongst its membership and felt strongly I had a duty to explain my decision. I thereupon submitted to the editor of the *Newsletter* an article for publication, in which I outlined my reasons for leaving the Society. Sadly, it was suppressed, never to see the light of day, and the membership was left to speculate over my withdrawal. For a Past President of an organisation to be denied such a right told me that my decision had been wise. Such suppression, I believed, could be neither ethically nor morally defended.

In spite of everything, I genuinely harboured no bitterness towards the Society and I clearly recognised that, to its members, it represented the best of Spiritualism. It was their path – it was no longer my path – I wished it well.

However, my resignation was not an isolated event. Excellent committee members had also gone before me for similar reasons, including the two people who had launched the Noah's Ark Society – Robin and Sandra Foy. With a constant leakage of members, I firmly believed that the writing was on the wall and that it would eventually collapse. Five years later it did so.

Chapter 7

A Dip into the Society's Archives

Some of the remarkable historic accounts of séances with legendary mediums originally published in the Noah's Ark Society's Newsletter.

In this chapter are a number of articles, first published on the dates shown by the Noah's Ark Society in its monthly *Newsletter*. Minor amendments to the originals have been made in an effort to make them more comprehensible to readers who may have little knowledge of physical mediumship.

The first, I personally wrote, based upon an interview I was privileged to have had with a Mr Norman Stacey, at his home in the North-East of England during the summer of 1990. Prior to publication it was submitted to him for confirmation of all the details it contained. The remaining articles were written by the gentlemen who had enjoyed the experiences reported. Over a period of several years, through personal contact, I got to know the first three well and I judged them to be sincere and truthful and I am therefore satisfied that the events related took place as described.

The final article was contributed to the *Newsletter* by a discerning and respected member of the Ark. Although I knew him only slightly, I have taken the decision to include his account because it detailed his sitting many years earlier with the medium William Olsen. Although today largely forgotten, during the 1950s he was well known and respected by Spiritualists. Yet accounts of his séances are comparatively rare when considered alongside those of other public physical mediums of the day. Olsen was one of the few trumpet mediums ever to travel the country to demonstrate publicly and the final account in this chapter will give readers an insight into what allegedly was a unique mediumship.

Lest We Should Forget

Originally published in *The Noah's Ark Newsletter*, September 1990.

Stewart Alexander, Archives Officer

To many present day Spiritualists, the medium Hunter Selkirk is largely unknown and yet, amongst a cluster of small villages south of Newcastle, he is remembered with considerable respect and has subsequently become something of a legend. People remember and refer to him with true affection. Remarkable accounts of his public clairvoyant demonstrations and of his physical séances regularly abound and stories are told and retold. If one visits the area, it is not at all difficult to find elderly people willing to share their personal recollections and they do so with both warmth and enthusiasm.

Hunter Selkirk's public demonstrations of mental mediumship at Spiritualist churches invariably saw them filled to overflowing with standing room only. However, it is with the startling physical manifestations within his séance room with which we are concerned here. During the war years a small book entitled 'Listen My Son'[1] (still in print today) was published by the Craghead Village Spiritualist Church of which Hunter, for a while, was President. It was written by a gentleman called Harry Emerson and gives a graphic, dramatic and often moving account of the medium's séances. The book was born out of a series of letters which were written by him to his soldier son who, at that time, was fighting overseas.

It tells of how, in the séance room, he had repeatedly witnessed extraordinary physical manifestations and met again his deceased wife (the boy's mother) who would materialise in solid form. Hunter Selkirk was an exceptional medium as made abundantly clear by the Foreword to the 1984 edition of the book, from which I now quote an edited passage :

'It is almost 40 years since the first publication of 'Listen My Son' by Harry Emerson and it is just over fifty years since the Spiritualist Church was first established in Craghead. Both church and book were influenced by the exceptional character and mediumship of Hunter Selkirk. Clothed in the unassuming mantle

(1) *This book is highly recommended to readers who may wish to learn more about Hunter Selkirk. Publishers; Craghead SNU Church, Front Street, Craghead, Stanley, Co.Durham - DH9 6DS.*

of a working man Hunter had been blessed with a gift of special dimensions'.

A few weeks ago I was privileged to visit a gentleman by the name of Norman Stacey who had invited me to his home in the North-East and who had known Hunter Selkirk well. I spent a full day in his company and was enthralled with his memories of Hunter the man and Hunter the medium. These were personal to him and could not be read in any book or published account of the mediumship. Two of those fascinating recollections I reproduce below with his consent.

One of the principal guides in Hunter's circle was a very young coloured girl known affectionately as Topsy. Clearly her responsibility had been to remove any tension amongst the sitters and this she did in a childlike way with good humour and sharp wit.

Stacey told me that occasionally she would fully materialise and leave the cabinet in which Hunter invariably sat in a deep state of trance. Often she would remain materialised for long periods and chat to the sitters. This would invariably take place in dim red light so that she would be visible to everyone within the séance room. Occasionally, whilst this was happening other voices could be heard speaking from within the cabinet and periodically additional materialised Spirit people would emerge from it thereby proving that fraud, as a possible explanation, was certainly not a tenable possibility.

Sometimes little Topsy would be asked questions and I was told that often her replies apparently belied her age and that one night this was pointed out to her. She was asked whether, in reality, she was really a small child. The sitters that night, which included my informant, wondered if she merely assumed that persona to best achieve her objective to eliminate understandable nervous tension which would have hindered the manifestations.

Topsy had been silent for a while before replying that indeed she was not. Upon being asked if the sitters would ever be allowed to see her as she really was she had replied that she would be happy to show her real self but warned that should she do so then the Spirit World would not be able to continue with the séance afterwards. By common agreement Topsy was asked to go ahead and everyone had waited in anticipation not knowing what to expect. Thereupon, in good red light, and in full view of everyone present, the little girl had raised her tiny arms at right angles to her body and then quite suddenly had begun to grow. Her features began to change and seconds later all found themselves gazing intently upon a fully formed white girl possibly in her mid to late teens.

Understandably, the passage of years since that phenomenal occurrence had in no way dimmed Norman Stacey's memory of that remarkable incident although another one was shortly to follow.

One summer's evening, he, Harry Emerson and Hunter Selkirk had held an impromptu table tilting séance. The medium who apparently was always 'matter of fact' about his own mediumship, suggested that they place their hands lightly upon the table top.

Within seconds his head had fallen upon his chest and he began to breathe heavily as he fell into the trance state. The other two had then watched as – in good light – a thick stream of ectoplasm had emerged from the medium's mouth and slowly descended to the table top.

Once there it divided itself into two streams and then slowly formed, at opposite ends of the table, into individual mounds, out of which animated forms had then started to manifest. One was that of a man and the other that of a woman. Both had attained a height of approximately twelve inches. One stood facing Emerson and the other faced my informant. Both were pure white in colour and were attired in 'Queen Anne' period dress. The two astounded men clearly observed details such as the lace of the female's dress and the male's shirt cuffs. The buckles and the boots were – like everything else – in miniature. I was assured that these tiny figures were alive and animated. The little figures had then bowed several times to the two men but they had been so incredulous that neither of them had been capable of responding. Then, as they watched, the materialised forms had quickly dissolved into the two component mounds which themselves were quickly reabsorbed back into the medium.

A short time later Hunter came out of his trance and with no conception as to what had just taken place, asked; 'Has anything happened?'

In 1965 at the age of sixty-five Hunter Selkirk passed into Spirit.

❖ ❖ ❖

Amazing Experiences I Have Enjoyed

Originally published in *The Noah's Ark Newsletter*, August 1991.
Gene Woods (From Kettering, Ohio, U.S.A.)

Throughout my lifetime I have been privileged to experience séance room work by some gifted mediums, and I am now seventy-four years of age. My brother, sister and I are third generation Spiritualists, beginning with my paternal grandparents in the mid 1870s.

I supposed that I had seen the best of mediumship throughout my life, until I discovered a man thirteen years ago whose gifts were so astounding that as I relate only a few of my experiences with him, the events may seem impossible to believe, as indeed they did to me at the time that they occurred. I may ask myself if those events actually took place, or whether I had hallucinated? However, as many as ten other people present would also have had to have shared the same hallucination if that were the explanation. All the séances were recorded on audio tape, and the witnesses are still living.

Sadly, due to ill health, the medium involved is no longer working and I do not feel free to identify him without his consent. At present, I am unaware of his location.

He was a physical medium and many of the materialisations that manifested at his séances were cloaked in a drapery of ectoplasm. Occasionally however they were fully developed and appeared in their natural colours such as an American Indian who appeared dressed in his full regalia. On one very happy occasion my sister and I had the opportunity to meet our fully materialised mother[2] and we were able to hold her hands and talk to her whilst peering into her perfectly formed face. The meeting ended as she kissed each of us on the cheek.

On another occasion we held a séance in the basement of our local Spiritualist church with seven people in attendance. The red

(2) *In describing this wonderful event to me on audio correspondence tape – Gene Woods insisted that his mother had been 'exactly' as he and his sister had remembered her. Her appearance and character had left them in absolutely no doubt that it was their mother as against some kind of mannequin or simply an impostor. The three of them had spoken together for some time about family issues etc and in his own words; 'Stewart, without any conceivable doubt, she was our living breathing mother and she had not changed in any way.'*

light illuminating the room was exceptionally bright making excellent visibility possible. Following the appearance of several materialised loved ones, we were told by the medium's control (Guide) that he would like to try an experiment. I was asked to bring a séance trumpet from across the room and place it on the floor between my knee and the knee of a fourteen-year-old boy who was sitting next to me.

The control then asked us to talk amongst ourselves whilst he returned to the cabinet. After about one minute, there came a sudden sound from the trumpet as a great sheet of ectoplasm whisked out of the trumpet top (small end) and the sound it made was very audible and very startling and this was captured on the audio tape.

This ectoplasmic sheet floated to the centre of the room, formed into a mass out of which slowly the control, who had earlier returned to the cabinet, built and emerged. With a chuckle he asked 'Now – how did you like that?'

During the same séance the medium's mother materialised and spoke to us about conditions in the Spirit World. I was asked to approach her where she stood in the centre of the room. Then she asked me to reach out and to hold her hands to verify how solid and warm they were. She then asked me to feel around her mid section to testify how solid her body was explaining that this was her astral body which was produced by a lowering of her vibrational rate. She then asked me to step backwards whilst she changed into her etheric body which took a few seconds. Neither I nor any of the other sitters present took our eyes off her and we observed no change whatsoever in her. Her appearance was no different and she remained animated and talking to us. Then she asked me to touch her again. As I reached forward so my hand swept back and forth through her body touching nothing but thin air. It was as if I was literally putting my hand and arm into a mirage! After we had thanked her for that remarkable experience she simply vanished before our eyes just like the turning off of a lamp. This was one of the most enlightening experiences of my life and is still vivid in my memory.

The medium held many séances in the cellar of my home using a makeshift cabinet. During one session my grandfather materialised and that was such a joy.

During a trumpet séance before the medium became entranced

we were all chatting with him. One trumpet suddenly rose into the air and moved around the cellar touching all the sitters on their heads. Then came the voice of the medium's control speaking to us through the second trumpet and talking to us whilst the medium was still conscious. This took place for several minutes before entrancement occurred – it was most enjoyable.

It is a well known fact that physical mediums have a fear of someone introducing a light in some way during a séance, or some sceptic trying to get to the medium hoping to uncover fraud with no thought whatsoever that their actions might result in harm to the medium's health. Because of this, on a few occasions, the medium asked me to sit at the side of the cabinet for his protection. In these situations the cabinet and I were at one end of the room with the sitters at the opposite end where the red light hung on   the wall above and behind them. Arranged like this, when the materialised Spirit people came from beside me and moved into the centre of the room, they were silhouetted against the light. Generally they were clothed in a drapery of ectoplasm, and through its translucence I could plainly see the nude body forms of males, females and children – tall, short, heavy, thin – all different!

Prior to his leaving our local church to move to another church in another city, the medium held one final séance. Instead of the expected ten or fifteen sitters, there were about forty and therefore too great a number to seat in our séance room. Therefore, several men went into the sanctuary of the church and moved all the pews to one end and created a makeshift cabinet in the centre of the room. The red light was then mounted in a less than ideal location. After a prayer and some singing, a cloud of ectoplasm was observed to rise from the top of the cabinet growing larger and larger before taking on the form of the upper half of a body until the head touched the twenty foot high ceiling. Its arms were seen to stretch from wall to wall. After about one minute, the form slowly gathered itself up and receded through the top of the cabinet. Then, this spectacle was followed by at least twenty separate materialisations some of whom seated themselves at the side of sitters to whom they chatted and who were their loved ones.

All the things reported in this article I personally witnessed in the presence of this man who was the most wonderful and complete medium that I have known during my seventy-four years.

❖ ❖ ❖

A Sitting With Helen Duncan

Originally published in *The Noah's Ark Newsletter*, August 1990.
William Cookson (From Perth, Scotland)

During the spring of 1947, in total ignorance of Spiritualism, I took part in a unique experiment. I was privileged to witness a very remarkable demonstration of physical mediumship by the famous materialisation medium Mrs Helen Duncan.

At that time I was a young man working as a builder in a place called Cowdenbeath and there I met a man called Mr Latimer. Little did I realise what an impact that meeting was to have on my long held religious beliefs. Spiritualism I had long regarded with cynicism and I was strongly opposed to what I considered to be its calculated nonsense.

One Saturday, shortly after our meeting, Mr Latimer invited me to a séance.

Following a great deal of hesitation and self-recrimination curiosity won the day and I decided to go. At the appointed time I stood at the door of a tenement building (No.5 Bain Street) in Lochgelly, Scotland, and found myself walking up a staircase still regretting my decision to participate in 'the unknown'. I was introduced to Mrs Duncan who was a very large lady (22 stones) and Mr Latimer took me through to a small room devoid of any furniture except for a large sideboard and a row of chairs placed in a circle. A wooden chair with open curtains in front of it stood in a corner, and there was a red light in the ceiling above. Eventually we took our seats and Mrs Duncan sat on the one behind the curtains which were then closed. The red light was switched on and we waited.

What can I possibly say regarding what then followed other than the fact that I found the experience shattering? Soon a very tall gentleman appeared from behind the curtains and introduced himself as Albert Stewart, Mrs Duncan's guide. He was slim, six feet tall, bearded and spoke with what I believe is often referred to as an educated Oxford accent. He was draped in a substance which I have since learnt to be ectoplasm and he invited questions from the sitters which he answered eloquently. He explained many aspects concerning the Spirit World and finally returned to within the cabinet and disappeared behind the curtains.

What happened next was to be the greatest emotional experience of my life, apart from the recent passing of my wife after thirty-five years of marriage. I saw a mother embrace her materialised daughter, who I later learnt had passed with tuberculosis at the local Hillside hospital, a fact that I recently confirmed by consulting the hospital records.

Both the mother and her materialised daughter were reduced to tears of joy during this reunion.

A small baby was carried forward by the entranced medium to an overawed mother.

A young girl appeared next with a bunch of flowers and embraced her mother and father who were amongst the sitters that night. A very old lady appeared, described by Albert Stewart as of the Catholic faith. She had a crucifix the length of her entire body and the lines and creases of her forehead were clearly visible.

Although I was there only as an observer imagine my feelings when Albert (from within the cabinet) told me that a Spirit visitor had come for me.

Then, from out of it strode my brother David, who had died aged thirteen but now showed himself as a twenty-six year old – the age he would have been had he still been alive. He made the conversation and because I was so scared I refused to take his hand when he offered it to me.

He said, 'What a surprise. When I was told that I could come I didn't believe it. How are you – and mother and father?'

Before he returned to the cabinet he said that perhaps one day we would meet again in the same way. We never have and since then I have never heard from him again.

We were then treated to a song and dance act by a little girl called 'Peggy', another regular control of the medium, and she sang 'Deep in the Heart of Texas'.

Ever since that remarkable evening, I have carried with me complete conviction and knowledge of personal survival beyond death.

❖ ❖ ❖

98

'Just William'

Originally published in *The Noah's Ark Newsletter*, October 1990.

John Squires

When the Noah's Ark Society Chairman asked if I would contribute an account of my past séance experiences I pondered a great deal over my lingering memories of a lifetime associated with psychic matters. For instance, I had, when seventeen years of age, sat in Manchester with Helen Duncan. I recalled my incredulity when I had observed the manifestation of seventeen materialised forms and how whilst still talking they had gradually sunk downwards through the floor and disappeared. But my awe and wonder at the sheer range of physical mediumship has always been accredited to the two sittings I attended in Birmingham with the Sheerness (Kent) medium, William Olsen.

By invitation of the church secretary I had taken tea with her, the church President and Mr and Mrs Olsen prior to the first séance. I admit to being a little apprehensive at meeting 'Willie' but I need not have worried. I found him to be a short, stocky, red-faced man in his fifties with a pronounced Geordie accent and a delicious sense of humour and fun. He kept up a flow of banter whilst his wife eyed him solicitously and watched how much he ate and drank. Never before had I seen such vitality.

Later, at the séance, twenty-five people were in attendance, sitting in a large circle configuration and I had a seat next but one to the medium. His seat was a simple wooden Windsor armchair which had a portable red light facing it, the intensity of which could be adjusted by means of a rheostat. Together with another sitter I was invited to an upstairs room to search 'Willie' to ensure that he took nothing (implement or device) into the séance and we checked everything. By this time his eyes were half closed and he was breathing heavily as he began to sink into a state of trance. We led him down into the séance room and to his chair where one of the lady sitters sewed his jacket from the bottom hem to his collar. He was then roped into his seat and the hall lights were extinguished leaving only the rheostat red light which illuminated the medium. At this stage he was seen to be swaying a little and he was breathing heavily. His wife then led us in song with her raucous voice and the séance had begun.

A few minutes of singing and then Mrs Olsen commanded

silence and Willie began to speak in a cut-glass public school accent and we were informed that he was being controlled by an entity who claimed to be a scientist. He spoke of his intention to demonstrate the extrusion of visible ectoplasm – the production of independent voices (voices independent of the medium) – the levitation of objects and finally the levitation of the medium in his chair.

Mrs Olsen then commenced singing once again and startled us all with her ear-splitting voice and we all joined in. Heavy sighs came from the medium and then as his head rolled from side to side we all went quiet. I leaned forward expectantly towards his contorted face which was well illuminated by the red light and saw a white filmy substance coming from his mouth and his nostrils. It grew quickly and extended outwards and downwards whilst constantly shimmering white. It spread into a wide semi-circle around Willie's feet only a few inches from my own. All was then still and I noted that the partly transparent gossamer-like substance was pulsing along its breadth and its length as if in unison with the medium's heartbeat. Then, quite suddenly, it vanished. I fixed my eyes on his face and saw ectoplasm once again emerging from it. This time it formed into a structure resembling an elephant's trunk and as it swayed in the air before us I noted tiny finger like grippers had formed on its extremity. Watching in amazement I observed the 'trunk' as it curled upwards and backwards over the medium's head and saw how the little grippers took hold of the jacket collar. Slowly the garment was drawn upwards until clear of Willie's head and then in a convulsive movement the structure flicked it onto the floor in the centre of the room before quickly disappearing. Turning to the medium I could see that his legs and arms were still securely tied to the chair.

A brief pause in the proceedings then followed after which a skipping rope which was on a small table near to me was lifted up and began to skip around the room. This was made visible by the luminous paint on its handles and everyone could hear it as it struck the floor. A tambourine then shot into the air and proceeded to play and two small bells with luminous dots tinkled merrily as they danced in the air. All this time I kept peering at Willie in the glow of the red light. The effects then subsided and we awaited the next phase of the séance which came quickly. The two trumpets with luminous markings zoomed straight up into the air like rockets and they proceeded to weave around each other near the high ceiling. They swooped down and all the sitters ducked as they hissed past us – so near that we could feel the wind they created. They flew, ducked, weaved and danced exuberantly for several minutes before finally each trumpet assumed positions on opposite sides of the room and hovered at head height. Now the voices began and I could hear the sounds from both the trumpets. All around the room sitters were responding to the voices of their loved ones. From the trumpets came male and female voices and the sound of children chattering enthusiastically. At one time three spirit voices were speaking simultaneously with William Olsen in good view of all.

Then, once again Mrs Olsen broke into song with everyone joining in and then the red light was extinguished. A few seconds later there came a blinding flash of light followed by a shattering crash on the far side of the circle. The lights were called for and as we all blinked in the light we saw that the medium, still firmly tied into his chair and entranced, had been levitated and deposited at the far side of the circle of sitters. He was in his shirt sleeves and the jacket upon being closely examined was found to be as before with the stitching undisturbed. The medium was released and taken out of the room leaving the sitters to chat excitedly amongst themselves.

Eventually he rejoined us and as we all enjoyed a cup of tea I noticed that he appeared to be as fresh as a daisy – positively glowing with health. Later, in his hotel room he regaled me with the story of his life – how he had discovered his powers following the death of his son due to a road accident. He told me of the fact that his mediumship had been tested many times but that nothing ever satisfied the investigators. He spoke of sceptics shining torches upon him during séances and of the frustration suffered and the dangers posed by those opposed to physical mediumship. Many were Spiritualists who considered that his mediumship was of a lower form as against the presentation of abstract platform philosophy.

Mr Olsen was finally dragged to bed by his wife in the early hours of the morning and I was left to reflect on this extraordinary man.

I believe that simplicity was the key to his powers. He was not interested in the mechanics involved with his mediumship and he did not allow speculation to get in the way of the phenomena. He was a descent, honest, humorous man who was simply an unquestioning channel. In fact … Just William.

❖ ❖ ❖

The NAS during its lifetime received many rich accounts of past séance room wonders but I believe that the ones included here are representative of the events that can manifest in them. Surely they can only be dismissed by objective readers who conclude that the informants were either gullible fools who saw what they expected to see, or that they were dishonest.

My close contact over a number of years with three of them leads me to insist that they were neither. John Squires, although not personally known to me, was highly regarded and respected by several learned members of the Ark's committee.

It is hardly surprising that such wonderful events remained crystal clear in the minds of those who witnessed them and that they could be recalled many years later with clarity.

Finally, if there is any virtue and veracity to be found in human testimony, then, at the very least, we must surely give serious consideration to reports included in this chapter whilst bearing in mind that they are but a few amongst the many.

Chapter 8

The Home Circle

Introducing members of our home circle ~ A member of my home circle tells of her experience when the Spirit team enabled her to feel the ectoplasm ~ Spirit people help a lady, deaf since birth, to hear clearly each time she attends the circle.

Although I had been sitting regularly in various home circles since 1969 it would not be until 1988, following our departure from the bike shop, that Ray and I would create our final circle. This has now been meeting in a small room on the first floor of Ray and June's home for the past twenty-two years. During that time its composition has largely remained unchanged with permanent members Ray (our circle leader), June, his wife, their daughter Denise and myself; together with my sister Gaynor[1], and my brother Michael, although sadly he was to leave the circle in the year 2000 when he relocated to Spain. However, in 2008 we were joined by Gaynor's daughter Lindsey and by York couple, Chris and Jane Jackson. In the following year the circle was to increase in size again with the addition of Carol Petch, but now I am ahead of myself and must return to 1993, for it was in that year that we were to be honoured by a visit from a gentleman called Tom Harrison.

I had first made contact with Tom, by letter, four years earlier, after reading his booklet 'Visits by Our Friends from the Other Side'. This was based on his diaries, records and recollections of his mother's materialisation circle from the 1940s and 50s. I was struck at the time by his obvious sincerity and by his extraordinary accounts of meeting, on hundreds of occasions, the solid materialised forms of the living dead.

Sadly, such phenomena, once so important to the Movement and regarded by many as the crème de la crème of mediumship, have, this

(1) *My sister Gaynor was tragically involved in a road accident, and passed into the Spirit World on Saturday, 7 February 2009.*

past half a century, almost died away. From him – as one of its last surviving witnesses – I knew that I could learn such a great deal.

Tom was born into a Spiritualist family in 1918 and his mother Minnie Rose had developed her natural mediumistic gifts from childhood. At the age of just four he sat on his mother's knee in the family's home circle. After he was demobbed from the army in 1946 with the rank of major, he returned home to Middlesbrough where, for a few years, he was to work in industry. Throughout that period however, and within weeks of his army demob, the home circle with his mother as the medium had begun. Perhaps, in view of later developments within it, he was therefore destined to devote his future life to the Spiritualist cause. Indeed, it would be in 1966, just three years after the launch of a family-run restaurant that fate would intervene. He was offered and accepted the post as Founder Manager of the Arthur Findlay College at Stansted Hall. During Tom's time there, it was suggested to him that he should travel the country to tell of his mother's remarkable mediumship and of her circle where he had been so privileged to witness such wonderful phenomena. (More about this in Chapter 14.)

In 1991 Tom and I finally met when I heard him give a talk at an early Noah's Ark Society Seminar and immediately we struck up a friendship. Then, on the 19th April 1993 he made the long journey from his home near High Wycombe in Buckinghamshire, to sit with our circle.

On that night, we all felt highly privileged that he had accepted our invitation and we welcomed him as a highly honoured guest. Although it is not for me to record here the events of that particular sitting[2], I can state that thereafter he regularly visited the North and our circle. These visits were principally to give his renowned and mesmerising talks about his mother's séances where, years earlier, he had enjoyed the unique experience of witnessing over 1500 materialisations – men, women and children – the 'living dead'.

It was to be at one of those talks that he was to meet his future wife, Ann, who lived in a village on the outskirts of my home town, Kingston-upon-Hull. His visits to the North and to our circle then became more frequent and in 1995 he finally moved into the area to live with Ann.

(2) *Interested readers will find a detailed account of the séance in Tom's book: 'Life After Death: Living Proof' published by Saturday Night Press Publications, 2008.*

Thereupon, to our delight, we were pleased to welcome them both as permanent circle members which they remained until they too left for Spain some five years later. However, in common with my brother Michael, they are now honorary members of the circle and visit us whenever they are back in the UK.

When Tom first brought Ann to the circle, she had never before experienced physical phenomena but it would not be long before she took to it like the proverbial duck is said to take to water. Her knowledge of such matters is today extensive and she and Tom now work closely together in the presentation of his talks.

But, back then, she sat with no practical experience but from her very first visit she sat with absolute sincerity. Four years later in August 1998 this was to be repaid when, in the absence of my sister Gaynor, she was invited to sit on my left hand side which was Gaynor's usual position in the circle. There she was to have a remarkable experience.

Ann's Account

Part of the way through the evening Freda (a Spirit communicator) asked us to test the red light (mounted on the underside of the glass topped table – situated in front of Stewart) so that they could assess the brightness that the ectoplasm would be able to stand during the séance. Then, as the ectoplasm was extracted from Stewart, via the navel we were told, we could hear it fizzing and crackling and Michael joked about it being the cheesecloth that mediums are supposed to secrete to produce their 'apparitions'. I commented that it sounded more like crinkly cellophane and Tom said that it was just as he remembered it to be 50 years before. That night we were able to turn the light up, brighter than ever before, and see an amorphous blob of ectoplasm, in silhouette, against the under-lit table. It then formed into a pincer with which a 'trumpet' could have been picked up.

Freda instructed us to turn out the light and asked me to put out my hand, but to turn it with the palm up. I held out my right hand towards Stewart. My wrist was grasped by strong fingers so that I could not move it. Stewart, as usual, was fastened into his chair with ropes, and his arms secured to the arms of his chair with strong cable ties so it could not have been his hand grasping my wrist. I then felt something moving across my fingers. In texture it was like a small, thin plastic bag full of wobbly liquid. The 'bag' rolled up and down across my fingers and then suddenly it was gone and my wrist was released. I put my hand back onto my knee.

Freda spoke, 'Again, Ann.' I held out my hand and again, fingers grasped my wrist. This time what seemed to be a piece of thin but roughish 'cloth' was laid and then pulled across my fingers. I told the others 'Something is lying across my hand. It's like cloth.' Immediately the response came from Freda, 'Like cheesecloth.' Yes it was!

And it felt quite different from a previous occasion when it had felt just like silk voile. As quickly as it had come, it was gone. We heard Freda again, 'Then let us try it in what, I suppose, could be described as its dematerialised state. That is to say the state before it takes on a solid form. Give me your hand again, Ann. You must tell everyone here if you are able to feel anything.'

When I put out my hand this time, as well as it being held at the wrist, other fingers grasped the tips of my fingers. There was a slight regurgitating sound from Stewart, and then across my hand came cool air. Very gently, a beautiful cool breeze was flowing across my hand. The feeling is difficult to describe because it was nothing like someone blowing on your hand, but more like the cold air that flows on to you when you open the freezer.

It continued for some seconds before I became aware that the coolness was decreasing and the 'breeze' was becoming quite warm. My hand was released and I lowered my arm.

Once again I had been honoured. They had given me the experience that so few people have – to know the feel of that most rare substance – ectoplasm. I had previously felt it as flesh when Walter, another member of the Spirit team, invited me to feel the back of his hand when he materialised it against the under-lit table. But to be trusted and loved so much to be given that evening's unique experience was a wonderment.

I feel I have been given these amazing 'close encounters' because of the contact I have with people when Tom gives his talks about his mother's mediumship, to be able to pass on to them how near our Spirit friends really are, and what is possible between us when there is dedication of purpose bonded with love, harmony and trust.

❖   ❖   ❖

Since 1988, with an established enduring circle and a permanent venue, my mediumistic development continued in an atmosphere of stability and with Spirit orchestrated direction. We had never thought in terms of 'us and them' rather it has always been a shared venture. Our Spirit friends have often spoken of 'our team' and 'their own team' and how, once the séance room door closes and we open the circle, the two teams merge to become as one. Always our combined intention has been to do all that we can to be of service to the great immutable reality. The Spirit World has consistently maintained that our work does not only benefit the people who come to us in the hope that their loved ones may communicate, but also people within their reality, within their world, who are just as anxious to make a connection. Over the years we have observed the slow but steady progress of the circle and how existing physical manifestations, whilst often repetitive, have expanded to include new levels of physical communication. Of course, there have been many occasions when home circle sittings have apparently been blank and I believe that it will always be so.

Two-world communication is tenuous – it is fragile, and frankly we have little conception of the conditions that may effect and influence it. All we can do – all we can ever do – is to work in full co-operation with the Spirit people and give always of our best.

Katie Halliwell

Within the home circle séance room, I have on occasions witnessed extraordinary occurrences that transcended the phenomena that we had come to regard as the norm. Whilst it is true that communication of any kind with the Spirit World is in itself wonderful, those events particularly impressed me because they were not only unusual but because they were remarkable even for the physical séance room.

One of those involved Katie Halliwell, who since birth has been severely deaf in both ears and depends entirely upon her hearing aids. Her story rightly falls into two parts and with her permission I reproduce below both her accounts in shortened form.

In the first, which appears in Part One of her trilogy of books 'Experiences of Trance, Physical Mediumship and Associated Phenomena with the Stewart Alexander Circle'[3] she tells of her first sitting with the circle in 1999.

_____

(3) *3rd Edition published by Saturday Night Press Publications. 2008 (1st & 2nd Editions published privately, 2003, 2004).*

Following further private and public sittings with the circle she was moved to write loose notes about her experiences for her family and friends only to discover that they failed to understand and appreciate the reality of her experiences – a common reaction. How indeed can those without knowledge or experience of such matters be expected to accept that the dead return in the séance room to speak in their own voices and appear as solid flesh and blood animated human beings! And so the idea of a book (as mentioned on the previous page) with an accompanying CD of recorded Spirit voices was born together with a transcript for the hard of hearing. First published in August 2003, two further books with CDs have followed and all three are now available throughout the world and together they present a sincere record of one woman's experience of physical mediumship.

I present below brief details of Katie Halliwell's first sitting with the circle. Not because it was in any way unusual as a séance but because it had a direct bearing upon the future course of her life and is directly linked to her second account which was published in Part Two of the trilogy[4]. In that report she informs her readers of a most singular phenomenon that has continued to repeat itself whenever she sits with us.

Hull Séance Report, 8th July 1999

Originally published in *Experiences of Trance, Physical Mediumship and Associated Phenomena with the Stewart Alexander Circle: Part One, 2008*

The time is 10am on July 9th 1999 and I am sitting in a picnic area glancing over the pond at the Burton Agnes Hall in East Yorkshire[5]. There is a lovely cool breeze and today is very special. I write these notes with a feeling of elation and with tears of happiness in my eyes.

For many years I have had an interest in the possibility of an afterlife. I have visited Spiritualist churches, had private sittings with mediums and I have read a great deal about physical mediumship. Earlier this year, I booked through the Noah's Ark Society a place in a HomeCircle. The medium was Mr Stewart

---

(4) *Experiences of Trance & Physical Phenomena etc.-Part Two:- Published by Saturday Night Press Publications: 1st edition 2006; Revised Edition, 2008.*
(5) *A beautiful Elizabethan house open to the public.*

Alexander. I had never personally witnessed physical séance room phenomena before and I had never sat in absolute darkness.

I wasn't nervous at that prospect but I was quite apprehensive although excited at the same time.

At this point I must mention that I am very hard of hearing and I was concerned that I might not have been able to hear the Spirit voices in the dark. I knew, of course, that lip reading would not be possible.

Yesterday afternoon I arrived at my hotel in Hull and following a meal I telephoned Ray Lister (the circle leader) to tell him that I had arrived. A little later he collected me from the hotel. To my relief I found him to be lovely and warm-hearted with a happy personality and straight away this put me at my ease. At his home I was introduced to the circle members and we chatted for a while.

Unfortunately I was unable to pick up group conversation and I was concerned that I would not be able to hear at the séance. However, Ray told me not to worry as he would be sitting next to me and would interpret for me if necessary.

At 8pm we all went up to the little room on the second floor where the séance was to be held.

Stewart was strapped firmly into his chair and I noticed that attached to his knees were two luminous tabs which I could clearly see once the lights were turned off. I could also see the luminous paint at the broad ends of the two trumpets and I was entirely satisfied that no one in that room could have moved around without bumping into things.

A member of the circle opened the séance in prayer and soft music was then played. Shortly afterwards the voice of the North American Indian, White Feather, began to speak, seemingly from mid air, and he gave his blessings to the meeting. I then commented about the loud volume of the voice which had so amazed me.

Ray replied that he was the quiet one. Then, a child began to speak. This was Christopher. A loving, cheerful, laughing soul who put us all at ease very quickly. The atmosphere was one of love and all my earlier apprehension simply faded away. Following the little boy another regular communicator, known as Freda, came and spent some time speaking to various people.

Then Ray was asked to play some music on the cassette player and soon one trumpet began to float in the air and shortly afterwards the other one joined it. Both moved around above us and one soared up to the ceiling. The other made rapid movements as it approached one sitter after another.

And then one slowed down and hovered in front of me. Ray remarked that it was looking at me and I replied; 'Yes it is.' Then the trumpet slowly and directly touched my left arm and gently stroked it whilst the bell that had been on the séance table top commenced ringing and the drumsticks began to play. Walter, another member of the Spirit team responsible for all the physical phenomena, called for the little table to be placed in front of Stewart.

I was called forward and was instructed to sit facing the medium at its other side. The table light was then switched on and I was able to see the ectoplasm roll on to the table.

It appeared to resemble thick paste, a kind of thick mist and in places it was transparent. I felt privileged to witness this and soon I saw a finger form out of the substance and then a thumb appeared and then another finger. Soon a fully formed materialised hand was before me and it touched my fingers and stroked the back of my hand. I expected the ectoplasm to be wet, cold and slimy, but to my surprise it wasn't. The hand – as Walter himself had said – would feel perfectly normal and indeed – it did.

I came away from that séance feeling wonderfully elated. I felt so privileged to have been touched by Walter's hand; to have been touched by the hand of a soul from the Spirit World. I close this report by emphasising the extreme love that the Spirit people expressed throughout and the care and consideration that they had for my hearing deficiency.

❖ ❖ ❖

Help and Healing from the Spirit World – 2000 to 2003.

Originally published in *Part Two* of the Katie Halliwell trilogy, 2006

As I recorded in Part One of my trilogy, I am severely deaf in both ears and can hear very little sound without my hearing aids. I have been deaf since birth but because my speech is quite normal people often fail to realise just how deaf I am. During my early childhood I could not speak properly and I had to have speech therapy which continued after I was transferred to Odsal House School for the Deaf in Bradford. Since I am unable to hear properly, I have developed the habit of picking up snippets of conversation and then I try to work out what is being said. However, because I am preoccupied in this way I often lose the flow of a conversation and as a result I am unable to join in as much as I would wish.

The Spirit people are very aware of this and they know and appreciate that my hearing is severely impaired. I recall just how apprehensive and concerned I was on the first occasion that I sat with Stewart, not knowing if I would be able to hear anything. I was worried because I knew that I would be sitting in total darkness and would be unable to use my other senses. I would be unable to lip-read and I would be unable to watch people's facial expressions and look for signs that people were talking to me.

However, I need not have worried. Freda would often ask the circle members if I could hear her and they would do their best to interpret for me. Little did I realise back then the amount of help and healing I would receive from the Spirit people in the future.

At a séance on the 4th May 2000 Walter gave me the news that whilst my words both spoken and written about survival would reach and touch many people it would never be possible to correct my hearing deficiency.

After hearing this I realised that I would never be cured and although Walter went on to say that they 'would do everything that could be done' my immediate thought was that they would help by always speaking slowly and by asking circle members to interpret. Little did I realise at that time what preparations were being made in the Spirit World.

At subsequent sittings my hearing improved by degrees within the séance room.

I understood that this was achieved by means of a hearing mechanism that had been created by the Spirit World and was described as tubes which originated within the cabinet and were connected to my ears. Whatever the truth is, the fact remains that whilst sitting in the darkness of the séance room, I invariably experience a strong sensation of pressure at the back and at the top of my head. I feel as if I am wearing a hat. The sensation is so strong, I instinctively want to put my hand to it but know that I must not do so when ectoplasmic energy is present. However, the fact is that within the séance room my hearing inexplicably improves to such an extent that I am able to converse with the Spirit people without any help from circle members.

During a séance on 13th May 2003 Walter explained 'Katie, you should understand that whenever we know that you are to join us, throughout the day we create special conditions within the séance room which later will enable you to hear'. He then continued by exclaiming, 'If only you could spend your entire life here you would have no problem with your hearing at all.'

Later in 2003 Walter addressed Tom Harrison, with these words; 'You know that our friend Katie is in many ways profoundly deaf. However, when she comes within this room, where our two worlds meet and blend together, then – because of the work she has done to inform people of survival and communication, and shall continue to do (the Trilogy) it is of vital importance that she should be able to hear all that transpires. For that reason the scientific people in my world connected to the circle have developed a method, by which, once she is here within, and the light has been extinguished, she will hear. That in itself demonstrates clearly the power of the Spirit.

We appreciate that there are many within your world who will always seek to advance normal theories and explanations to explain away séance room physical phenomena no matter how ridiculous or inappropriate.

But let them explain that, Tom!'

As a footnote I must mention that although I was assured by the Spirit World that a cure for my condition would not be possible, it appears to have improved. In the year 2000, I was supplied with a set of digital hearing aids which, unlike the old analogue ones, did not have a manual control function. These had been set by a computer to match my degree of deafness and the chip inside them regulated the sound level.

Until June/July of 2004 I was quite happy with them and then the right one became uncomfortably loud. Manually I could not reduce the volume level and as a result I often had to remove the aid. It showed no malfunction and because problems arose (particularly at work) arrangements were made to have my hearing tested again and this revealed that the hearing in my right ear had improved. As a result the aid had to be reset by computer to reduce the sound level. Since then I have been left wondering whether the improvement had occurred as a result of spiritual healing! Certainly I am not a person who reaches conclusions easily and I accept the fact that in all probability I will always   remain deaf. However, I cannot disregard the outside evidence which indicates that a gradual improvement has occurred.

❖   ❖   ❖

Having now given the reader a taste of the positive and constructive aspects of the home circle, and of my mediumship, in the next chapter I intend to deal briefly with one aspect which some readers may consider to be somewhat unsavoury.

This, however, will be balanced by Chapter 11 in which I present a paper, first published in the *Paranormal Review,* the journal of the SPR. It describes in some considerable detail the typical events of one of my own public séances and the protocol and the conditions within which they are held.

Readers may then understand more fully the nature of my mediumship.

Its author, retired electronic research engineer Lew Sutton, has been at my public demonstrations many times over the past fifteen years.

Chapter 9

An Endemic Problem

I answer past critics of my mediumship and address the possibility that allegations of impropriety may be levelled against it in the future.

In this chapter, I intend to answer past accusations of impropriety levelled against my mediumship. I also address the distinct possibility that at some future time, further allegations of dubious practice could arise thus casting a shadow of doubt upon my work as a medium. Knowing that to introduce such material here would almost certainly prove controversial, and might reflect negatively upon the entire book, I hesitated considerably before finally taking the decision to include it. Reason informed me that I had no option but to face the facts surrounding such matters irrespective of how difficult and uncomfortable they might be. On that singular basis I really had no choice – there could be no middle ground – no alternative – the matter simply could not be ignored or avoided. That said, it is my fervent hope that in addressing such vitally important issues, I will ensure that I have a voice in the future which may perhaps go some way towards countering and answering past critics and pre-empting prospective ones.

As I have repeatedly pointed out, where physical mediumship is concerned, and the dark séance room, it is understandable why controversy has never been far away and alas I imagine that it will always be so. As history clearly and repeatedly illustrates, this is regrettably endemic to such mediumship. While fully accepting this, my fear is that, at some future time, possibly when I am no longer here to defend myself, allegations involving my own mediumship might arise, and indeed, I would be rather surprised if they did not. The fact is that anyone can allege fraud and will do so for a variety of reasons most of which I have mentioned elsewhere. With my own mediumship, if I ignore the eminent SPR investigator of whom I wrote in Chapter 5, insinuations have been made on only two other occasions with many years between them. To demonstrate that nothing has been omitted from this book – that I have not sought to hide uncomfortable facts – I shall briefly touch upon them now. In so doing I am happy to leave you – the reader – to decide if either, or both, had any merit. However, what I cannot possibly convey is the feeling of utter devastation and emotional turmoil that they caused, not merely to me personally, but to all the members of the home circle. Indeed, as we were quickly to discover, it only takes one single accusation to unbalance and outweigh a thousand positive reports gained over a period of many years.

The first involved two ladies from the same family who came to our guest circle some years ago. They were accompanied by an unrelated, elderly gentleman who just happened to live close to them and who coincidentally had booked a place at the circle for the same night. Therefore they had travelled together. What we did not know was that some months earlier the old gentleman's wife had passed away. The circle that night appeared to go well and towards its conclusion the man's wife had manifested and spoken to him. Understandably, he was ecstatic and after the séance had ended he bubbled with joy. A few words from his wife had literally meant the world to him. Of course, we all shared in his pleasure and we parted company that evening knowing that this event, like many others that we had witnessed before, had fundamentally changed his life. However, our delight was to be short lived. The following afternoon one of the ladies telephoned our circle leader Ray insisting that they had seen through it all that the séance had been fraudulent from beginning to end. She informed him that she had spoken to a friend of hers who just happened to be a psychical researcher.

Apparently he had asked her to explain in detail the events of the séance. She informed him that Ray and I had gone into the séance room first – several minutes before the sitters had been invited in. 'Well then, that's the answer,' explained the researcher.

It had apparently been blatantly obvious to him that whilst alone, Ray and I had made our preparations. The trumpets had been attached to wires, and then, under cover of darkness, that is how we had manipulated them.

Other similarly ridiculous explanations had been suggested to account for all the events that had taken place, and predictably yet unsurprisingly, the phenomena that he had been unable to dismiss with a cursory explanation (including the personal communications) had conveniently been ignored.

My own distress upon hearing this was considerable but what upset me the most was the very thought that such cursory silliness would have impacted upon the old gentleman had they chosen to share it with him and might distress his wife, who, the evening before, had made such valiant efforts to communicate with him from the Spirit World. Whether he was informed I have no idea but if we assume that he was then it would be impossible to even imagine the mental turmoil that he must have suffered. Perhaps it matched my own!

Indeed, I was so distressed that I immediately ceased all public work for almost a full year until finally the realisation dawned upon me that these people had, at a stroke, halted all that was good and precious. In effect, I had stopped because two ladies, and a so-called researcher, who had not even been present and had never sat with me, had presumed fraud.

Eventually however I came to realise that in refusing to sit again for the public I was, in effect, depriving the Spirit World of the opportunity to reach a great many people with their glorious message. Shortly afterwards I began to sit again.

The second more recent allegation was to come from a Spiritualist group who themselves had been sitting over a long period to develop physical mediumship.

Indeed prior to and following the sitting they had with us they liberally regaled us with accounts of the wonderful phenomena that regularly manifested at their weekly circles, including the exceedingly rare phenomenon of materialisation. At the time I thought it strange that they had chosen to travel a considerable distance to attend a sitting with me when, seemingly, they were regularly experiencing, within their own circle, such wonderful manifestations.

Following the séance that night they continued to describe in some detail their own phenomena whilst their medium said precious little and simply smiled throughout. Again I wondered why they had come to us. Whatever the reason (and here I have my own thoughts) a few days later our circle leader received a communication from them effectively expressing their disappointment with the sitting and insinuating fraud. After reading their email several times I was, apart from my feelings of utter inner turmoil, uncertain as to whether they were suggesting that I was solely responsible or that it had been a kind of combined effort – that my own circle members present that night had conspired with me to produce dubious and/or bogus manifestations and that we were all complicit in what they were clearly alleging had been a kind of deception.

They spoke of having heard footsteps around the séance room. They claimed that in some way I had released one hand from my neighbour's at the illuminated table so that the hand that appeared upon it, rather than being Walter's, had in reality, been one of my own, or perhaps, one which belonged to another circle member.

They further claimed that the alleged Spirit people had appeared to follow a kind of script, which in content had varied little from an earlier occasion (some months or years before) when one of their group had sat with me, and based upon that experience, the physical phenomena and the manner in which they had been presented were said to have followed a similar format. Personal communicators were also dismissed because apparently they had failed to sound as they did when on earth.

With incredulity I read and re-read the analysis of the séance and finally felt impelled to write in reply, as did our circle leader.

It would serve little purpose to detail here my response but suffice to say that I learnt a valuable lesson from the entire episode and it was this:

If people attend a physical séance looking for 'loopholes' they will find them. If none are to be found then they will create them. In finding them or in creating them the accusers will refuse to face the facts which fail utterly to fit neatly into their own conclusions.

And neither will it occur to them that literally thousands of sitters before them had failed to identify their imagined loopholes.

Supposition, in their minds, becomes certainty. Mere conjecture conveniently converts to fact. Whether this can be considered a purely wilful act concealing hidden motives or an unconscious one I have no idea – I only know that common sense suggests that in such matters, where human nature is concerned, there are no easy answers.

In such situations previously published reports concerning the protocols and controls imposed at my séances will amount to nothing. They will be ignored. For example; in the matter of Walter's materialised hand, often both of my own are clearly seen to be held by my immediate neighbours. But the critic(s) will pay no heed to this if he/she/they fail themselves to observe it. In the case of the 'armchair critics' they will not trouble themselves with such inconvenient facts. Consciously or unconsciously they would simply ignore them refusing even to acknowledge them.

Similarly, voices of personal communicators may be cursorily dismissed (as in this case) on the basis that they failed to match their earthly ones, little or no consideration being given to the difficulties involved in communication of which we know virtually nothing. Such a standpoint 'beggars belief' since, to my mind, it is akin to a miracle if communicators manage to utter a single word. And, although it can be said that at public séances there are occasional similarities in verbal communication content and also in the presentation of physical phenomena, legitimately it may be argued that such is not exactly surprising.

The facts are that over a period of many years the Spirit people have developed 'a formula' and whilst there is always a variation in séance content they do tend to follow an established pattern.

The critic will also readily ignore that over a period of forty-two years I have given my life to 'the great cause' – and served the Spirit World to the very best of my ability. For twenty-five years my circle leader Ray and his wife June have sat loyally at my side doing exactly the same. For almost eighteen years I have, in addition to the home circle, sat weekly for the public in our home circle séance room and also in venues throughout England, Scotland and Wales.

I have sat in Sweden, in Switzerland, Germany and Spain. I have sat for groups of people ranging from ten to over a hundred. I have sat for Spiritualists – for sceptics – for individual researchers and para-psychological organisations.

I have sat in ideal conditions and in conditions not exactly conducive to séance work.

I have sat in Spiritualist churches, lecture halls and private houses. Repeatedly I have witnessed how lives have been changed and yet such critics clearly have the confidence, following a brief association with my mediumship (or none at all) to accuse and to state that *they have seen through it all*. Readers may form their own conclusions!

Although I should be proud that accusations of impropriety – imputations of doubt of any kind have rarely been attached to my mediumship the fact is that I consider any allegation to be highly disappointing and distasteful. However, in the arena of public physical mediumship a relatively clean reputation is indeed remarkable and for that I must be grateful.

And so to my critics – past and future – I simply say this:

this book from its first word to its last presents all that I wish to say on the contentious matter of physical mediumship and particularly in respect of my own.

You are entitled to your views, but respectfully, I would ask you to consider the feasibility of your adverse conclusions against all that is contained herein, for it is my sincere hope that this book will, at the very least, appeal to all reasonable minds.

I can say no more than that!

Chapter 10

Evidential Communications

Reports of my mediumship from America, Israel and the United Kingdom during my years in the Noah's Ark Society.

During my Noah's Ark Society years, there occurred several notable highly evidential communications delivered at our home circle but only confirmed at a later date. Although others could have been included in this chapter, I have selected just three which I consider to be somewhat unusual and which I feel deserve to be recorded for posterity. The chapter will then be concluded with accounts of two rather unique experiences – not verbal post mortem séance room communications but events which strongly support the supernormal reality of particular aspects of the physical phenomena manifested.

However, before continuing, I must first briefly mention the interaction of the two worlds as it existed and manifested through my mediumship throughout my involvement with the Society and which still exists up to the present day.

White Feather, who for some years was our single communicator, was joined in 1982 by the larger than life personality Lila Josephs whom I introduced in Chapter 3. A year later she was replaced by the colourful chatterbox, little Christopher. He gave the age at which he passed into the Spirit World as 'six and a bit'. For the next nine years, he was a veritable spiritual Jack-of-all-trades.

Following White Feather's opening blessing at every séance Christopher was solely responsible for providing survival evidence and in addition he answered the sitters' questions. He also relaxed any tension amongst the sitters in his own inimitable style. He entertained and seemingly produced all the physical phenomena, although of course, he was merely the presenter and the mouthpiece for the Spirit World.

Then in 1992 we were introduced to a new communicator – the singular Walter Stuart Stinson. Students of Spiritualism and of psychical research will know that the name of Walter Stinson was, during the 1920s and 30s synonymous with the Boston (USA) medium known to the world under the pseudonym of 'Margery the Medium'.

Her real name was Mina (Stinson) Crandon – Walter was her brother and the principal communicator at her well publicised séances. In Part Two of this book I have included an appraisal of her mediumship since it is, in many ways, central to my own. That he should have broken his long silence (following the death of his sister in 1941) by choosing to manifest thorough my mediumship, was wonderful but not exactly a surprise.

The Margery mediumship had fascinated me for many years. I had studied the entire case and read copiously the views of its supporters and its denigrators. I had long considered that she had been a sacrificial lamb on the altar of psychical research.

Evidently, and according to his own words, he was returning to do all he could to complete the task that he had commenced so long ago and at the same time to vindicate his sister from claims that she had perpetrated the greatest psychic fraud in history.

Walter was to immediately take full charge of the physical manifestations at our séances refining and extending the existing phenomena and soon he also introduced new forms. Christopher, until the arrival of Freda Johnson in 1996, was left solely to concentrate upon the easing of tension and the presentation of evidence.

When however Freda became a permanent fixture at the circle, the presentation of evidential communication fell upon her shoulders so leaving Christopher to do the job he clearly relishes; relaxing tension and dispelling fear amongst first time sitters – neither of which is conducive to successful séance room physical communication.

So – with this gradual construction of the circle it was very evident that slowly the Spirit World had created a special team to work with us and to take advantage of the conditions that we habitually offered to them.

And then finally, in the year 2000, the Spirit team would be augmented yet again with a Dr Franklin Barnett who arrived with the intention of stabilising and developing the phenomena of materialisation. Therefore, the evolution of my mediumship since its inception in 1971, up to the present time, can clearly be seen to have been one of measured pace and intelligent fixed direction.

To illustrate this, I now present in some little detail a small selection of examples which readers may find of interest.

Accounts of all three were first published by the Ark in their *Newsletter* under the headings and dates shown. Where I have felt it necessary to edit the original scripts I have done so, hopefully to make them more understandable to readers unfamiliar with the séance room. Also, original text has been removed where I have deemed it to have little relevance to the incident under review. However, I have throughout endeavoured to restrict all editing to an absolute minimum and to remain faithful to the originals.

A Séance with Stewart Alexander

Originally published in *The Noah's Ark Newsletter*, November 1993.
Douglas Glasby (From York, England)

On the evening of June the first of this year (1993) my wife and I had the privilege of attending Stewart Alexander's home circle. We had sat with them a number of times previously but that was three years earlier. Consequently, it was with visions of past sittings, and joyful anticipation that we were introduced to the present circle prior to taking our seats in the séance room. When everyone was seated, the light was extinguished and following a short opening prayer we listened to taped music. In a very short time Stewart's guide White Feather spoke through Stewart in trance assuring us that the power was good and giving greetings to us all. He was quickly followed by young Christopher who soon had the sitters in near hysterics with his antics. Then, as the taped music was again played, the two trumpets – luminous around the wide ends – began floating around the room swinging to the music and occasionally rapping on the ceiling. One trumpet tapped me on the head and then gently stroked my cheek. It then hovered in front of my face and I heard a voice coming out of it – no more than a whisper. Because of my partial deafness, I was only able to make out a few words, but I was assured by nearby sitters that my late wife Joan, was speaking.

After a few minutes the voice faded out but before it did all sitters, myself included, heard a resounding kiss from the trumpet.

Then, the trumpets came to a rest on the small table within the circle and two regular communicators (guides) spoke to the circle through the entranced medium. When they eventually left the two trumpets again commenced their gyrations until one, once more, floated in front of me and out of it I heard the name James Hudson. For me this was wonderful evidence, and I keenly listened to the voice of my one-time friend. James Hudson was a Spiritualist/researcher friend of mine who, in the late 60s had suddenly departed this life, suffering from a rare form of cancer. After a short chat, the voice got fainter and the very welcome communicator left.

Now followed – for me – a startling incident. Through the trumpet, still in its position near me, I heard a slightly stronger male voice. The name 'Changi' and 'you sweat blood' came through with the name 'George Clarke' and other words relating to South East Asia.

When the short communication was over, and the trumpet floated away, my mind was left in turmoil. Thinking back in time some 50 years or more, I felt that once again I was back in Changi Jail, Singapore, a reluctant guest of the Mikado!

But George Clarke – where did he fit in? There were huge gaps in my memory and I could not place the man. Yet by his words I knew that he knew, as I did, the 'score' out there all those years ago. My mind flashed back to the present, and I became aware of Christopher bidding us a fond farewell and then White Feather returning with kind salutations and so ended – what for me – was to be a remarkable sitting.

At home the following morning I feverishly searched through my Japanese memorabilia, but alas, no joy. But wait – the tiny cupboard in the hallway. In no time at all I was rummaging inside and finally I discovered a small cardboard box which once held Christmas cards. I looked inside, and there amongst some papers was a folded card, approximately 3 by 4 inches in size. In colour on the front had been drawn a palm tree and over the palm were the words 'P.O.W. Changi Camp 1944'. Carefully, I lifted it from the box and just as carefully I opened it. Inside was the word 'Menu' and beneath it, in coloured wording an exotic choice of dishes.

Slowly I began to remember – seven young men thrown together in adversity – a planned meal. Bits and pieces of food, all rice based, collected, scrounged, appropriated – all end products given classy names by the cook and written neatly in the menu. He had even written at the end of the menu; 'Coffee and Cigars'. Full marks for imagination! My eyes were moist as I turned the card over.

There on the back were seven names, encircling the gun emblem of the artillery. Halfway down on the left was the name 'Gunner Clarke'.

Now it was clear in my mind. The war was drawing to a close and the Japanese could not then win it. We all suspected that no POW would be allowed to survive – no matter how the war ended. To hell with it – with physical and psychological pressure mounting – we would have one last get together. But we were never to meet again.

My search was over.

❖ ❖ ❖

The Transatlantic Séance Experiment

Originally published in *The Noah's Ark Newsletter*, March 1995.

Noel Riley Heagerty (From Oswego, New York, USA.)

The following is an account of a séance – a transatlantic experiment – that took place on the 1st November 1994. The circle sat in its usual séance room in Kingston upon Hull,England. The remote sitter, Noel Riley Heagerty, sat at precisely the same time at his home in Oswego, America.

Stewart and Mr. Heagerty had first made contact with each other some years earlier as a result of their common interest in the medium Mina 'Margery' Crandon and had corresponded since then.

Noel Heagerty Writes

I suggested the experiment to Stewart to see if his spirit team could lock into my vibration from a lock of hair and a small picture of myself which I duly sent to him. Stewart's circle arranged the séance procedure. I sat at precisely 3 o'clock in the afternoon, and the circle, allowing for the time difference, sat at 8 o'clock. Therefore we were sitting at the same time. Throughout I played the exact same music as they did.

I simply concentrated my thoughts on the circle guides; White Feather, Walter and Christopher. That is all I did. I had absolutely no idea, until I received the tape recording of the sitting that Walter and Christopher had actually come to my house. Stewart and I had never once considered that they might do that and had simply expected that they would offer their impressions from the lock of hair and the photograph.

I was absolutely wondrously stunned when I heard the tape – absolutely shocked.

There has never been a Spiritualist in my sitting room and I had never described it to any person on earth, nor my house, or any of its contents or structure. I have known Stewart for about five years. Our interests are in research and physical mediumship. We have shared very little on a personal level outside those specific interests.

Stewart Alexander Writes

The idea of attempting such an experiment came to me from Mr Heagerty several months ago. My initial reaction to the proposal was that the possibility of achieving any success would be somewhat unlikely. During the twenty-four years that my mediumship has functioned I had never before attempted to participate in such an ambitious experiment and indeed, I had never previously heard of a similar experiment having taken place. However, because I felt unable to disappoint Mr Heagerty – whose friendship I highly value – I agreed to try and I wrote back to him nominating a date.

I suggested that both parties should play my circle's séance music whilst the experiment was taking place and I sent a copy of our cassette music tape.

The Noel Riley Heagerty Report Received by Stewart Alexander

Introduction: First, I must say what a tremendous mature and powerful circle you have; one shining light in the firmament of reality. I thank you with my heart and soul for trusting in me and, of course, words fail me in trying to thank White Feather, Walter and Christopher.

Now, let me tell you that I was sitting at the exact time for the experiment – I consulted with the international operator and set my clock accordingly. My thoughts were centred upon your circle your energy and Spirit guides and I tried to visualise a white beam of light from here to your circle room. I had the exact music playing softly and sat in a dim red light throughout.

Core Specifics: I intended to wait until the end of my report before I commented upon the accuracy of the experiment but have decided not to do so. Analysing the recording again I rate content accuracy at almost a clear and total 100%. I shall now look at each specific statement.

Walter's Input

1. A large house – *Correct. I live in a very large, pre-Civil War house built in 1847.*

2. Five steps up to the front door before entering the house – *Correct.*

3. A very large door – *Absolutely correct.*

4. Natural wood railing and stairs – *Explicitly correct; these are pure mahogany.*

5. Stairs continue, turn and continue up – *Correct.*

6. Home of peace – *Absolutely correct.*

7. Proceeding down a long corridor with rooms at each side – *Both correct.*

8. At the end of the corridor there is a room – *Correct.*

9. We now walk up to the very top of the house – *Absolutely correct. I live in the attic of the house.*

10. The room is rich. It is filled with the Power of the Spirit. There are several pictures on the wall. – *Nothing could be more correct about these statements.*

11. Opposite the door to the right is a desk – *Perfectly correct.*

12. Above the desk there are bookshelves – *Correct.*

13. To the right there is also a bookshelf and all are filled with books – *Correct Again.*

14. Walter states that a great deal of development has been done in this room – *No one knew before that.*

15. A burial ground not far from the house – *Absolutely correct. It is a beautiful place and I visit it most days.*

16. Opposite the door to the left a window which is covered over – *This is astonishingly correct. I have permanently covered over the left window.*

17. The gentleman sits without shoes – *For this experimental séance absolutely no shoes were worn.*

18. The name Cecilia – *Is the name of Cecilia Butler who is buried in the cemetery. She passed in 1848 and her presence did not come as a surprise to me.*

19. An irritation in the right arm – *On the very day of the sitting, I was in the back yard trying to get our snow-blower working. I pulled the rope with full force trying to start it and hit a pile of wood directly behind me with my right elbow. I thought that I had broken it and in trying to type this letter it still hurts.*

20. The significance of the letter 'B' – *My father's best friend committed suicide this year – his name; Bob Baker.*

21. Walter's reference to a strange smell – *The room is filled with the smell of cranberry.*

Christopher's Input

22. A large bookcase with lots and lots of books – *Perfectly correct of course.*

23. Third shelf down. 14th book in from the left is a pamphlet and next to this is a book and the cover is torn – *The pamphlet, my friend, is 'Visits by Our Friends from the Other Side' which was written by Tom Harrison about his mother's mediumship back in the 1950s. Readers should know that Tom Harrison was due to attend this particular sitting but at the last minute had to cancel for personal reasons. This, of course, made this entire experiment even more extraordinary. Next to the pamphlet is indeed a book with a torn cover. This was all quite astonishing.*

24. Christopher refers to the drawing of a sailing ship – *Most Incredible. There is a painting of a group of sailing ships right above*

my old leather chair. If one were to step back and see it as a young child would it appears to be one ship.

25. A lady in a long dress – *If you move to the left of the sailboat picture along the wall there are four ladies in long dresses.*

26. Dogs barking – *They are barking all the time over here* – *the four houses that surround my house all have dogs.*

27. Slight step up into the room – *This has to be the floor in front of my door. Because of the chimney, the floor goes up like a hill and then down again. Amazing indeed.*

❖ ❖ ❖

Personal Evidence

Originally published in *The Noah's Ark Newsletter*, December 1997.
Dr Adrian Klein M.DD. (From Israel)

In this open letter to members of the NAS I wish to share my thoughts after attending a most remarkable sitting in Mr. Stewart Alexander's circle earlier this year.

Twenty-three years ago I left Romania for Israel as a young dental surgeon and found freedom there to extend my deep interest in the possibility of an afterlife. Following my father's death in 1978 I became deeply involved in the fairly new field of EVP[1] and enjoyed great success. After a long illness my mother also passed into Spirit in May 1995 and words cannot possibly convey my distress over that unbearable loss. Soon however, it became clear to me that in addition to my continued involvement in respect of my own particular field of survival research, I must also make contact with leaders of modern investigation. This, in terms of mediumship and instrumental communication and with principal authorities and scientists involved with such research.

As a result I duly made the necessary contacts including one with the NAS General Secretary who, following an understandable

---

(1) *EVP (Electronic Voice Phenomena) Said to be communication between two different planes of existence by means of tape recorder or radio but unheard by anyone until the recording is replayed.*

delay, finally put me in contact with Mr. Ray Lister – Stewart's circle leader. Some time later, towards the end of August of this year, I found myself in Kingston upon Hull where the Stewart Alexander circle has now been meeting for many years. Although a little tired, after my long trip to England from Brazil (where I had attended the second ITC[2] World conference in Sao Paulo) I had the opportunity, the day before the scheduled sitting, to meet with Mr. Lister. We debated highly interesting aspects relating to modern physical mediumship and I express here my gratitude for the long hours he spent with me and for the hospitality that I received from him and his wife, June.

The following evening I joined the members of Stewart's home circle and entered the séance room – the light was extinguished and the séance started in an atmosphere of total harmony. Soon, White Feather, the circle's old friend and main spiritual guide communicated in his deep wise voice and I was greeted cordially. Imagine my amazement when I realised that he was aware of my own active involvement in survival research.

A most useful and friendly conversation between us then followed before finally Christopher arrived and I shall never forget his extremely kind behaviour and willingness to answer my various questions. Then, for me, the climax of the entire evening – the most wonderful contact with my own dear mother whose passing was not even known to Stewart. However, as previously advised by Ray, I had, up to that point, refrained from making any request for her to come. My excitement can easily be imagined when Christopher suddenly informed me of the presence in the room of both my parents and I shall never forget the undeniable evidence he gave for my mother's identity complete with a description of her physical stature. But Christopher's input was not restricted to that first piece of information; he went on to say that she came from a country utterly unknown to himself (obviously Israel – the country of her last residence) and then went on to say that she had been born in a different one. Her birthplace had been Czechoslovakia.

At that moment I lost control of my previous reticence to speak up and I asked Christopher if he could help her to speak directly to me. He agreed to try. Just a few seconds later I perceived a

(2) *ITC (Instrumental TransCommunication), said to be communication between two different planes of existence by means of tape recorder, radio, telephone, computer and TV etc.*

whisper a few centimetres away from my right ear, to the right and slightly in front of it.

The room quickly sank into a deep and respectful silence and only my dear mother's whisper could be heard. For me it was the same familiar whisper which I had heard many times during my own ITC recordings but much quieter and slower.

That I was unable to understand her words was hardly surprising for at that moment I was extremely tense and emotional.

Nevertheless, I realised that the speech was performed in a different language from the English one and this was to be confirmed by all the sitters. Sadly, at that time I had assumed that since my mother's voice had been of such low volume intensity the séance room microphone would have failed to register it and I would be denied a recording.

However, the extremely sensitive equipment had indeed succeeded in recording in high fidelity range the whisper thus allowing for subsequent analysis and digital filtering systems back home. After denoising (reducing recorded background noise) and with selective amplifying procedures using the software used in my own ITC research, I have now succeeded in deciphering a short sequence of her séance room speech. She spoke to me in our routine conversational language – Hungarian. The English translation being 'tell me something' (mondjal nekem valamit) pronounced very slowly and with an obvious excruciating effort.

I am confident that I shall soon be able to successfully 'clean' and reveal some further fragments of her long message to me.

And so I end by thanking Mr and Mrs Lister for offering their home to host that unique event.

Thank you also the NAS for their kindly introduction to the circle and finally; 'I thank you, Christopher for being as you are. There is no earthly terminology which would adequately express my feelings and my thoughts.'

❖ ❖ ❖

Some Unique Experiences

Of the following experiences with physical phenomena the first took place in our home circle séance room and the second at a Spiritualist church. Both were witnessed and recorded by future Ark President Alf Winchester.

In his own words:

Matter through Matter

On 22nd February,1994 my wife and I, together with our friend Jonathan Dorrat, attended a Stewart Alexander séance and were treated to an amazing sight, the passage of matter-through-matter in good red light. This phenomenon is a regular occurrence at Stewart's séances but these experiments are held (certainly in public demonstrations) in total darkness. The practice at that time was for the medium to be trussed up by means of strong rope (at the very least 6mm thick) which firmly bound his arms, legs and torso to a chair and was securely knotted. I carefully observed the ropes being applied and was satisfied that there was no way that the medium could release himself from his bonds. As an added precaution there was a metal plate fitted to either side of the chair back.

The plates had deep indentations on their edges that the ropes fitted into. These prevented the medium being able to wriggle out of the ropes that were around his chest and also stopped the ropes from slipping downwards. Walter Stinson, through the entranced Stewart, instructed Ray (the circle leader) that when he heard the sound of a knock he was to switch on the red light for five seconds. We were told to look towards Stewart's right arm and observe.

When it came on, I clearly saw the medium's arm shoot up into the air directly passing through the ropes that bound it securely to the arm of the chair. Simultaneously there was a loud noise similar to the cracking of a whip. The ropes which had secured the medium were left intact but loose on the chair arms.

The experiment was then repeated with the left arm. I had had no preconceived idea as to what to expect and certainly considered that it was not possible to pass an arm through a rope.

Obviously on the second attempt, knowing what to expect, I watched extremely carefully. I have absolutely no doubt that I saw the medium's arm pass through the rope. My wife's and my friend's observations were identical to mine.

Invisible Ectoplasm

At a séance held at the Sleaford Spiritualist Church (England) I was again privileged to be seated behind Stewart during a séance. Immediately in front of him there was a small table which had a red cloth covering its glass top and that was under lit by a red light, the brightness of which could be controlled through a rheostat. With the room in darkness, apart from the glow from the table, a small bell was levitated from the table top and rung above it. Other sitters saw what appeared to be a bell floating in mid air with no means of support.

However, from my vantage point, I was able to see over the medium's shoulder an ectoplasmic rod silhouetted in the very low red light and it headed towards the bell but where it passed over the illuminated table top it disappeared. The bell reacted to every movement of the rod. It was never more than 6 inches (15cms) from the edge of the table and that 6 inches (15cms) was always invisible. I can only conclude therefore, that the missing end of the rod had been composed of invisible ectoplasm.

Chapter 11

An Academic Treatise

An academic paper on the public séance room protocols and manifestations (physical and mental,) which occur in my presence; first published in July 2009 in the Journal of the Society for Psychical Research.

The following paper is reproduced *exactly* as it was published in July 2009 by the SPR in their quarterly journal, *Paranormal Review.*

It was written by retired electronic research engineer Lew Sutton, an established writer on the subjects of Spiritualism and altered states of consciousness. I thank him and also the *Paranormal Review* for allowing me to include it here. Readers should find the report both interesting and informative irrespective of their knowledge of physical séances. Unlike other accounts included within this book, it records in some detail the protocol involved whenever I have sat for the public. Descriptions of the physical phenomena contained herein will allow a better understanding of their nature and of their manifestation.

Contemporary Physical Mediumship,
Stewart Alexander Séances

Lew Sutton

Several accounts have been published in *Psychic News* and *Psychic World* over the last seventeen years of public physical séances held with physical medium Stewart Alexander from Hull, Yorkshire (e.g. Sutton, 1997; 2007). However, a really thorough description detailing the phenomena, procedures and conditions under which the séances are held has never previously been published.

This comprehensive report seeks to rectify that situation and covers the last four years. Significant advances were made in the development of the phenomena and its presentation in these recent years. Stewart's mediumship is continually developing and those who have not attended a séance within the last year or so will not have experienced all of the phenomena described in this report.

The conditions under which these séances are conducted will not satisfy outright sceptics. Stewart's reluctance to submit to scientific investigation is explained in this report. His overriding aim is to encourage others to develop this form of mediumship, which has become quite rare.

Venues

Over the past four years Stewart Alexander has given about 200 public séances of which the majority have been held in Hull, Yorkshire. Other locations have included the Cober Hill Conference Centre in Yorkshire, Norfolk, South Devon, York, locations in Scotland, and on the Continent (Spain, Sweden and Switzerland). Stewart has recently cut down on travelling and his demonstrations are now predominantly held in his home county of Yorkshire.

Venues have included rooms in private houses, churches[1], large hotel rooms, and lecture rooms in conference centres. Attendance has varied from sixteen to one hundred plus, the larger numbers being at seminars.

Initial conditions

A room is completely blacked out and a curtained cabinet installed, usually against a wall. The cabinet structure varies depending on where the séances are held but is a simple framework supporting dark curtain material. The cabinet is at least large enough to allow the medium to sit in his chair without his feet protruding through the curtain, and sometimes is somewhat larger.

At some locations a curtain is hung across a room corner to form a triangular cabinet. The curtains meet in the middle when closed. Luminous tabs are attached near the top of the curtains

---

(1) *Spiritualist churches. (Stewart Alexander)*

and close to their opening edges so everyone can see whether they are open or closed.

A chair with wooden arms is provided by Stewart Alexander (this can be freely examined by sitters). It is placed just in front of the cabinet and later moved back into it for the materialisation part of the séance. Occasionally the chair has been initially placed elsewhere and then moved into the cabinet after the 'materialised hand experiment' (discussed below).

Chairs for sitters are placed in a circle configuration and if the room is large enough, extra concentric circles may be added. The chairs are usually packed closely together.

A low wooden table with an oval top measuring 58 by 46 cm and standing 47 cm high is placed in front of the medium's chair. The table weighs about 8 kg and has a translucent red panel set into its top. The table is boxed in so that a light bulb mounted inside only illuminates the top. The light bulb is controlled by an electrical dimmer switch mounted on the side of the table.

On the table top are placed strong electrical plastic cable ties[2] which are used to secure the medium to his chair and a pair of pliers to release him at the conclusion of the séance. Additionally, two small drumsticks, a small hand bell and a torch emitting a red light, for use by the circle leader, are also placed on the table top. An extra chair is placed on the opposite side of the table facing the medium.

All séances are invariably recorded in stereo using portable audio digital recorders. A stereo microphone is placed near the cabinet, or if the cabinet structure is suitable, it is fixed to the top front edge of the cabinet.

Preliminary procedures

Sitters are always searched immediately before entering the séance room. They are not allowed to wear or take in with them watches, large items of jewellery, coins, anything capable of emitting light, or any other object deemed to be inappropriate. Sitters are placed in positions considered conducive to a harmonious séance, with experienced sitters normally interspersed amongst newcomers.

---

(2) *Referred to hereafter as a 'Strap' or a 'Wrist Strap'. (Stewart Alexander)*

Sitting next to the medium, one either side, are placed two experienced lady sitters who are well known to the Spirit controls. Next to the two ladies will normally be: on one side the circle leader and on the other side an experienced male sitter, also well known to the spirit controls. Stewart's Spirit controls insist that they can use these sitters to supplement the psychic energies supplied by the medium (apparently this also applies to other nearby sitters).

Once the sitters have been seated the medium enters the room with both ladies who will sit next to him for the duration of the séance. Except that the lady on his right moves temporarily to a spare seat in order to make room for the participant (a person selected from the sitters) in the matter-through-matter experiment (described below), or any other activity that requires the participant to be next to the medium.

The medium is then secured in his chair by two of the plastic straps taken from the six or so that have been placed on the table. The straps pass around his wrists, securing them to the chair arms. His arms cannot be freed from the chair by normal means – the straps must first be cut with the pliers. Whilst it is possible to force a thin needle into the ratchet locking mechanism to unfasten a strap, it would be extremely difficult to do so, particularly in the dark. Even in the light the author has found it difficult to undo one, requiring nimble fingers and patience.

If a strap were surreptitiously unfastened, attempts to reassemble the strap (so as to leave it at its original setting) would produce a very audible and distinctive sound as the tongue of the strap slides against the ratchet mechanism. In the séance there is insufficient time for such a fraudulent act.

A volunteer is called forth to examine and verify that the medium is secured to the chair by his wrists. The volunteer returns to their chair and retains the pliers in order to release the medium at the end of the séance.

The lights are extinguished and only visible are the luminous tabs attached to the medium's trousers at knee height plus the two tabs on the cabinet curtain which allows the sitters to determine at any time whether the curtains are open or closed.

The séance

Trance communications

An opening prayer is said, followed by music played at a moderate level from a small portable CD player. A spirit control known as White Feather speaks through Stewart Alexander, who is apparently in trance, and gives an opening greeting.

Spirit communicators Christopher, Freda Johnson and Walter Stinson follow and speak in turn, using Stewart's vocal apparatus, who allegedly remains in a deep trance. Personal communications and/or the answering of questions may form part of this stage of the séance. Freda normally introduces loved ones who wish to communicate with sitters and acts as go-between when they have difficulty in getting their message across via the medium in the deep trance state.

The 'matter-through-matter' experiment

A sitter is invited by Spirit control, Walter Stinson, to sit next to Stewart on his right-hand side. The person selected may be chosen for some specific reason, or, more usually, is selected from those who have spoken to him earlier in the séance perhaps to pose a question. The lady originally occupying the chair on Stewart's right then moves to the spare chair at the opposite side of the table to Stewart.

The participant holds Stewart's right hand with their left hand and is instructed to keep hold of his hand for the duration of the experiment. Then by Walter's invitation, they are asked to feel with their right hand to confirm that Stewart's right arm is still secured to the chair arm by means of the strap. Within a few seconds of hearing confirmation of the arm being still secured, a noise is heard very briefly – like the sound of the plastic strap being jolted against the wooden chair arm. Almost instantly the participant exclaims that his/her left hand is now up in the air and is still holding Stewart's hand tightly. The participant, as instructed by Walter, then feels the chair arm with their right hand to ensure that the strap is still there.

Within a few seconds the red light is switched on by the circle leader at the request of Walter. All can then see Stewart's and the participant's interlocked hands in the air and the chair arm with dangling strap, thus confirming what has occurred. The light is switched off and the participant, holding Stewart's hand, feels the arm dropping back down.

Within a second or so Walter asks the participant to use their right hand to feel along Stewart's arm and place their hand firmly on the strap which once again is found to be securing the medium's arm to the arm of the chair.

They are instructed to press down upon the strap thereby ensuring that it is under their control at all times. This is important in terms of what shortly follows. He then asks the participant if he/she would like the strap as a small memento. Then, usually almost immediately, once again their hands rise into the air but this time the strap remains on the medium's arm and, of course, it is still looped.

The participant is then instructed to take the strap with their right hand whilst still holding the medium's right hand with their left hand. Participants describe the strap as being pushed against their hand as the medium's arm drops down.

The medium's right arm comes to rest unsecured upon the chair arm. It must be stressed that from the very beginning to the very end of these experiments, the participant has retained Stewart's right hand in his/her left.

Walter then announces that he will use one of the spare straps on the table to re-secure Stewart's arm. Within a matter of a few seconds the sound can be heard of one of the spare straps being dragged across the surface of the table followed shortly by the very distinctive clear sound of the plastic strap being tightened up. This sound is loud enough for everyone to hear.

The participant is asked to confirm that Stewart's arm has been re-secured to the arm of the chair after which the red light is switched on so the participant can return to their own chair.

This experiment is usually repeated with one or more of the sitters, who are usually ladies, as it seems to be rarely successful using men. Walter claims that this is because female energy is more conducive to the experiment than male energy.

The 'materialised hand experiment'

This experiment is usually performed with the medium sitting in line with the front of the cabinet. Occasionally he has sat against a wall away from the cabinet to give sitters a better view of this experiment, due to the shape of the room.

The table with the translucent top is placed close to and in front of the medium and the interior red light is switched on. The light intensity is adjusted as per Walter's instructions. A sitter is invited to sit on the spare chair opposite the medium and to put a hand on the table so that those nearby can see it silhouetted against the red light. Often those further away are allowed to stand to get a better view.

After a few moments a blob of what is announced to be ectoplasm is seen to appear on the illuminated translucent table top on the edge nearest the medium. Slowly it forms into a large hand – which Walter claims is his. It is certainly larger that Stewart's hand. The materialised hand moves towards the sitter's hand and then strokes and/or grasps it before withdrawing and melting away. The hand is invariably reported as feeling normal and warm. In the early years the hand that materialised was said to be ill-formed compared to that which now appears.

For the last year or so it is now usual for two more sitters to be called to the table and then for Stewart's hands to be paranormally released from the straps and his hands placed on the table together with the three sitters called forth for the experiment. Thus four sets of hands can be seen on the table with finger tips touching adjacent sitters' finger tips[3]. The extra materialised hand then forms in the gap between the medium's hands and may touch some or all of the three sitters' hands before melting away again.

It may be claimed that the materialised hand could be that of the male circle leader or any other gentleman sitter. However, with three sitters and the medium tightly packed around the table an accomplice could only be positioned behind the medium. This is clearly impossible when a corner cabinet is used or when the medium is sited against a wall.

It is now common at the end of this experiment for the table to appear to levitate up to about 30 cm clear of the floor. Levitation now happens with the participants' hands firmly linked together and all clear of the table top.

(3) *Following the original publication of the report this phenomenon has developed further. Often, Walter now calls for the temporary introduction of an additional overhead red light so that everyone can clearly see the four pairs of hands resting in close contact upon the translucent table top. (Stewart Alexander)*

Trumpet phenomena

For the demonstration of levitating trumpets the table used in the previous experiment is moved to one side and two trumpets are placed on the floor in front of the medium. The position of the trumpets with their luminous tabs is clearly visible to all the sitters. The aluminium trumpets are about 0.5m long and weigh about 100gm (4 oz).

Unaccompanied singing commences by attendees and continues until one of the trumpets lifts up and becomes airborne. Walter claims that sounds are extremely important to the production of physical phenomena. Singing stops and music is then played at low volume. The trumpet appears to float around the room, often responding to comments from the sitters with appropriate movement.

The trumpet's motions can vary from performing fast intricate patterns to slow graceful glides around the room giving the impression of weightlessness. There have been reports of seeing the outline of what is taken to be ectoplasmic rods controlling the trumpets when a small amount of light has entered the séance room.

Occasionally the trumpet will shoot towards someone and stop dead millimetres from their face and then sometimes caress their head or gently traverse around them. They have also been known to land on people's hands. All these actions indicate a controlling intelligence with a great spatial awareness in total darkness.

After a while the second trumpet usually becomes airborne and may manoeuvre several metres away from the first one.

The second trumpet rarely moves with as much vigour as the first one to become airborne. After a minute or so both trumpets land on the floor and one is seen to slide inside the other. They then take off together and the combined weight of both being locked together seems to produce slower movement around the room.

The trumpets will often deliberately touch the ceiling in rooms of normal ceiling height. In rooms with exceptionally high ceilings the trumpets have reached a height of over four metres.

Unlike the early days, Stewart is now normally conscious throughout most of the trumpet phenomena and is able to appreciate watching them, making comments whilst the trumpets are airborne. He has said that the only discomfort he feels is when one trumpet is inside the other and they move as one – possibly due to the extra weight on the end of one ectoplasmic rod.

Sometimes voice phenomena are heard through the trumpet as loved ones try to communicate with the trumpet hovering just in front of the recipient. The voices through the trumpet are instantly recognisable as not being by independent direct voice[4] through having that distinctive metallic megaphone type of sound.

Partial materialisations

Independent direct voice phenomena invariably follow the display of trumpet phenomena. Sometimes this starts before the trumpets have finally come to rest. The voice commences as a soft whisper and is often first heard by the lady sitting on Stewart's left side, or by Stewart himself, who is frequently conscious at this stage of the séance. The independent direct voice phenomena usually increase loud enough for everyone to hear what is being said. It is usually a Dr Barnett communicating, but it could be a personal communication for one of the sitters. Dr Franklin Barnett is said to be the nineteenth century Scottish physician who claimed to work through the famous early twentieth century American trumpet medium George Valiantine[5] (Bradley, 1924).

After a few minutes the voice fades and Walter briefly returns to request unaccompanied singing, which continues until signs of physical phenomena occur in what is taken to be partial materialisations. The first signs are those sitting nearest to the cabinet report experiencing gentle touches followed by voice phenomena.

In recent years it has been Dr Barnett who announces himself as he wanders around the séance room touching sitters gently on the head or touching/holding their hands whilst speaking to them. He also addresses the sitters in general. Amazingly, in total darkness, he displays a great spatial awareness as without fumbling he touches sitters. On one occasion he gently removed the author's glasses to administer healing. The glasses were placed in the author's hands.

(4) *Independent direct voices speak from a point in space close to but separate from the medium's vocal apparatus – hence 'Independent'. A trumpet, which is used to amplify Spirit voices at a séance, is not utilised. (Stewart Alexander)*

(5) *See Part 2 Chapter 3. (Stewart Alexander)*

Whilst away from the cabinet Dr Barnett has been known to invite one of the ladies seated next to the cabinet to reach into the cabinet with their hand to confirm that the medium is still sitting there.

For some time now Dr Barnett almost without exception announces that he has helpers with him who he says, are like himself, only partially materialised. The presence of additional helpers is confirmed by exclamations from sitters of simultaneously feeling hands touching them.

The author has personally felt two hands touching his head whilst his wife experienced the same as Dr Barnett spoke to her. Simultaneously, exclamations of feeling two hands came from the other side of the room.

Other phenomena

Briefly during a séance it is usual to hear the small hand bell being rung and to hear the drumsticks beating against something hard − probably the small table. These activities often happen simultaneously.

Paranormal lights are frequently seen, usually appearing just in front of the cabinet, or occasionally, a soft light is seen originating within the cabinet. It has become common in recent years for Dr Barnett to declare that it is he who cups a light in his hands and moves around the room to display it closely to sitters in the front row.

The orb of light has been seen to change in size and intensity, from a dull orb approaching the size of a tennis ball to shrinking down to a smaller more intense light.

In recent times, towards the end of the séance, whilst Stewart is within the cabinet with the curtain open, he is seen to levitate up to approaching 90 cm from the floor, this height being estimated from the fact that the luminous tabs just below his knees (attached to his trousers) are at least at eye level to the surrounding sitters. Stewart is conscious when this occurs and invariably utters a few exclamations − no doubt feeling a bit precarious!

Dr Barnett occasionally administers healing by the laying on of hands. The author's wife had a medically incurable problem that was leading to loss of sight in one of her eyes. She could not, with that eye, see the eye chart let alone the lettering on it. It was over three years ago that she received healing from Dr Barnett and she has had excellent eyesight with that eye ever since.

There have been other excellent reports of healing such as an impending operation being averted, much to the shock of the patient's consultant, who found the condition had mysteriously disappeared.

Survival evidence

The physical phenomena demonstrated at these séances does not on its own constitute survival evidence. Spiritualism is primarily concerned with providing evidence of an afterlife so there is always survival evidence in the form of communications from loved ones who have passed on.

As the majority of the phenomena occur in the dark, the evidence is of an audible nature, apart from when a sitter is touched or stroked in a particularly distinctive and significant way associated with the discarnate person claiming to communicate.

The audible evidence takes the form of personal communications from loved ones who have passed on and can be by direct voice (via trumpet), by independent direct voice, or by trance via the medium's vocal apparatus. Sometimes this evidence is outstanding, for example, when a father communicated one day after his funeral and signified that he knew what had happened at the funeral. No one present, apart from the recipient, knew of the unfortunate and particularly sad event that had occurred at this funeral (Sutton, 2007).

On several occasions outstanding survival evidence has been reported using 'book tests' (Farrow-Topolovac, 2007). These were similar to those produced through the mediumship of Gladys Osborne Leonard in the early part of the last century (Gauld, 1982). The latest tests, in 2006, involved three sitters, each attending different séances (held in Spain, Switzerland, and for one sitter, several séances in the UK).

All of the books successfully selected by Stewart's Spirit controls, when found and identified by explicit directions, were discovered to have a particular significance to the participants. Two of these books were in foreign languages, one very poorly known to the sitter. The overall success rate was excellent. Great success is also reported by Farrow-Topolovac (2007) with locating photos[6] instead of books.

Séance closure

Séances end with a prayer and then time is allowed for the medium to return to normal consciousness from his previous apparent state of deep trance. A fairly low intensity red light is switched on to allow the sitter, who checked the medium's straps initially, to confirm that they are still in place.

Although the medium was paranormally released from both straps for the 'materialised hand' experiment, he will have been paranormally strapped in again at the end of that experiment. This fact is observable when the red light is switched on for the participants to return to their normal places.

The wrist straps are cut and the medium, who is usually a little disorientated, is then guided out of the room. The circle leader then brings the proceedings to an end.

Verification of phenomena

Stewart Alexander is happy for psychic investigators to attend his séances. Indeed, prominent SPR members attended and contributed to a seminar with séances in 1997 (Sutton, 1997). Since then there have been major advances in his mediumship.

However, Stewart (personal communication 2008) has made clear he will not subject himself to the never ending scrutiny of sceptics who can never be satisfied. He said:

'When I first began to sit for the public, and for several years, I insisted upon my arms, body, legs and ankles being bound to my chair, but even that was not sufficient to stop criticism. I finally decided to abandon such methods of control since experience proved they were a fruitless path to pursue.

(6) *See:- 'New Wonders in Yorkshire' – Farrow-Topolovac (References). An example of this phenomenon; at a séance at the Edinburgh College of Parapsychology, (in 2006) the location and description of a photograph was given by Freda to a sitter who had just communicated with her deceased grandmother. She described it a group photograph – three ladies all wearing hats. The following day this was confirmed by the recipient and a copy of the picture was presented to me. (Stewart Alexander)*

Having studied extensively the history of physical mediumship over the past forty years, I am very aware that almost without exception those mediums who cooperated with the researchers, in the hope of establishing their mediumship on a scientific level, invariably failed and were forever surrounded in bitter dispute and allegations of fraud. In cases where tests were inconclusive (the usual case) and/or the tests were favourable to the medium, then more tests were demanded. In short, from beginning to end they found themselves in a no-win situation.

I therefore have no intention of proceeding down that well worn path feeling that to do so would simply be negative and pointless because almost certainly history would repeat itself (the recent Scole experiment[7] being a perfect example). My intention in holding public séances has always been to encourage others to sit for development of physical mediumship, now exceedingly rare, and to help bring reassurance of survival to sitters.'

❖ ❖ ❖

I suspect Stewart's attitude is partly influenced by the experiences of his main spirit control. Walter Stinson[8] has provided ample evidence to satisfy Stewart and others of his authenticity. Walter allegedly spent many years trying to prove the mediumship of his sister, Mina 'Margery' Crandon[9], when he operated through her, just as he allegedly does through Stewart. Mina's experiences are précised well by Fontana (2005)·

So often investigators have ignored a fundamental principle of science – to examine the evidence without prejudice. In their eyes it can't happen so it must be fraud. Open-minded scepticism on the other hand is to be encouraged and helps prevent us from following false trails.

---

(7) *The 'Scole Experiment' revolved around a circle based in Scole, Norfolk. During the 1990s, over a period of several years, they regularly enjoyed quite extraordinary physical phenomena. By invitation some Senior Council members of the SPR attended the sessions on many occasions. Their detailed findings when published were favourable to the phenomena. Included in the report were a number of criticisms from fellow Council Members which resulted in some controversy and dispute. (Stewart Alexander)*

(8) *Walter Stinson is largely responsible at my séances for the creation and presentation of the physical manifestations but he is not, as implied here, my main spirit guide. (Stewart Alexander)*

(9) *Mina Crandon was known under the pseudonym of 'Margery'. (Stewart Alexander)*

Summary

The procedures and controls under which Stewart Alexander's séances are conducted is likely to be as far as the medium will go towards satisfying any restrictions or conditions that sceptics would wish to impose on his séances. Mina Crandon's extensive co-operation with investigators, like many other mediums, came to almost nothing. Stewart has made it clear that he will not follow that same 'fruitless path'.

Stewart Alexander's reluctance to participate in scientific tests is a great loss to psychical research but who can blame him? Prejudiced investigations over the last 100 years or so have sullied the name of paranormal research in the eyes of many a physical medium. It is so easy to hint at fraud without justifying such suggestions. The fact that there have been fraudulent mediums should not taint them all. The media of course headlines the negative report and so often neglects the substantial amount of research completed by open minded investigators.

Rather than attempting to satisfy the sceptics, Stewart holds public seminars and séances to instruct and encourage others to sit for developing physical mediumship – which has become so very rare.

References

Bradley, H. Dennis (1924). 'Towards the Stars'. London: T. Werner Laurie Ltd.

Farrow -Topolovac, S. (2007). 'New wonders in Yorkshire'. *Zerdin Buzz Sheet*, 13, p30-31. (now known as Zerdin Phenomenal)

Fontana, David. (2005). 'Is There An Afterlife? A Comprehensive Overview of the Evidence'. Ropley, UK: O Books 13, 300-307.

Gauld, Alan. (1982). 'Mediumship and Survival'. Series editor Brian Inglis. London : William Heinemann Ltd (on behalf of SPR), 47-49.

Sutton, L. (1997). 'Noah's Ark seminar at Cardiff'. *Psychic World*, October 1997, 46, 1.

Sutton, L. (2007). 'Séance contact day after funeral'. *Psychic World* January 2007, 157, 2.

❖   ❖   ❖

Chapter 12

I Visit Switzerland

A report by the Swiss Journal of Parapsychology (Basler Psi-Verein), patrons of Europe's largest parapsychology congress, covering the séances I gave in Switzerland in 1999.

Several months before I resigned from the Noah's Ark Society in 1999, I began to conduct for members regular weekly guest séances in our home circle séance room and also private one-to-one trance sittings. These small intimate séances were to prove to be an unqualified success.

I believe that principally this was due to the size of the room which could only accommodate about twelve people. Everything therefore – communication and phenomena – were far more concentrated with all participants having a ringside seat.

On the other hand, I felt most uncomfortable with the private one-to-one trance sittings which I gave each Thursday afternoon throughout that year. Today, with hindsight, my dislike of them is not difficult to understand. My many years of mediumistic development and my public work as a medium had, until that time, conditioned me to work only within darkened rooms. Everything had been geared towards physical phenomena. Then, following innumerable requests, I had taken the unfortunate decision to give private sittings and did so not in darkness but in red light. Always I faced them with apprehension and misgivings and the repugnant feeling that I would be 'on show' as against being a part of the darkness within which I had habitually and comfortably merged.

Those private sessions lasted on average for sixty minutes. Always I arrived at Ray and June's home at 1pm and by 1.30pm I would be in the trance state and remain within it for many hours to be visited by a succession of clients. It all seemed most strange to me. It was trance to order – it very quickly became a job and there was no joy in it for me.

Inadvertently I had become a professional medium, and that ran contrary to my nature.

I found that under those circumstances, the imposed load of responsibility was far too great to bear, as people arrived from home and abroad with such expectations. I longed to be free of it all and to return to working solely within the dark séance room. That was my comfort zone; that is where I belonged and so it would not be long before I took the decision to fulfil my commitments of private sittings for the remainder of the year, then to accept no more.

In May of that year I was also to demonstrate my mediumship in Switzerland, having accepted an invitation from Dr Hans Schaer – a Swiss lawyer and a member of the NAS. This would be my first work outside the UK and I was accompanied by my wife and by Ray and June Lister. Throughout our stay we were guests in the home of Dr Schaer who had kindly taken on the responsibility of organising arrangements for my work for two Swiss Parapsychological organisations with which he was connected. The Zurich-based 'Schweizer Parapsychologische Gesellschaft' (Parapsychological Society of Switzerland) and the Basle-based ' Basler Psi-Verein' (Basle Psi-Association).

In total I was to give three séances with the first two held in Zurich and the final one in Basle. I also gave a small number of private one-to-one trance sittings.

The following report[1] of my visit appeared in the August 1999 issue of the PARA Journal (Swiss Journal for Parapsychology and Esotericism) published by the Basler Psi-Verein.

This international organisation are patrons of the noted Basler Psi-Tage (Basle Psi-days) which is Europe's largest congress in respect of all areas of parapsychology and the border areas of science. The article was written by the association's president Lucius Werthmuller with additional contributions by two sitters who participated at the Zurich séances.

Spirit Hands and Flying Trumpets

Introduction

Physical mediumship is the most spectacular but also the most controversial form of mediumship. Since the very beginning of

(1) *This has been partially condensed from the original.*

modern Spiritualism up until the middle of the twentieth century there were endless controversies as to whether it was genuine.

Since then little had been heard about it but during the last decade (the 1990s)[2] it would appear to have gone through a renaissance. The best known exponents of this revival being represented by the Noah's Ark Society based in England. For the past few years we have heard and read astonishing things about the Society which now has members in 22 countries and so the debate about such mediumship is very much alive again.

Stewart Alexander is a former president of the Noah' s Ark and at its seminars has often produced amazing phenomena. He trained and developed his mediumship in the English tradition for more than 30 years during which period he sat at least once a week in a home circle. In the middle of May this year Stewart, and members of his circle, held three experimental séances in Switzerland – their first outside Great Britain.

I had the opportunity to participate in two of them.

Prior to each séance he addressed his audience through a translator about the history of Spiritualism and also about the various forms of mediumistic manifestations.

He also spoke of his own development and how physical phenomena had gradually unfolded within his circle.

Following his talk, people were asked to vacate the room which was then prepared for the séance and chairs were arranged in concentric circles. Participants were then asked to return one by one and were checked to ensure that no one brought in with them anything that could produce a light. Cameras, matches, lighters, etc were not permitted. Such a safety check was most important due to the fragile state of the medium's body during the séance. The sudden introduction of light of any kind could apparently cause serious damage to the medium's health.

Stewart prepared himself in a side room and when he returned he already appeared to be in a state of disassociation. He took his place in a chair with wooden arms and both his arms were secured to them by means of strong plastic cable ties. After the séance, Ray Lister, a member of the medium's circle, used wire cutters to cut through them and thus free him. The securing of the medium and his later release were controlled by a participant.

(2) *This report was written in 1999.*

The Séance Begins

At both of the sessions that I attended the first 'being' who communicated was 'White Feather'. After a few words of welcome a communicator calling himself Christopher then spoke and with his humour and child-like loving manner he quickly eased tension amongst the sitters. The change in the medium's voice from a deep baritone to the high pitch of a child was amazing. The next 'being' was Freda Johnson who talked about the Spirit World and its connection to us.

It was she who later conveyed personal evidential messages to some of the participants. The fourth Spirit communicator was Walter Stinson who is mainly responsible for the production of the physical phenomena.

Soon the medium's arms were paranormally freed from his plastic cable restraints and then – without human intervention – were once again secured. The later personal account of this experiment by participant Tina Luscher explains the phenomena in some detail.

A lady (see Gabriella von Glasgow report below) was then invited to sit at the medium's small table which had a glass top and which was positioned immediately in front of him. A red bulb mounted beneath was then switched on and a cloud of ectoplasm was seen, out of which a hand materialised.

This took the lady's hand and turned it around. Then, several sitters claimed that they too had been touched by a hand. However, this phenomenon only happened at the first séance that I attended which was held in Zurich.

At both séances (Zurich and Basle) trumpets (cones of lightweight aluminium marked with luminous paint) rose into the air and flew through the room. First they knocked on the floor before rising hesitantly and then flying at high speed through the entire room. In Zurich, where the séance room was around six metres high, they flew up to the ceiling, knocked on the walls and completed the most exciting flight manoeuvres at breathtaking speed. They also touched several of the sitters. At the séance in Basle they also flew for a while but remained in just one part of the room where the medium and participants sat. I myself was touched twice in a very gentle way by one of the flying trumpets. Whilst, as requested by the trance communicators, all participants sang in order to heighten the atmosphere, Christopher tapped out the rhythm of the song on the table with the drumsticks that had been provided. Two additional phenomena occurred in Basle. One was a faint voice calling a participant by name but it was very soft and could not be heard throughout the room. During the séances Stewart came out of the trance state on two occasions but strangely the phenomena were still taking place – the trumpets were still flying and a direct voice could be heard. At the end of the Basle séance when the light came back on there was another surprise waiting for us. The shirt that the medium had worn under his pullover at the start of the séance was now seen to be lying on the floor in front of him at a distance of one metre. This happened in spite of the fact that his arms were fixed with plastic cable ties to the chair arms. It seems that his shirt had been dematerialised and then rematerialised and left on the floor.

Following a short break Stewart was available for questions.

These séances impressed me deeply. However, it has to be said that the arrangements left room for sceptical speculation. But for me personally, I am convinced that I witnessed genuine paranormal phenomena. The sincere and modest behaviour of Stewart Alexander and his fellow circle members convinced me even further.

❖ ❖ ❖

The Tina Luscher Report

The trance personality Walter Stinson asked me to sit at Stewart Alexander's side and to grasp his right hand which was secured to the chair arm. I took hold of it with my left hand and with my right I felt the plastic band that was tight around his arm and the chair arm rest.

Suddenly there was a jerk and my hand together with his own shot up into the air. There they stayed for a couple of minutes. During this time I felt the chair arm with my right hand and realised that the plastic band was no longer there. Suddenly there was a further jerk – our interlocked hands went down and by feeling Stewart's arm I discovered that again it was fixed tightly with a plastic band. Then I was seized by a hand and it was obvious to me that it could not be that of anyone else in the room. I was certain that it was a materialised hand. In one respect this was a shock to me but on the other hand I was deeply touched.

Some weeks earlier I had really desired to have a substantial contact with the Spirit World. Therefore, after the initial shock I was smiling and I was very happy with that solid touch particularly since I had participated at the séance with no expectations.

❖ ❖ ❖

The Gabriella von Glasgow Report

During the séance I realised that we have to encourage and communicate with the Spirit World in order to develop and maintain a strong connection. As the flying trumpets came to me I talked with Christopher who was speaking through Stewart Alexander. Then I was gently touched on the nose and on the cheek by them. Not long afterwards Walter enquired who the lady was who had spoken to Christopher. He wanted to know my name and he invited me to sit at his table. I accepted his invitation and he asked me to report out loud everything that I could see and feel. I placed my hand palm upwards on the table top which was illuminated with a red light from below. Soon a black mass appeared on it out of which fingers and a hand slowly formed. A warm, soft and pleasant hand of a man then grasped mine. It was not bony but fleshy. It pressed my hand, caressed it and left me with a firm handshake. It then dissolved and again became a black mass.

Walter then said to me; ' I hope that you had as much pleasure from that as I did' and I replied 'Sure did'. I was very touched and happy. It was my first experience of physical séance room contact with the Spirit World.

❖ ❖ ❖

That first visit to Switzerland proved to be a wonderful experience during which we made many new friends. More importantly, the séances I gave there introduced participants to physical phenomena and enabled them to witness the reality of such a dynamic and tangible form of two-world communication. That first visit created so much genuine interest that it was to lead to further visits until my final one in 2008.

However, those early séances in Switzerland proved to be amongst my last under the auspices of the NAS from which I resigned in 1999.

And After the Ark

Following my departure from the Ark I almost immediately began to receive invitations from far and wide to demonstrate my mediumship. Of course, these could not be accepted lightly. The safety aspect had to be the circle's principal consideration, because there is always an element of risk involved whenever the Spirit World withdraws from the medium the vital substance/energy known to Spiritualists as ectoplasm and then utilises it to create physical manifestations.

As I stated earlier, physical phenomena rest and depend entirely upon it. It is a living energy and it is a part of the physiology of the medium and its externalisation is safe providing the strict conditions of the séance room are not violated.

For example; the sudden introduction of light (artificial or natural) at a time when physical manifestations are occurring would cause the highly light sensitive ectoplasm to recoil and rapidly return to its source (the medium) with potentially catastrophic consequences to his/her health. Such dangers are inherent and therefore it required no great intellect for my circle and myself to realise that without the protection of the Society, which always went to considerable lengths to ensure the safety of its mediums, we had to consider all invitations with considerable caution.

History can teach us such a great deal and if we are wise, then we must always heed its warning.

Additionally, as a very private man, who courted neither notoriety nor publicity, I personally had no particular desire to continue to work in public and was content to simply disappear from the public arena and retire back into the obscurity of my home circle.

We also had to consider the fact that séances undertaken for the Society had, for some years, held back developments within the home circle. Such a sacrifice we had accepted simply because we had all felt that it was for 'the greater good'. They were opportunities for the Spirit World to reach a considerable number of people. It was hoped that in witnessing and experiencing what we always referred to as 'the great reality' sitters would be inspired and motivated to form their own circles and indeed many were.

So we felt that the slowing of progress in our circle was a small price to pay when balanced against the positive achievements born out of our public work.

These then had long been our major considerations. We also believed that without the burden of outside influence and concern our withdrawal from the Society had left us free to chart our own course and our future as a circle.

However, in spite of our good intentions we were soon to find that it was impossible to turn our backs on the many friends that we had made within the NAS who constantly enquired about possible future public sittings and also about the established Thursday evening guest circle. We were also receiving enquiries from other sincere Spiritualists who had never had the opportunity to witness physical communication with the Spirit World. So, whilst at that time I felt somewhat obliged to continue to sit for the occasional guest circle and large séance, we, as a circle, felt it important to sit away from the public arena for a while. This, we hoped, would give the Spirit World the opportunity to further develop the mediumship.

Unfortunately, this would not in reality prove entirely possible as invitations continued to flood in from home and abroad and I felt overwhelmingly obliged to comply.

Although we tried very hard to limit such demonstrations, in the next few years I was to work throughout England, in Scotland and in Wales.

I travelled to Switzerland again on several occasions and now I was also able to visit Sweden. However, I did turn down offers from Australia, America, Argentina, Canada, Finland, Denmark, Norway and Germany, mainly because until 2006 I owned an extremely busy company which required my continuous presence and input. On the few occasions that I did have time away from it I first had to make involved, difficult and elaborate arrangements. Therefore, I strenuously limited my absence from my company.

In the next chapter I include a selection of previously published séance reports which, I consider are largely representative of the mass public demonstrations that I gave in both England and Scotland following the NAS years.

Although I could with ease have filled many volumes with similar reports in my possession, it would have served no purpose.

By including such material, my sole intention is to impress upon the reader the truth of all that I and others have written about. As I pointed out in my letter to my readers at the beginning of this book, nothing contained herein is a matter of egocentricity.

Rather, it is perhaps my final opportunity to leave on permanent record a rare insight into my world of dark rooms and of people who, having once walked this earth, have returned to share with all who will listen their own glorious message of survival.

Within these pages, I have endeavoured, mainly through the words of those who have attended my public séances, to give the Spirit World a voice which may influence the lives of all who read this book both now and in the future.

That is all.

Chapter 13

Here, There and Everywhere

More previously published reports of my public séances in Bristol, Scotland and Norfolk.

Always when I travelled in England, Scotland and abroad I was most fortunate not to do so alone. For that I have long been indebted to my loyal, dependable friends – Ray and June Lister who, as the leaders of the home circle, have long been at my side. Whenever they were unavailable, then my friends June and Alf Winchester invariably took their place. As the ex-president and vice-president of the NAS their knowledge of physical mediumship is considerable. Because of the nature and inherent dangers attached to the demonstration of such mediumship then wise and reliable support is crucial. It is to such a person or persons that the responsibility falls to ensure the safety of the medium who, when in the trance state is unable to protect him or her self. Such support is without price and throughout the history of modern Spiritualism invariably it can be seen that physical mediums who demonstrated in public deemed it essential. They rarely travelled alone and they rarely exercised their mediumship in the absence of their dependable companions. The crucial task of controlling the conduct of sitters fell directly upon them. Ray and June and/or Alf and June, in being always at my side, have long performed that role.

In respect of large public séances the quality of phenomena and evidential communication will always vary considerably but never – to my recollection – did we ever have a totally blank sitting where nothing whatsoever happened. Evidently, the Spirit people would move heaven and earth not to disappoint. On the occasion of my very first large public séance, I had mistakenly entered into it believing that for the Spirit World it would have been quite a simple affair.

In my ignorance I had imagined that with so many people present, and therefore all the extra energy available, the usual difficulties would be removed. There would be an inexhaustible amount of energy, with which they would be capable of moving mountains. Sadly, I could not have been more incorrect. I soon came to realise that within the home circle the Spirit workers were very familiar with the energy of all the individual members. On the other hand, large groups presented them with energies with which they were unfamiliar. It was therefore remarkable that they were able to produce any results whatsoever.

At such events the obstacles that faced them were many and although now, all these years later, it seems so obvious to me, it was, back then, to be quite some time before I recognised my own profound ignorance in such matters.

So I now present a small selection of public séance reports which I believe readers will find to be of interest. From them a clearer insight may be gained into my life as a medium and the manifestations associated with it. For brevity all the accounts have been edited. All are included courtesy of the journals in which they first appeared.

Music, Trumpets and White Feather

Originally published in *Psychic News*, 9th December 2000, Issue No. 3574.

The members and friends of the Redland Spiritualist Church had the privilege of welcoming medium Stewart Alexander to Bristol on the 9th and 10th of October. On the Monday evening Stewart and twenty-five guests sat for a private materialisation circle at the home of well known local Spiritualist Doug Powell. This proved to be a wonderful experience for all present. For those who have never attended such an event, here is a brief description of what took place. The medium was securely bound to his chair at the ankles, wrists and waist with heavy-duty cord. No sitter was allowed to take into the séance room cameras, torches or matches since any light could cause serious damage to a materialisation medium's health. However, Stewart is well protected by June and Ray Lister, his minders, organisers and circle leaders. His safety is of paramount importance to them and their devotion to him is plainly evident.

After an opening prayer it was only a matter of minutes before Stewart's guide White Feather began to speak in his Native

American accent. He welcomed all present and expressed his joy at the opportunity to build a bridge of communication between the two worlds. He then congratulated Doug Powell on his careful preparation of the séance room and said that the conditions were excellent for the purposes of the séance.

Then little Christopher 'popped in'. Everyone was delighted to hear the voice of the small child and the atmosphere was charged with great energy due to the laughter as Christopher proceeded to charm the sitters with his light hearted humour. The little boy assured anyone who might be nervous that there was no need to be since 'if a ghost appeared in the room now – I would be the first one out of the door'. The next communicator was Walter Stinson, brother of well-known Spiritualist pioneer, Margery Crandon. He wasted no time in telling sitters that if they expected wise and elevated speeches, they would be disappointed as the purpose of the sitting was simply to link the two worlds together in love and harmony.

Again, the atmosphere was lightened by laughter as Walter flirted with the ladies present! He explained that the energy needed from the medium for physical manifestations would take time to generate and could not be rushed. Many, he said, would feel uncomfortable around the solar plexus as energy would be 'borrowed' for the same purpose. However, he assured everyone that it would be returned later. He then asked if anyone would care to ask a question. A lady responded and was immediately invited to sit beside the medium and hold his right hand with her left. Then she was instructed to feel with her right hand the strap which bound his hand and arm to the chair. She then announced with excitement that he had raised his hand above his head which, she exclaimed, 'is quite impossible'. Walter explained that she had witnessed the passing of matter-through-matter – i.e. the medium's arm through the restraining strap. Permission was given for the lights to be slightly raised and all were astounded to see that Stewart's arm was quite free of the strap which had been left firmly tied to the chair arm. Walter explained that this was no miracle but a demonstration of natural law. The lady participant was again excited to report that a third hand had materialised and was patting her arm and this was audible throughout the room. She was then invited to remain behind after the circle for a private sitting as there was a 'football team' of loved ones in the Spirit World waiting to speak to her. Music was next played to heighten the energy and two trumpets, edged with luminous paint, began to proceed around the room.

As they did so they began to touch the sitters one by one on the hand, knee or face as they effortlessly floated up to the ceiling and around the room accompanied by sounds of 'Ahhh! – Oh! – Lovely etc' as everyone was simply entranced by the experience. Even the medium was allowed to 'wake up' for a few moments to see the trumpets. Very soon after this, a 'speaking mechanism' was created by the Spirit people from ectoplasm for the purposes of direct communication. This mechanism (a so-called voice box) was quite separate and therefore detached from the medium and the voice that began speaking from it was audible to all from a different location. This communicator spoke articulately about the wonderful reality of Spirit communication and went on to explain that by working together we become as a united team – that we become as one in service. He spoke of taking our experience out into the world to share it with all who would listen. 'We cannot do this alone my friends,' was his message, 'and with a greater understanding and knowledge regarding the very nature of life itself then you would truly attain heaven upon your earth.' At this point the voice box began to fail and it became too weak to function and communication was transferred back to the medium. The next communicator introduced herself as Freda Johnson in a very 'school-marmish' voice.

All were called to attention as she explained that although she was female the voice had male intonations, as she was speaking through Stewart's 'bits and pieces'. She wanted us all to know that it was an extremely uncomfortable process. She then went on to pass various messages through to several sitters including one lady who was given a message from her mother. This included many intimate details known only to the two of them. Freda then allowed the mother to attempt to speak directly to her daughter. A very emotional exchange then followed after which the lady was left in no doubt that her mother – with considerable effort – had indeed spoken to her. Later in the séance Walter organised a demonstration of materialisation and the lady was able unmistakably to recognise her mother's hand which was displayed upon the under-lit glass table top. Then a further hand was materialised in the centre of the table which many sitters were able to see because of its luminosity.

Before White Feather's final words of blessing, Walter closed the evening by thanking everyone present for supplying the necessary energy through their love and kindly thoughts. He apologised that on this occasion, due to conditions beyond his control, he had been unable to leave the cabinet and walk amongst us. Nevertheless, everyone present was very pleased with the wonderful experience gained and all left the room in a buzz of excitement.

The following day Stewart gave a short talk to a packed Church Guild explaining how his mediumship had developed. He, Ray and June had been sitting in a circle together for almost thirty years. Following this he briefly left the room to compose himself and upon return quickly slipped into trance. Again White Feather, Walter, Freda and Christopher were in attendance with the same high standard of communication. The Church Secretary and her mother were given the opportunity to speak to their father and husband who spoke through the medium. A very emotional conversation resulted which had the entire audience in tears as indisputable evidence was given. This included the name of the gentleman (and the name of his mother-in-law who apparently had accompanied him) and he recalled incidents relating to their lives together.

Stewart Alexander is a self-effacing, non-egotistical, genuine person whose warmth and charisma permeated the room. Those in attendance at these two events thank him and his supporters June and Ray Lister, for sharing their knowledge of the great truth of survival.

❖ ❖ ❖

Stewart's Scottish Tour

Originally published in *Psychic World,* June 2005, Issue No.138.

Mary Armour

Returning home physically tired, but spiritually enriched, the team (Mary and Joe Armour, Alf and June Winchester and, of course Stewart Alexander) parted company in Glasgow on Saturday 7th May, with many requests having been made for a return visit in 2006.

The medium and his entourage commenced this exciting eight-day tour, at the College of Psychic Studies[1], Melville Street in Scotland's capital city Edinburgh. On the Saturday morning at a one-day Seminar Alf was the first to speak and supported his talk, about famous physical mediums from the past, with photographic slides. Stewart followed him by relating the marvellous and miraculous story of his development, an incredible journey of happiness, tears, hard work and dedication. In the afternoon Mary Armour spoke of 'Science in the Séance Room' and discussed the work of past SPR researchers.

This highly successful seminar was indeed a wonderful beginning to what would prove to be an unforgettable phenomenal week. And just when delegates thought it could not get any better, in the evening there was a deep trance demonstration by Stewart.

Many attending receiving glorious, tear-jerking and also happy communications from their loved ones from the higher realms – the evidence being 'out of this world'.

On the following day the team began to blackout the College library and arrange seats in readiness for the evening séance. Several hours later the room became a sanctum where the two worlds met and for over two hours we were to witness many things including the passage of matter-through-matter. In red light we all observed ectoplasmic hands and viewed trumpets dancing high in the air. The evidence given to sitters, by direct or independent voices, being instantly recognised and verified by the recipients. One outstanding materialisation was a Dr Barnett who gave healing to me and advised that the benefit would only be felt two or three days later. Many were physically touched in love by the solid warm hands of the Spirit people. A wonderful experience for all who attended the event.

The next day we travelled on to Portobello to meet our hosts where, in their church everyone enjoyed another outstanding evening of trance by Stewart. The following day (the Tuesday) we found ourselves back at the College in Edinburgh for another remarkable séance, this time for East Lothian Spiritualists who were privileged to witness the truly wonderful manifestations, phenomenal demonstrations of the power of our Spirit communicators.

(1)Renamed as Edinburgh College of Parapsychology in 1974 but still referred to by many as the College of Psychic Studies.

Wednesday found us heading off to one of Scotland's islands. We were literally going 'Doon the Watter' to the beautiful island of Rothesay. Mary Armour's 'White Rose Group' presented a night of healing, clairvoyance and trance, the energy and loving atmosphere within the room being dynamic, which is so seldom apparent within today's Spiritualism.

On the following day things were to get even better. Having sat with Stewart since 1993 the writer found the séance on that evening was to be his best ever. With only nineteen sitters present we were able to form one reasonable sized circle where everyone literally had a ringside seat.

The séance began with the usual phenomena and then one young lady was called forward by Walter Stinson to sit by Stewart's side. He impressed her so much (as she did him) that she later requested a picture of him. Walter, of course, was the brother of the famous 'Margery' and he lost his life in a railway accident at the age of twenty-eight in 1911. Just over ten years later he began to manifest through his sister's outstanding mediumship and today, he has continued his work through our own Stewart Alexander.

The palpable energy in that room was such that after the demonstration of all the usual phenomena there was still sufficient to levitate the table to a great height. This had been standing in the middle of the floor and was illuminated by red light. Indeed, the icing on the veritable cake.

After the séance we all enjoyed a buffet supper at the nearby tearooms to marvel at, and to discuss the intertwining of the two worlds we had just witnessed. This, incidentally, had not been the first time the island had been visited by a physical medium. Between the years 1913 and 1919 there had been séances in Glenbeg House the home of ardent Spiritualist James Coates who owned the Coates Mill in Paisley. The medium was the renowned Mrs Etta Wriedt of Detroit, Michigan, U.S.A. The coincidence does not end there. Mrs Wriedt was often conscious at her séances as is our medium. She used to go to Berkley Street in Glasgow following her sittings in Rothesay and folks, just guess where Stewart's next venue was?

Our journey to Berkley Street Church the following day was to be somewhat historic as we went via Callander, Perthshire, the one-time home of Helen Duncan who, of course, many believe had been the finest materialisation medium in history. There we visited one of Helen's nieces and a good friend of mine, Mrs FlossieMacfarlane. For two hours we sat enthralled as we listened to her childhood memories of her Aunt Helen, or Nell, as the family affectionately called her. Late in the afternoon we finally and reluctantly bade Flossie a fond farewell and set off on the last leg of our odyssey to the Association of Spiritualists, Berkley Street, Glasgow.

Arriving that evening somewhat exhausted, we partially prepared the blackout for the Saturday evening séance which would be held following a full day seminar.

This commenced with Alf once again sharing with students his extensive knowledge and recollections of spiritual mediums. He was followed by Stewart who had people sitting on the edge of their seats as he told of 'his journey' of development. The morning closed with a choice of workshops, the development of mental mediumship (clairvoyance etc.) conducted by excellent young local medium Stewart Esler and yours truly taking a trance development class. The afternoon was filled with most interesting lectures and a demonstration of mental mediumship by three mediums working in unison – excellent young mediums Stewart Esler, Peter Gough, and myself.

And then, as a climax, and as the zenith of all our expectations, the two worlds once again merged at the evening séance. White Feather eventually, and reluctantly, closed the circle and what was the experience of a lifetime drew to a close with yours truly still overawed at the visible levitation of the table in red light.

❖ ❖ ❖

Materialised Hand in Red Light

Originally published in *Psychic World*, August 2007, Issue No164.

Denzil Fairbairn (Oxfordshire)

The following experiment took place at the Cromer, Norfolk, home of Alf and June Winchester on the evening of Friday 4th May 2007. The purpose-built room, where various types of mediumship are demonstrated, is roughly square in shape and large enough to seat twenty people comfortably around its perimeter. The physical medium, Stewart Alexander, was seated in his own chair at one end of the room within the area known as the medium's cabinet.

This consisted of two lightweight curtains, suspended from a ceiling-mounted curtain rail, which were at times drawn to form an enclosure with the wall directly behind Stewart.

Prior to the commencement of the evening's proceedings the room in which the demonstration would take place was thoroughly searched for any wires or contraptions or devices which conceivably could be considered to aid the phenomena that we hoped would manifest later that evening. This was carried out by a company director from Northamptonshire along with myself (I am a fourth generation Spiritualist and highly experienced in matters of physical mediumship). Also present was the venue owner Alf Winchester who was on hand to answer any questions we may have had. Our search revealed no surreptitious devices within the room and we were both satisfied.

Following communication at the séance with Stewart's regular Spirit team of communicators and various significant demonstrations of the matter-through-matter experiment and trumpet levitation, Alf Winchester was requested to switch on the light-box. This piece of equipment is made from what appears to be a converted coffee table approximately 24 inches in diameter with solid sides and an opaque top which allows varying degrees of light to filter through it. The light mounted inside is operated by a remote dimmer switch. I have personally seen the box utilised on numerous occasions at Stewart's demonstrations but I have to advise that I have never witnessed as high a degree of luminosity as was displayed that evening. Indeed, there was sufficient light, at times, to see the sitters on the opposite side of the room, some 8-10 feet (2.5-3 metres) distant.

Then the alleged materialised hand appeared on the light-box top whilst the medium's wrists were securely attached to the arms of his chair, with no means of escape save by cutting through the plastic cable ties with pliers. Following this experiment, Walter, one of Stewart's main controls, asked for the people sitting either side of the medium to move their chairs so that they were sitting facing each other at opposite sides of the box.

An additional lady was then called forward to sit at the far side of the light-box facing the medium. Each person was then asked to place their outspread hands on top of it so that their fingers were touching. Walter then released Stewart's hands from their restraining ties (we were led to believe that this was through the process of passing matter-through-matter' as no other means of escape was viable) and placed alongside those of the other participants' hands so that they were all touching. This was done within the red light emitting from the light-box beneath their hands. With confirmation given that the hands of all four people were in contact with each other, several of the sitters closest to the experiment were able to confirm that they could also see clearly that all hands were in place and touching. I myself was one of those close enough (24 inches – 60cm) to observe very clearly what happened next. A sense of anticipation filled me. However, before moving on I shall reiterate – there were four pairs of hands clearly visible showing in strong black silhouette against the background of the red light emanating through the top of the light-box. Then, within a matter of seconds, a mass began moving on to its surface from the direction of the medium and as it passed his hands so it began to metamorphose, gradually changing from a shapeless mass into that of a hand. Before taking full form, those of us close by could see a gradual change in the density of the mass, particularly that located between each of the fingers, which changed from obscure, to opaque, to the appearance of sheer gossamer. And then finally it disappeared to leave a fully formed hand in the middle of the box which was wholly animated, knocking vigorously on the box surface to create a rapid audible tapping sound.

Now, readers must ask themselves a question. Where did the hand come from?

Those seated next to Stewart guaranteed that at all times they were in contact with his hands and this we as observers could clearly see.

The materialisation process of the hand was also played out in full view of all the participants who were close by.

Therefore, unless Stewart is able to grow, at will, an extra appendage, and then cause it to disappear once the experiment is over, then one is forced to the inescapable conclusion that what took place was one of, if not the most remarkable piece of life continuation evidence produced in a demonstration of physical phenomena in modern times.

It was a privilege to observe, witness and be a part of this small experiment. It just shouts to the world that there simply must be a continuation of intelligence and therefore life beyond that of the physical which, under suitable conditions, can manifest to prove its own existence.

❖ ❖ ❖

People unfamiliar with the Spiritualist séance room invariably imagine that the proceedings are sombre affairs which are generally revered by apprehensive participants.

Some may feel that such things ought not to be 'messed with' whilst others are convinced that they harbour tom-foolery orchestrated by bogus unscrupulous mediums out to make a fast buck. That the dead are dead and therefore that there cannot be communication between our world and a mythical spiritual one. Such arguments are generally based upon ignorance of the facts. Within this and previous chapters I have endeavoured to show that, contrary to such widespread impressions, in reality the physical séance room is a place of joy, laughter and wonderment. I also hope that I have now successfully made a *prima facie* case for survival and communication and that readers will be encouraged to read on.

In the following pages I intend to illustrate further that death is a mere fleeting event in life and that given the opportunity the so-called dead can and do return to our world with their glorious message of continuous life.

Chapter 14

The Seminars

Annual weekend residential physical phenomena seminars ~ Previously published reports from a French scientist and a Canadian medium on the séances they attended at the seminars ~ Code word proves survival at York.

In the year 2000, in response to a considerable number of requests, I decided, together with my friends Alf and June Winchester, to conduct a weekend residential Seminar at a North Yorkshire Hotel / Retreat. Our carefully considered intention was to base its programme around quality mediumship, both mental and physical, and to include demonstrations of both. Additionally, we planned a variety of lectures about séance room phenomena both historic and contemporary and offered a choice of workshops designed to constructively help those individuals with mediumistic potential to develop their abilities. We also decided that on the Saturday evening there would be the opportunity to attend an experimental physical séance with myself as the medium. Considerable thought was given to the creation of what we hoped would prove to be a varied and interesting programme of events. The mediums and speakers invited to demonstrate and lecture were chosen with great care. Furthermore, based upon our own convictions and the experience that we had acquired during our NAS days, we suspected that there would probably be considerable interest in a seminar which promised to exclude the kind of fringe subjects which had gradually infiltrated and attached themselves to present day Spiritualism.

So-called 'New Age' activities and 'channelling' and the kind of nonsense that had gradually corrupted and brought Spiritualism to its knees. These would have no place.

It would be back to basics – it would be free of what we believed to be absurdity.

And within days of the Seminar being advertised under the title

'Stewart Alexander and Friends', it was sold out with a long waiting list of people who had been unable to secure a place.

When the weekend finally arrived we were delighted to welcome and renew friendships with many people who had been, or who were still members of the NAS together with those whom we had not previously met.

At the very first session, which followed dinner on the Friday evening, I personally welcomed all the participants and introduced to them our team of speakers and mediums.

I also reminded them just how important it was for us to create between us a warm and harmonious atmosphere within which the team could best work and which would enable the Spirit World to draw close. I pointed out that this could not be over-emphasised and it behove us all to leave outside the hotel, for the duration of our stay, our everyday problems and concerns. Quite simply they did not belong there. Ambience would be everything and if we could function as a united team then we would be doing everything that our Spirit friends would expect of us.

As it was, I need not have worried. Everyone enjoyed a most wonderful invigorating weekend and left feeling physically and spiritually rewarded and fulfilled.

Indeed, if our success that weekend could be measured against the public response to the announcement of our next seminar planned for the following year, then it simply could not have been better. Again, it would be fully booked within days of it being advertised. This then would be the pattern for all subsequent seminars and indeed such was their success that it was not long before one seminar a year quickly became two. In the world of informed Spiritualism they soon became known as being inspirational and educational and also as wonderful social events. Today, we invariably welcome people not only from all parts of the UK but also from all over the world. The seminars have become truly international with people journeying from America, Australia, Canada, France, Germany, Sweden and Switzerland. Perhaps this endorses my belief that today there is indeed worldwide disappointment in Spiritualism as it now exists.

Somehow the way has been lost and with it a widespread belief that physical mediumship – once the flagship of the Movement – is of the past and as such is no longer welcome.

Following that first seminar the responsibility for arranging accommodation at the venue and organising subsequent programmes, speakers and mediums fell directly upon Alf and June Winchester. I myself have played a very minor role in spite of the fact that they still carry my name. Over the years we have been most fortunate to have had many excellent speakers but perhaps one of the most engaging and hugely popular has been Tom Harrison who, now in his nineties, is considered by many to be Spiritualism's elder statesman. From such a credible witness, his talks about his mother's circle, of which he had been a part, have been unique. They have been inspirational, emotional and dramatic, leaving one in no doubt that he has spoken from the heart.

His vivid recollections of astounding events simply captivate his audience for he is a living witness to the kind of séances, which today, we can only read about. Always he speaks with patent sincerity and humility. Enthralling the listener he takes them back to 1946, to a sitting room at the side of a baker's shop in Middlesbrough, the home of fellow circle members, Sydney and Gladys Shipman. What they witnessed in that circle every week for the next ten years was, by any stretch of the imagination, remarkable. For within that room the dead materialised in solid form and could be seen by all present. They could be felt and they could converse with the sitters. Little wonder therefore that Tom in the years that have since passed has remembered it all in detail. Indeed, how could he ever forget? However, of all his spellbinding tales, my own particular favourite has long been his description of the evening when the circle witnessed its very first materialisation. Never have I tired of listening to his emotionally charged account and I believe that it is worthy of a place in this book. With that in mind I approached Tom who, upon my request, kindly wrote the following which I am now happy to share with readers.

A Breathtaking Experience

We had been sitting for only eight months when, during a sitting on 7th December 1946, we were astounded to have such a phenomenal and breathtaking experience; truly 'out of this world'. Here in this everyday friendly sitting room adjacent to Sydney and Gladys' shop, with the door and windows locked, we opened and closed our sitting that evening with seven of us around the fireplace. Yet, for a few precious minutes during that sitting there had been eight of us, all clearly visible to each other in the red light.

This illuminated the room during the whole forty-five minute séance with my mother on her usual dining chair at the end of the semicircle of sitters around the fireplace in full view of everyone in the room. I always sat immediately opposite her at the other end of the semicircle and could clearly see everything that happened.

We sat for at least half an hour and nothing had happened, which was most unusual, and we had begun to think that there would be no phenomena that evening. Then, we saw on the floor between my mother and myself a white disc about two feet in diameter. Because of the smallness of the room I was never more than five feet from her and I could clearly see that the disc was linked to my mother who was in deep trance and knew nothing about what was happening. We were all very excited of course and as we chatted we saw this disc begin to evolve into a vertical white column which built to about five feet of solid ectoplasm. 'Amazing!' we said. The column remained still for a few minutes whilst we stared at it, getting more and more excited. Then, as I was watching, the top part of it began to twist towards me and I could see that there was a semblance of a face within it, but I could not recognise who it was. From the body of the column there then appeared two hands and arms covered by the ectoplasmic 'robes'. As the hands reached forward and approached me, I instinctively stretched out my hands towards them – not in any way frightened as it all seemed so natural. But still apprehensive, I suppose, about meeting a materialised Spirit person so close for the very first time. Then, our hands engaged and I realised that in my right hand I was being given four beautiful carnations – apports. As I grasped the flowers tightly, my two hands were firmly held by the warm ectoplasmic hands in front of me. I then heard, quietly but clearly, from the face above me, the words 'For you, for you'. The hands and arms went back into the column of ectoplasm which then shrank slowly to the floor as the ectoplasm returned to my mother. We were all left exceedingly breathless after such a unique experience. As for me, there I was sitting on my chair opposite my mother, with my mouth wide open, still tightly grasping the four carnations that I had received a few moments earlier and trying to appreciate the meaning of my 'brief encounter' of a most wonderful kind! We later learnt that our first visitor had been my mother's sister, Aunt Agg[1] who, because of her mediumistic qualities and

(1) *Mrs Agnes Abbott was a highly regarded professional medium at the Marylebone Spiritualist Association (MSA) in London, during the 1930s and 1940s.*

empathy with my mother, was thereafter to act as the 'test pilot' in the development of the phenomena. However, that night I found it difficult to fully comprehend the significance of her visit although there was no question about her presence as confirmed by the carnations I was still grasping minutes afterwards. We shared them amongst us and mine still has prime position in my folder of memorabilia, which I invariably take with me whenever I deliver my talks about our 'wonderful circle'.

❖ ❖ ❖

Wonderful indeed. Thank you Tom.

With each successive seminar, I have, as mentioned earlier, sat for the Saturday evening experimental séance with generally ninety plus people in attendance. At each we have enjoyed communication on a physical level with the Spirit World and whilst it would be a simple matter to now include innumerable past reports, I have chosen just two. Both were written by overseas visitors. The first is by a French researcher, who, whilst not a Spiritualist, attended because of his lifelong interest in physical phenomena and the second is by a Canadian visitor. The latter I chose simply because it illustrates so powerfully the impact that such phenomena can, and regularly do have upon people's lives.

I have concluded the chapter with a report in respect of a séance which, although not held at the usual venue in North Yorkshire, produced an exceedingly rare communication. This involved the transmission of a single 'code word' from the Spirit World which effectively proved survival.

The French Researcher

In March 2006, Dr Michel Granger, accompanied by his wife, travelled to the north of England and to our seminar from his home in Chalon-sur-Saône, Burgundy, near Lyon, France. Having researched in depth the phenomena of Spiritualism for many years he has been a member of the English SPR since 1981. His great interest can be traced back to the mid sixties when he was studying for a doctorate in physical chemistry at Montreal University.

Dr Granger, a chemist, has since written extensively on the paranormal with 12 books published and with over 1400 of his articles appearing nationally and internationally.

This was to be his very first personal experience of a physical séance.

His account of the event, under the heading; 'Mystery', was to appear in the French weekly newspaper; *'Dimanche – S & L'* (Saône et Loire) and an approximate translation into English now follows:

Mystery – Did I Shake the Hand of Someone who died in 1911?

A tangible hand with five fingers – warm – clearly alive and animated, with a benevolent attitude towards me! No, I have not lost my mind. I refer to the amazing experience I had when I witnessed this in person on Saturday, 18th March 2006 at a spiritual seminar held at a hotel in Northern England. I will now recreate for you the details that will be engraved on my memory for the rest of my days.

At a séance I was asked to place my hand on a little table which had an illuminated glass top. And with no one in front of me apart from a man sitting opposite in a state of trance, and immobilised in his chair, a hand, at first floating in outline and then much better formed, came and placed itself on the table directly in front of me. I had a sense of a normal human hand – firm and solid – a materialised ectoplasmic hand belonging to a 'guide' who was speaking through the medium and giving me the remarkable privilege of shaking the hand of a dead man.

Walter Stinson, in this case, was the Spirit guide of the medium (one of four who, over the next two hours, came one after another). He claimed to be a young Canadian who had been killed in a railway accident in 1911.

At the end of a long journey last weekend, my wife and I arrived at the hotel in North Yorkshire on the East coast of England having travelled by car, plane, train and taxi.

A trying and tiring journey but at least we were promised to be welcomed as privileged participants in a physical circle consisting of Stewart Alexander, one of the last mediums in England to produce physical psychic phenomena. Alf Winchester, the leader of the circle that night, transmitted to us in the afternoon indispensable important instructions for a successful séance. The 'circle' was arranged in several concentric ones more and more removed from the cabinet – a sort of alcove hung with curtains in front of which the medium sat. We were placed in the inner circle three places to the right of the medium. The main lights were turned off, and in the sem-darkness, Stewart was fastened to his seat by means of plastic ties that secured his wrists to the chair arms and which could only be removed by the use of pliers to cut through them.

Two phosphorescent strips were stuck to his knees to reveal his position at all times.

The main lights were then turned off to leave us in complete darkness.

I will pass now to the manifestations which then happened but, in passing, it should be noted that no entities spoke in French. We were impressed by the direct voices (alleged Spirit people who spoke from a point in space removed from the medium) that we only understood in snatches. We were dumbfounded by the parade of guests to the central chair (an empty chair in the centre of the circle) who came to meet again their deceased friends and loved ones. We were surprised by a fleeting glimpse of white ectoplasm thanks to the brief introduction of red light and we were intrigued by the flight of 'trumpets' (megaphones often used to amplify the volume level of direct voice manifestations).

These trumpets, made visible by phosphorescent paint, traced surprising arabesques in front of our flabbergasted eyes. We had not been sitting for long when 'Walter' desired to make a gift to the person who had come such a long way to be present, and he asked me to sit in the empty chair facing the little table which was positioned in front of the medium.

I was happy to oblige and, as requested, I extended my hand, palm downwards, on the illuminated table top. Captivated I then watched an indefinable mass extending out from the medium rapidly change into the form of a hand. I was asked to take it which I instinctively did with the impression that I described earlier. Later in the night, the energy developed in the circle permitted an ectoplasmic materialisation to manifest and to move around with audible footsteps. This was akin to the past experiences of physicist Sir William Crookes meeting with the materialised Katie King; with the psychic researcher Harry Price and the

Rosalie manifestation and physiologist Charles Richet confronted by the materialised priestess Phygia.

So – here I am – possessed forever by the question; 'Did I really shake the hand of someone who has been dead for ninety-five years?'

How I would truly love to know for certain. How this would help me to confront the issue 'what happens after death?' How I would love to be in a position which would enable me to convince readers of the reality of all that I witnessed. Without wishing to be trite, I pose this question and ask readers to reflect as I myself shall do. I see no motive that we should have travelled 2000km to be deceived and I thank Stewart Alexander and his friends for their warm welcome as extended to two people from France who were so unfamiliar with our hosts' language and beliefs ...

❖ ❖ ❖

The Canadian Visitor

Toronto based Carolyn Molnar has thirty years experience as a psychic medium and spiritual teacher and has conducted 'personal growth' seminars and workshops. As a highly respected international medium and spiritual author she has been featured on Canadian radio and television. The following report dated 2nd June 2008 was first posted on her Spiritual website (www.carolynmolnar.com) and I republished it below in abbreviated form. Later it was to appear in her book, 'Compassionate Messenger, True Stories of a Psychic Medium'[2].

After my last psychic development class, one of my students joked that, after working as a medium in Canada for twenty-eight years, there was surely nothing under the sun that amazed me!

'Not true,' I told her. In the first place life itself is a miracle and when you are into the flow of the joy of living, you notice amazing things all the time.

But in terms of sheer wonder, one of the most astounding things I have ever witnessed was in a séance led by English physical medium Stewart Alexander. Not only was I able to see a hand made from ectoplasm grow from the medium's chest – but it touched me.

(2) *Publisher; Dundurn Press - 2010*

Ectoplasm is a cobweb-like white substance that a medium releases which is then used by the Spirit people to assume a physical form. Think of breath on a cold night.

The Lily Dale museum, in Lily Dale, New York – the largest Spiritualist community in the world has several wonderful pictures of physical mediums exuding ectoplasm.

Some witnesses have described it as looking like 'cheese cloth' and smelling like ozone.

Last October, at a spiritual retreat in the North of England, Stewart demonstrated the art of physical trance mediumship. I had looked forward to the séance for two principal reasons. On a past occasion I had sat with him and I was aware of what we might expect.

And secondly, because one of his controls named Walter is a Canadian and therefore one of my fellow countrymen. Having met him at that previous séance I knew that he was charming and he had been delighted to meet another Canuck from across the pond.

At this séance none of the ninety or more people attending were to be disappointed.

Trumpets danced across the ceiling, and the Spirit people made their presence known through a variety of phenomena. But the highlight of the evening for me was when Walter called out 'Carolyn ma'm, come and sit with Stewart at the table'. Two other ladies were also called forth. The medium was sitting within his cabinet but his hands joined ours to form a circle of hands upon the glass table top which was lit from beneath with a soft red light. As we sat quietly in the darkness, a mist – a concentrated thick fog – appeared to leak from Stewart's solar plexus. 'Oh my God,' was my immediate thought as I stared intently at the glowing haze as it slowly coalesced into a mass. Then it evolved into a hand with webbed fingers and finally into a fully formed male hand. And this all took place right before our eyes. I heard gasps of surprise from those people sitting nearby.

'Hold still ma'm,' Walter said and with that, this ectoplasmic hand moved across the table and gently tapped the top of my hand. It was large and well defined. 'Not bad for a man who passed away a hundred years ago, eh?' Walter quipped. I felt light-headed and a little fearful and apprehensive to have been touched by the Spirit realm. It felt so – otherworldly. That is the best way that I can describe it. The 'skin' was warm – warmer than my own hand. Then a sensation of warmth flowed into my hand, up my arm and into my heart. I felt at once giddy and happy and I began to weep. I had an urge to grasp the hand more firmly and to really experience the connection with Spirit, but I resisted. After all, the ectoplasm was coming from Stewart and I knew that any firmness could harm him.

The next few minutes passed in a blur. Slowly the hand began to withdraw, back towards the cabinet. I was sorry to see it go. One of Stewart's 'aides' helped me back to my seat and the séance continued. Walter withdrew and Freda (another of the controls) took over the remainder of the evening by connecting audience members with their loved ones who had crossed over. In a daze and excited I was later unable to sleep. The experience of physical mediumship had been profound and at the same time a little sad because such mediumship is now a disappearing art. So few mediums now seem to be practising it.

❖ ❖ ❖

Secret Code Word Proves Survival at Séance

Originally published in *Psychic News*, 23rd August 2008, Issue 3968.

There is a saying beloved of those who know the truth of communication between this world and the next; 'It only takes one word'. Many people agree on a private word or message to be imparted by a loved one or friend after their passing. Sir Oliver Lodge did it – a thousand others have done it. But it is oh-so-rare for that precise communication to take place.

Former president of York Spiritualist Centre, Gerald O'Hara, made an agreement with Michael Cunningham, a long-standing friend, to communicate such a pre-arranged word. Gerald and Michael had been friends for twenty-two years at the time of Michael's passing in 1995.

Though he has often returned and given Gerald proof of his survival, it would not be until 2008, some thirteen years after his death, that Michael would manage to communicate the agreed code word. At a recent séance given by Stewart Alexander for a group of German Spiritualists, his circle guide, Freda Johnson, spoke to Gerald and said just one word – 'Marmalade'.

Michael had endured a lengthy period of ill health before his passing, and at times he tired easily. Well-meaning friends would visit him – some would inadvertently drain him, others would lift his spirits. Gerald was in the habit of telephoning Michael regularly, and over time a coded conversation evolved between them when others were present. If Michael had visitors but was feeling drained and unhappy, his telephone code word to Gerald would be 'Jam'. If on the other hand his visitors had enlivened him and made him happy, his word to Gerald would be 'Marmalade'. The pair agreed that Michael would use one or other of those words after his death, to prove his identity to Gerald.

Gerald told PN, 'In using the word 'Marmalade', Michael was not only saying, 'It's me,' he was also letting me know, 'I am happy.' Definitive proof of his survival and happiness in the next world.'

❖ ❖ ❖

In taking the decision to republish the above article it occurred to me that some readers, understandably, may take the view that the 'code word' was common knowledge.

I therefore requested a statement from the recipient to clarify this important issue. This is what he had to say:

'The 'code' was fixed by Michael and myself as a harmless way in which he could let me know if he was fatigued by visitors. It was 'Marmalade' if he was not, and it was 'Jam' if he was. Eventually we agreed that he would use it as a 'postmortem' communication to identify himself should the opportunity present itself.

I had never told anyone including my partner who, as a medium, I did not want to compromise, just in case the code word came via him. I was the only person living who knew the code and I wrote it in the last book that Michael gave to me so that, should it eventually be transmitted, I could prove the authenticity of the communication'.

Truthfully,

Gerald O'Hara

❖ ❖ ❖

Chapter 15

Touching the Soul

The moving story of a visitor who came to sit at a home circle guest séance and returned to sit many times.

Although my large public séances enabled sitters to witness phenomena and two-world communication on a physical level, and no doubt encouraged many people to form their own physical circles, unfortunately they would seldom produce the kind of results regularly achieved in our guest circles. As I wrote in an earlier chapter, with a great many people present at large meetings, and therefore a great many unfamiliar energies to contend with, the miracle was that the Spirit World actually managed to communicate at all. Therefore, it is not difficult to understand why, in comparison with the large séances, our Thursday evening guest circles, held in our own small séance room, regularly produced and still produce far better results. Because of its size, all participants are close to the cabinet and therefore, unlike the large meetings, they have a ringside seat. Secondly, with such a small number of participants, and with less unfamiliar energies, the Spirit people are evidently better able to work. And finally, communication tends to be far more concentrated. Over the years, the circle has received innumerable cards, letters and e-mails of thanks from people who have attended those special séances. Many reunions between the living and the dead have taken place and sitters have derived from them comfort on many levels and in a variety of ways.

In this chapter I would like to highlight the experiences of just one lady who, like most people, came to us as a total stranger. Of all the incidents and events that have been played out in that tiny first floor room, hers proved to be amongst the most exceptional and profoundly moving. Like others who came before and were to come after her, what she witnessed and experienced would ultimately prove to change the entire course of her future life. Perhaps therefore, this one single case, first published in part by the Zerdin Fellowship[1] in June 2006, exemplifies that truly the physical phenomena of Spiritualism can – as she so eloquently wrote later, 'touch the soul'.

This then is her story;

Some Reflections on a Personal Journey

Susan Farrow Topolovac (London)

Picture this: You are a happy forty-something woman, you are in a deeply loving and supportive relationship with your partner. Life is wonderful. You are both fulfilled in your work and at peace with each other and the world.

He dies. Overnight. You are picturing me.

Words: Shock, desolation, excruciating pain, loneliness, confusion, anger, resentment, guilt, rage.

They do not come close to expressing how it feels.

What does someone do if, like me at that time, they have no real belief in survival after physical death? They believe their loved one is gone forever. The End.

They have options of course, none of them very attractive. A bottle of pills; a retreat to bed for a year; a nervous breakdown; or perhaps a grief counsellor can help. They have another option too: a visit to a physical séance. This is my story: The pain of my sudden loss in November 2004 was so unbearable to me that I could neither sleep nor eat. Night and day I searched the internet and read every book I could find on the evidence for and against the survival hypothesis. I became absolutely determined to find out the truth for myself. I knew nothing whatsoever about mediumship, let alone physical mediumship. By the time February came I had absorbed a mass of information and research and I decided to begin putting it to the test.

I made an appointment with a well-known mental medium and vowed to myself that I would at least go with an open mind.

I arrived for the sitting and told the poor woman that I had no

---

(1) *Afterwards changed to Zerdin Phenomenal*

definite belief in the world of Spirit but that my mind was as open as I could make it. Fine, she said kindly, no problem. This lady knew my first name and nothing more about me. There followed an hour of impressive evidence, the majority of which could not have been attributed to research, cold reading or lucky guesswork. This did not fully convince me, but it certainly made me think. Sceptic that I am by nature, I resolved to visit another medium. And another, and another.

By now it was June and I had been given so much evidential information that I was beginning to believe that Spiritualism might actually have a point. Still, I continued to read more and tried to address my remaining doubts. One night, searching the internet again, I came across a reference to a website entitled 'physical mediumship'. Intrigued, I clicked on the link and began reading. I looked at the séance reports and could hardly believe my eyes: direct voice, materialisation, flying trumpets... What on earth?

I explored the website further and clicked on the 'circles' link. Surprise, surprise, there was a circle based near me searching for one more female sitter. To this day I do not know why I did it, but I immediately e-mailed the circle leader to enquire further. A reply came back by return inviting me to meet the circle members. I did this two days later, and three days after that began sitting in the circle myself.

One evening, a few weeks after I began sitting, I came across a magazine on physical phenomena. I devoured the contents avidly, including reports of a Stewart Alexander physical séance. I remember thinking, 'If all this is true, it has to be the most priceless thing in the world.'

And then I saw it, in very small print right at the back. I will always remember these words: 'Visits to Stewart's home circle are possible.' I don't know why, but the words affected me so much that I read them out loud. I knew then that I would go there. Plucking up my courage I phoned Ray Lister, Stewart's circle leader, and asked if it would be possible to come. Rightly, he spoke to me at length, and it was eventually agreed that I would sit as a guest on 13th October.

The date dawned and I got up exhausted because I had been too excited to sleep. I arrived at the appointed time and was given the warmest and most generous of welcomes.

The séance was a life-changing experience for me, the atmosphere full of love and laughter, kindness and compassion. I should say at this point that no one in the room had the slightest idea that my beloved partner had passed to Spirit. Imagine then, after almost a year of searching, what it meant to me when one of Stewart's Spirit team told me that someone was waiting to speak with me.

My heart rate was off the scale as I went to sit beside Stewart. And then it happened – my darling partner spoke to me, lovingly and evidentially, from beyond the so-called grave. There are no words in any language to describe the peace and joy this brought me.

Now I eat, I sleep and I am living again. The physical loss of someone so beloved will always be hard to bear, but I know now that it is only a physical loss, that our love survives and that we are just as closely connected to one another as we ever were. This knowledge is beyond price.

All who are grieving deeply would benefit enormously from such precious gifts. But there is a problem. Physical mediumship has always been rare, but in contrast to earlier times, we have fewer developed physical mediums than ever. And it's not surprising, is it? A developing physical medium must dedicate him or herself to years of patient sitting. They must find sitters who are similarly patient and dedicated. They must juggle the many distractions which prevail in modern society: television, computers, movies and so on. They must balance family and work responsibilities also. If there is a moral to my story, it is that those who sit in development circles must do so with all the dedication they can muster. There are people out there with a crying need for the powerful evidence of survival that physical mediumship can provide, and it is our job to ensure that it becomes more widely available and more widely accepted among the population at large.

Physical mediumship at its best can change lives; it can heal and restore hope like nothing else. Yes, grief counsellors and therapists have their part to play and they fulfil a necessary and important role for the bereaved, but if we can help the next generation of physical mediums to develop, we can change the world. In the words of Freda, a wonderful member of Stewart's Spirit team: 'If you have a bereavement where great love is involved, it makes no difference whether you are a Christian, a Buddhist or a Spiritualist. You will grieve. But later, if you are a Spiritualist and you know the truth concerning life and death, it can be a great comfort.' It's the understatement of the century. Everyone deserves that comfort.

* * * *

Since writing the above article, I have been privileged to sit with Stewart Alexander on literally scores of occasions. In December 2006, Stewart and his dedicated home circle members, all of whom had by that time become trusted friends, did me the enormous honour of inviting me to become an honorary member of their circle. I accepted this invitation with alacrity and the greatest pleasure. Thereafter, I began to sit regularly until, in January 2008, I was appointed editor of the weekly Spiritualist newspaper, *Psychic News*, a job whose considerable demands made it impossible for me to attend as often as I had previously been able to do. My consequent inability to take a regular part in the circle has been the only true down-side of a job to which I am passionately committed.

Nevertheless, during the brief period when I was sitting regularly as a member of the home circle, I was privileged to witness things that were both precious and extremely rare.

For reasons of space I will single out just two of those many extraordinary experiences.

From January 2007 to January 2008 I sat with the circle at least fortnightly, sometimes weekly, and my beloved partner – referred to at length in the article above – seized that opportunity to acquaint himself fully with the Spirit-side mechanics of communicating through an ectoplasmic voice box, a phenomenon known as independent direct voice.

Over time, he became an expert communicator, able to convey quite complex ideas along with subtle nuances. An accomplished linguist in earth life, he seldom disappointed me when, through Stewart's mediumship, I addressed him or asked him questions in languages other than English.

My questions were invariably understood and, without exception answered in English. Not only did this confirm that he had retained his linguistic expertise beyond the grave, it also reassured me that his earthly personality was very much intact. In earthly life he had always had impeccable manners, and when speaking with a linguistically diverse group of people would always choose to express himself in the language of the majority present at the time. He continued this habit within the séance room, mindful of the fact that, had he replied to me in a foreign tongue, my fellow circle members would have been completely excluded from the conversation.

On more than a dozen occasions it has been my great privilege to sit next to Stewart during séances. Each of those experiences yielded a unique insight into the workings of his mediumship. On one memorable evening I was holding Stewart's left hand while June Lister, wife of his circle leader, Ray Lister, held his right. Stewart was in deep trance at the time, while one of his controls, Walter Stinson, spoke through him. Walter finished speaking, and at this point would ordinarily have instructed me to release Stewart's hand in order to ensure his safety as ectoplasm was drawn from his body. Imagine my surprise, then, when instantaneously, and within a very hot room, my hand, still attached to Stewart's, was immersed in freezing cold as what I can only imagine was ectoplasm poured over it with an audible 'whoosh'. Few have been fortunate enough to experience this with any physical medium, and it is an event I shall never forget.

On a later occasion when I was seated next to Stewart, Dr Barnett, a regular and much-loved member of the Alexander Circle's Spirit team, had manifested in the séance room and was addressing the assembled sitters. Dr Barnett, a Scottish physician while on earth, has been responsible for the ongoing development of an ectoplasmic voice box, through which he now communicates with considerable skill, on occasions speaking for almost twenty minutes at a time. He is always eager to experiment with ways in which Stewart's mediumship can be further developed, and on this occasion caused me some concern when he asked me to perform a most unusual function.

Sitters at physical séances are repeatedly warned that the medium must not be touched at any time, and never more so when a materialised figure is abroad within the séance room. Many physical mediums of the past have been injured when reckless sitters have disregarded this warning. You will readily imagine, then, that when Dr Barnett stood amongst us in the room and asked me to reach inside the cabinet, grasp Stewart's hand and verify that he was indeed seated within it, I felt torn. I knew the rule; Do not touch! But I trusted Dr Barnett implicitly, as did all the circle members. Double checking with the doctor that I had heard him correctly, and receiving his assurance that I had, I reached slowly and carefully into the cabinet. I found Stewart's hand, as I had known I would, and held it for several seconds before withdrawing my own from the cabinet.

It was an extraordinary experience from an evidential point of view, but was also a test of my trust in the Spirit World and, indeed, theirs in me. The memory will stay with me forever.

These, and many other séance room experiences with the Alexander Circle, would enable me to take the witness stand at the Old Bailey and state without the slightest hesitation that Stewart Alexander is that rarest of creatures – a true physical medium.

❖ ❖ ❖

Chapter 16

The Beginning of the End

My decision to cease sitting for large public séances after 2008 and the reasons which led to it ~ A report of my final work abroad, written by a German journalist / TV. editor who attended two of the séances.

Throughout my life as a physical medium I have always known that every time I gave a public séance the possibility existed that one day the unthinkable could happen.

Although I understood that the externalisation and usage of ectoplasmic energy within the darkness of the séance room posed no danger, I also knew and lived with the thought that the sudden unexpected introduction of light would almost certainly have a catastrophic effect upon my health. Whilst recognising that critics and cynics will disagree and dismissively claim otherwise, in Part Two of this book I consider the position of the sceptic and also the matter of fraudulence within the séance room.

But in this chapter I shall concentrate upon the decision that I took in late 2007 to bring to an end my large public meetings and consequently free myself of thoughts that if I continued indefinitely, the inevitable would occur at some time in the future.

It was a most difficult decision to make and although it was an illogical premise I instinctively felt that having demonstrated in safety for so many years, the odds against such an unthinkable event occurring were growing progressively shorter. History I have always heeded and learnt from – only a fool would fail to do so. To illustrate this I shall give just one example by citing the case of Alec Harris, one of Spiritualism's most renowned materialisation mediums, who sat in perfect safety for a considerable number of years. One day, however, the unthinkable did occur with terrible consequences to his health. I was not rash and foolhardy enough to believe that such a dreadful event would not arise at one of my own future public séances. History told me that should I continue then it would only be a question of time. On that basis and following consultation with the circle and the Spirit World, I determined that the following year (2008) would be the final one in which I would demonstrate outside the safety of the home circle séance room. The only exceptions would be the few sittings I gave and still give each year in Norfolk at the home of Alf and June Winchester and also the seminars that I help to organise with them each year.

And so as 2008 began I was to face it with a measure of relief knowing that the proverbial 'finishing line' was within sight but understandably those feelings were also tinged with sadness. Over the years I had served many organisations and the thought that I would be informing them that I would be doing so for the final time was far from easy. In a way, and because I had never previously been able to say 'no' – I felt as if I was letting them down. But then my wife reminded me that people would still be able to sit with me but that they would have to come to me as against the other way around. Still, throughout that year I had to engage in several difficult and painful conversations when, following séances, I informed people whom I had come to regard as friends, that I would not be returning – that I had worked for them for the final time. To me it was akin to bereavement – a cutting off – a finality.

Switzerland was the country where I first worked outside the UK and therefore it was perhaps fitting that in that final year I should have returned to give one of my last demonstrations abroad.

Again it was for the Basle-based 'Basler Psi-Verein' (Basle Psi-Association) and on that final occasion, such was the friendship that I had built over the years with the organisation, that I took the decision to visit them accompanied only by my wife, and for the very first time, without my usual support.

Upon arrival at their headquarters, we soon found that the room to be used for the séances had been extensively prepared and that the organisation for the events could not have been bettered. Lucius Werthmuller, president of the association, his wife Sabin and my old friend (by then an honorary member of my home circle) Dr Hans Schaer had shared the responsibility for ensuring that my safety was paramount and that the conduct of the sitters at the séances was exactly as it should be. Nothing had been left to chance and so it was that for the very first time I sat without the presence and protection of Ray and June Lister

186

or Alf and June Winchester and although I was a little apprehensive at first, the entire trip proved to be most memorable.

Switzerland has always held a special place in my heart. Its significance upon my work as a public medium had been considerable and therefore it is perhaps fitting that I have chosen to reproduce, in abridged form, a report of those final séances. Written by German journalist and TV. editor Kai Muegge it appeared on the internet in April 2008 under the heading:

Powerful Séances with Stewart Alexander in Basle, April 2008.

On the 18th and 20th of April 2008 I had the opportunity to witness the famous Stewart Alexander at two of his very last sittings outside the UK. I am a thirty-nine year old social-pedagogue and film maker by profession who has studied the history of Spiritualism and associated phenomena for over twenty years. We Germans once had an intensive connection to physical mediumship through the work of past German researchers such as Baron Albert von Schrenck-Notzing and Friedrich Zöllner. So my assistant Marita and I were pleased to have the opportunity to witness the 'grand old gentleman' of English physical mediumship on two occasions during this, his final working visit to Switzerland.

And, despite people whose opinion I trust (Hans Schaer and Lucius Werthmuller) regarding the medium as genuine; I found it interesting to witness him performing outside his safe environment. We all know that physical mediumship and its alleged phenomena were, and still are, regarded as suspicious by many, because of the charlatans who in the past were exposed in fraud. So – one of the first positive surprises was that Mr Alexander had travelled only with his wife and had no supporters from his home circle with him.

I mention this only because had he been accompanied by members of his circle then some might have considered this as suspicious since alleged phenomena would seem impossible to present without the direct aid of others. However, the transparency of his sittings was then further heightened by several other factors which I shall share with readers from the start of my account.

Stewart's wife was NOT with him whilst the séances took place. The only people, in a large room full of strangers, with whom he had any connection were Dr Hans Schaer and Sabin and Lucius Werthmuller, who may be regarded as totally creditable and honest.

Stewart sits bound by plastic cable ties to the chair arms and this is checked by several sitters before the lights are switched off. He sits outside and in front of the cabinet so that he is part of the circle and for most of the séance both of his hands are held by the person on either side of him.

On his knees he has luminous strips to identify his position.

Frequently a red light is introduced to guide sitters to a seat at the medium's side where they participate in several physical phenomena experiments.

On those occasions when the light is switched on the medium is seen in a trance state in his seat, bound with the cable ties.

Stewart's Spirit controls occasionally request sitters to quieten down whilst phenomena such as faint direct voices appear to speak from different places in the room.

There were only two instances when a song was sung by the sitters and the cassette player played and then for no more than five minutes in a two-hour séance. So any accusation that loud music would cover audible fraudulent acts cannot be levelled at all. On the contrary, several times the attention of the sitters was directed by the medium to forthcoming manifestations. Illusionists would surely have endeavoured to distract the sitters' attention away from them just before they occurred.

Whilst some of the most baffling phenomena were taking place i.e. with the alleged ectoplasm morphing and forming in the illuminated space above the table located in front of the bound medium or in full view of his hands – people were allowed to stand up to get a better view.

Fraudsters would endeavour to keep people at a safe distance to avoid exposure whilst manipulating their tricks. All objects, as well as the cabinet, the medium's seat and the well-known little table upon which ectoplasm becomes visible and develops into the hand of one of Stewart's controls, were accessible for inspection prior to the séances.

Therefore, prior to the second séance that I attended, I thoroughly checked everything for twenty minutes. I was alone with all the equipment. I checked the structure of the medium's chair to establish that there were no hidden mechanisms which would release the ties which are used to restrain the medium. I checked the rings through which the arm ties would later be anchored and which were fastened beneath the armrests. I checked the cabinet from all sides, the curtains, the bell, the drumsticks, the cable ties and the specific construction of the little table with the under-lit red top (onto which the ectoplasm flows) and I found nothing suspicious.

Séance, 20ᵗʰ April 2008.

White Feather opens the Evening.

In the final few minutes before the white light is switched off (approx. 6pm) we observe the medium inducing his trance state with deep breathing and abnormal facial expressions. Sabin sits on Stewart's left side and Bea (a well known medium in Switzerland) sits on his right and opens the sitting with a beautiful prayer. The lights are then extinguished. Music plays on the cassette player and in less than a minute, the first control addresses the sitters with a warm welcome. It is the typical trance voice of an old man. He introduces himself as 'White Feather' a North American Indian who acts as a 'gatekeeper' supervising forthcoming communications and manifestations. He stresses the importance of the moment, when the veil between the two worlds would, for a short time, be lifted to demonstrate the wonder that 'there is no death'.

Then as White Feather retreats, a second personality, Christopher, speaks through Stewart's physical voice apparatus. He presents himself as a young boy and talks in a childish voice. His task is to reduce and calm the emotions of the sitters since some who are sitting for the first time are a little nervous. 'I know that this is not what you were expecting,' he proclaims speaking in a fast excited voice whilst frequently laughing at his own jokes. Sitters laugh when he then continues, 'I know that you were waiting to hear the higher teachings but instead you only have me ...'

He addresses several people whom he already knew, and then he leaves, being replaced by the distinguished Walter Stinson.

One of the most powerful Spirit controls who manifests through

Mr Alexander, Walter is responsible for building and harmonising the sitters' energy and then conducting several supernormal experiments that appear to defy the laws of science.

While he chats in his rich and unique way of speaking and flirts with a number of ladies – a very clear and lifelike vision of his trance personality develops and lingers in everyone's perception. He speaks with a Canadian accent which seems to suggest a strong, subtle and humorous character.

A seating change is now requested as Walter invites a lady to come and change places with Bea who is sitting on the medium's right side. The red light is switched on and the ladies change places.

The light is then turned off. Walter addresses the lady with compliments and requests Lucius to switch the light on again so that everyone can see that the two plastic cable ties are connecting the medium's arms to the chair armrests.

Everyone is able to physically see this whilst the ladies at each side of Stewart are also able to confirm it by touch. Then the invited lady holds the medium's right hand with her left and the light is again turned off. She then feels for the tie with her right hand and is able to confirm that it is firmly in place. Immediately after she has done this, there is an indefinable noise and the lady announces that their interlinked hands have risen into the air. Walter calls for the red light and we can all see that their hands are now at head height whilst on the chair arm rest the tie hangs unopened. Stewart's left hand is still bound and held by Sabin. The lady, at Walter's request, reaches out and checks that the tie is firmly connected to the chair arm before again darkness is called for. An immediate noise follows and the sitter confirms by touch that the medium's arm is back in its original position bound as before, all this happening within a couple of seconds. The red light is then switched on and all can see for themselves that Stewart's arm is again secure.

This experiment is then repeated in a slightly different manner. His arm is lifted into the air still holding the lady's hand but on this occasion the cable tie has passed through the armrest and is mysteriously now dangling on the medium's arm and is taken by the sitter as a souvenir.

The red light is again introduced. It can be seen that Stewart's arm is now unsecured – his right hand held by the lady and his left still controlled by Sabin. Light out. We then hear a cable tie being dragged across the table top (where it had previously lain) and we hear it being tied around the medium's arm and chair arm rest. Both sitters, left and right, confirm that Stewart's hands were not involved in any of this action taking place. Red light on again reveals that his arm once again is tightly fastened. During this entire experiment the medium is in trance and Walter Stinson has been fully in charge.

Walter directs trumpet and direct voice phenomena.

Following the cable tie experiment Walter explains how he will now collect energy from the surrounding space, including from the sitters and how this could lead to subtle changes in perception. The room is in total darkness. Everyone is instructed to lay their hands upon their laps with palms upwards. The trumpets are called for by the control and are placed by Sabin on the floor between the medium's feet. Walter asks for people to join together in song while he gathers the required energy. During this process he brings the medium out of his trance to enable him to observe the levitating trumpets. In the inner circle the sitters discern a clear drop in temperature at ground level up to about knee height.

Within a few moments the trumpets began to vibrate and move between the feet of the medium. The first then majestically rises into the air and with it the singing changes to 'wows' and to 'ohs'. Lucius addresses Stewart who is awake and answers sleepily whilst coughing. The position of the trumpet at any time can easily be determined by the illuminated rings at its broad end and is observed by all present as it floats around the room.

Meanwhile Stewart talks with the sitters and then the second trumpet vibrates on the floor and appears to be attempting to levitate.

During this time the airborne trumpet knocks on the ceiling, shoots in front of sitters' faces, touches them gently and all this at an approximate distance of 3 metres from the medium's chair. Some sitters have the impression that the second trumpet lacks sufficient energy to lift into the air and suggest singing again to assist it. However, the fully awake medium, still observed by means of the luminous strip on his knees to be in his seat calls for quiet because direct voices could, at this juncture, manifest. Often these come through the trumpets and sometimes directly beside the ear of a sitter. As silence falls so the second trumpet finally rises and whilst Stewart is engaged in conversation both of the trumpets appear to move independently and in quite different directions with a different manner of moving.

As an example; whilst one slowly rises to the ceiling at one side of the circle above sitters' heads between the inner and outer circle, the other gently touches sitters' heads at the other side of the circle.

Occasionally one of the trumpets would tumble and crash to the floor only to be lifted again a few moments later. Suddenly a bell rings at head height in front of sitters in the inner circle, about 3 metres away from the controlled medium and then it falls to the ground.

Whilst I am listening to Stewart speaking, I can hear – simultaneously – the typical breathing sounds of a direct voice manifesting. He also hears them and directs the sitters' attention to them.

Dr Barnett speaks through the ectoplasmic voice box and Freda Johnson connects people with their deceased loved ones.

Suddenly a faint voice is heard and we are told it is the direct voice of Dr Barnett, another alleged Spirit personality. In a quiet voice he explains through the ectoplasmically formed voice box that he intends to reserve necessary energy which, later, he will use to materialise in physical form. Additionally he will build up healing energies. The voice box, he says, has been successfully constructed and is positioned about 30 centimetres away from the medium's left shoulder.

We hear the medium breathing deeply whilst the voice is speaking. Dr Barnett gives encouragement to sitters who may wish to experiment in physical circles and promises to support them and help in any way he can. Some sitters thank him and then he withdraws.

A trance personality then presents herself in extremely typical voice mannerisms that appear to be female although, of course, it comes from the medium's vocal cords.

Freda Johnson, we understand, had been a teacher in Manchester, England when on earth and it is her task to reunite sitters with their deceased relatives and friends and to provide evidential communications. She then addresses a female participant and relays information about her grandmother. And so it continues.

Walter withdraws ectoplasm from the medium's body in red light and invites sitters to stand up and bend forward to observe everything clearly.

Walter invites a lady forward to sit at his table facing the medium. Lucius Werthmuller switches on his red torch light to enable the lady to find her way. The medium is now visible in his trance state and clearly bound tight by the plastic cable ties with his hands held by Sabin and Bea who sit at either side of him.

The glass table top is illuminated by a red bulb under its surface and the intensity of light adjusted by a rheostat (operated by Hans Schaer) according to Walter's wishes.

Within 30 seconds of the torch light being switched off, when the medium was last seen controlled by ties and with hands held by his neighbours the ectoplasm becomes visible – 'living energy' – as Walter refers to it. He informs us that out of this undefined black mass he will attempt to create his own hand.

I myself am able to observe clearly the illuminated table surface. The lady sitting at the table is then instructed to place her hand on the table with her palm downwards.

The energy then seems to gradually swell before reducing in size until a very large hand emerges with no defining features. Everyone is then given permission to leave their places and stand around the table and observe the developing process at close quarters.

The energy then appears to reorganise itself and clearly I can then see something like a claw or a malformed hand. But then again it changes and a clumsy semblance of a hand becomes more and more visible until it appears and behaves like a human hand. Its fingers move and turn from side to side so as to be observable from different perspectives. The hand then takes the lady's hand and she reports it as dry, warm and seemingly a male hand. It shakes her own and Walter asks; 'Didn't you ever wish to shake the hand of a man who has now been dead for 100 years?' Everyone laughs.

The hand then retreats from the table; the performance has lasted no longer than two minutes. Almost immediately Walter asks for the torch light and the medium is seen, as before, still bound and held. He then states that he wants to be certain that everyone in the room has been convinced and will leave the room free of any suspicion. However, he goes on to say that it would be understandable if some wondered whether, in reality, it was merely the hand of the medium.

Therefore – to eliminate any such doubts he has a further experiment and invites two additional ladies to the table. With all three then sitting around it he asks them all to place their hands on the illuminated table top so that all their fingers are spread out and touching. Stewart is released (by the Spirit World passing his arms through the ties) and his hands then join theirs so there is a complete chain of hands – all four pairs clearly distinguishable one from another. Walter requests the torch light to be turned off.

Within a few seconds from the medium's end of the table suddenly a ninth hand appears and all the ladies at the table confirm this by sight and by touch. This extra hand touches and manipulates theirs and again it is reported as large, dry and male. And all this, the substance on the table, the morphing, the movements of the hand, are clearly observed by myself and by my assistant.

Our attention has never wavered for a second and we have a good direct view of the table top.

Stewart's hands are then returned to their original position upon the chair arms, secured by the cable ties. The red torch light is again introduced so that all the participants can see that this is so and Walter wants the cable ties thoroughly checked by Sabin and Bea. The light is then switched off.

Dr Barnett materialises and lays his hands on the head of a sitter while the medium's hands are secured

The medium is then moved back into the cabinet by supernormal means and the curtains are closed and Stewart's knees with their luminous strips vanish behind them. We then hear the curtains being manipulated again and the muffled voice of Dr Barnett from inside the cabinet.

Sabin, the sitter to the right of the cabinet, suddenly informs us that two warm hands have been placed upon her head and that they remain there. At the same time we hear footsteps in the free space in the centre of the circle.

Another lady seated approximately 2 metres from the cabinet and 3 metres from Sabin then informs us that two hands are also on her head and that someone is standing behind her massaging her back.

Two minutes later we hear footsteps moving towards the cabinet and at the same time the ladies report that the hands have disappeared from their heads.

Walter's voice speaks again and stresses that they themselves have enjoyed the séance as much as we have. And then, he tells us that Stewart will be brought back into the circle and we hear his chair being pushed or pulled out of the cabinet.

He bids us farewell and the sitters thank him and say goodbye.

Bea gives a closing prayer.

The séance is at an end.

Upon reflection, I would like to express how unlikely it was that the entire modus operandi of the séance could be due to fraud. The frequently lit red light, introduced repeatedly, confirmed that the medium was sitting in his chair. He was held by his hands during most of the phenomena and this alone makes it almost impossible that we were victims of an elaborate hoax. Sitting in the circle between two people with his hands controlled and his legs visible through fluorescent markers make such an explanation seemingly untenable.

It was a most satisfying and persuasive evening of rare manifestations – the product of physical mediumship.

❖　❖　❖

Chapter 17

The End of an Era

I share my thoughts from 2008 as, for the final time, I sit publicly for large groups ~ I include previously published reports of these séances in Devon.

And so in October 2008 I undertook my final work away from home when I visited Devon to give two séances at a Spiritualist church and also a demonstration of trance. I faced them with a sense of relief because with the exception of the 'Christmas Tree' séance that I was due to give at the York Spiritualist Church that year, and my own residential seminars each year, that visit would mark the end of an era. Never again would I risk or compromise my wellbeing and never again would I have to take upon myself the overwhelming burden of responsibility that I had always felt on such occasions. Throughout my years of public work I had faced each séance desperately hoping that sitters would see, witness and experience for themselves the wondrous reality of two-world physical communication. As I left home to make the long journey south I did so knowing that forty years had passed since my introduction to Spiritualism and sixteen years since my public work had commenced. Understandably, such sittings had always been given in atmospheres of high expectation and excitement and never had the Spirit World failed to manifest. But I went into those Devon séances wanting them to be extra special. I wanted them to live on in the minds of all the people who would participate and so it proved to be.

Below I reproduce an abridged version of the first of two reports in respect of my visit. It was published by *Psychic News* on 6th December 2008, and they have graciously given their permission for me to include it in this book.

Stewart Alexander in Devon

A personal account by Lew Sutton

Although Devon is renowned for its rich cream teas, some of its Spiritualists were in for a different type of treat a few weeks ago with the return of physical medium Stewart Alexander to the area – a treat for the soul rather than the taste buds. His third visit to South Devon, and most likely his last, resulted in two extremely successful séances, a trance demonstration and a very informative seminar for West Country Spiritualists.

Stewart had announced some time ago that he intended to cut down on travelling, so we were honoured to host his last public events to be held hundreds of miles from his Yorkshire home.

The First Séance

The October visit began with a séance in Paignton which lasted for an amazing three-or-so hours. The time flew, as did the levitated séance room trumpets with their graceful movements in a display lasting for several minutes. The levitated trumpets appeared to float gracefully around the room as if they were weightless, passing close to several of the twenty-three sitters present. Two or three times they rubbed against the ceiling of what is a large domestic room.

In contrast to the earlier days of his mediumship, Stewart is usually awake during the trumpet phenomena and is able to appreciate and comment upon the movement – which he did on this occasion. The only time he seems to experience any physical discomfort whilst the trumpets are whizzing around is when one trumpet positions itself inside the other and the two move around as one.

Two sitters in turn experienced the now famous matter-through-matter experiment in which a strong plastic cable tie is momentarily dematerialised to free one of Stewart's arms from being secured to his chair. As his arm becomes free of the strap and is raised up, the sitter holding his hand then uses their other hand to check that the tie is left dangling on the chair arm still fastened. A light is then put on for a few seconds so that all can see his arm is free of the tie. Within seconds of the light being switched off, Stewart's arm is re-secured paranormally under the supervision of his main Spirit control, Walter Stinson.

It is worth pointing out that sitters selected to take part in this experiment hold Stewart's hand throughout and use their other hand to confirm what has occurred. His left hand remains secured to the chair throughout these experiments.

The next experiment involves ectoplasm being made visible in a low intensity red light. Three sitters experienced seeing and feeling a hand created from a blob of ectoplasm before their very eyes. It is usual now for Stewart's hands to be freed paranormally for this experiment, as in the matter-through-matter experiment, and be placed on the illuminated table top to prove where his hands are during the materialisation of the Spirit hand.

After the experiment is completed, the medium's hands are then paranormally re-secured to the arms of his chair.

Invariably there are ladies sitting on both sides of Stewart so there is no question of any human hand being substituted for the large materialised hand, which by the way, is significantly larger than Stewart's own.

Once again, Walter stressed the importance of these experiments in demonstrating a remarkable control of physical matter by those living in the world of Spirit.

The highlight of the evening for one of the sitters, Joan Boydell, was to speak to her mother and also to her daughter who passed on as a baby. It was announced that her daughter was now a young lady in the Spirit World. Then it was husband Alan's turn to speak to his father. Alan and Joan confirmed to me afterwards that the mannerisms and vocabulary were just as when their loved ones were alive in the physical body.

Other sitters also received communications from their loved ones via Stewart in trance, with Spirit control Freda Johnson helping to establish the link.

Dr Barnett, a nineteenth century physician and regular communicator, then announced himself and spoke to us for over five minutes by independent direct voice (not through the medium's own vocal apparatus, and without a trumpet). He later moved around and told us that he was only partly materialised. Several reported feeling his touch. As is usual these days, he brought a helper with him, as at least two pairs of hands were being felt simultaneously by sitters. For a short while Dr Barnett appeared to be cupping a psychic light in his hands. Only those directly in front of him could see it clearly, and those behind not at all.

In the past he has moved around the whole circle carrying a light, but this time he stayed close to the cabinet.

Trance Demonstration

The following evening, Stewart gave a short talk on how he became a physical medium and related tales of some of the mediums he had met and heard about along the way.

The audience at the Paignton Spiritualist Church was enthralled by his enthusiasm for physical mediumship, which brought the subject matter to life.

The talk was followed by an hour-long demonstration of deep trance, during which most of Stewart's regular controls spoke to us. They demonstrated that they are very much alive in the next life and have certainly not lost their sense of humour.

As in the previous night's séance, personal communications were given, with Freda Johnson acting as the go-between to establish the link and help get the message across when the loved ones in Spirit had difficulty in communicating.

The Newton Abbot Seminar

The following day the action moved to the Newton Abbot Spiritualist church which hosted a one-day seminar on physical phenomena, culminating in an evening séance. About forty attended the very instructive seminar which began with a detailed talk by Alf Winchester on various types of physical phenomena.

Next, Peter Egan spoke about the importance of integrating mediumship into Spiritualistic philosophy; mediumship should not be viewed in isolation but as an integral influence in how we live our lives. It was a thought-provoking talk that reminded us what Spiritualism is all about, and of the part we should be playing in advancing the Movement.

After the lunch break, Stewart Alexander was back in action with a talk entitled 'My Journey' – covering his mediumistic development and experiences along the way. No one could have been more amazed than Stewart to discover all those years ago that he was a physical medium. The seminar ended with a question-and-answer session, with all three speakers addressing questions on aspects of physical mediumship.

The Newton Abbot Séance

As in the previous séance, Stewart was soon in deep trance and regular communicator Christopher, who portrays himself as a young boy, played his usual part in getting everyone to relax with his jokes and happy disposition. He has an important role in séances, particularly for newcomers who may be a bit apprehensive not knowing quite what to expect. This séance produced similar phenomena to that just described at the Paignton sitting (the first séance) with two ladies, Linda and Christine, participating one at a time in the matter-through-matter experiment. Later, Christine from Brixham, received a communication through Stewart in trance from her grandmother, to whom she had been very close. Freda Johnson again acted as facilitator and provided additional evidence. Christine told me afterwards that she received very good evidence, relevant to recent events in her life. Linda was also to play a further part by witnessing the hand (which Walter said was his own) materialising in red light. As in the first séance, the experiment ended with four sets of hands on the table, the large hand of Walter visible at the same time. The other hands belonged to Stewart Alexander, Louise and Ken from the USA.

Again, we witnessed the trumpets flying around the room with their luminous bands distinctly visible. However, as the room was considerably larger than that of the previous venue, the trumpet phenomena took place over a greater area and probably extended over 3 metres horizontally from the medium.

The room used had a very high ceiling and the trumpets shot up much higher than I had seen before – probably four metres or so above floor level.

After the trumpet phenomena Dr Barnett apparently wandered quite a distance around the room speaking, touching and shaking hands with several of the thirty-six sitters. Christine, mentioned earlier, was about three metres from the cabinet housing Stewart and reported that the doctor had gently touched her head, shaken her hand and spoken to her.

As in the first séance, one other Spirit visitor (or more) must have been present, since several sitters called out simultaneously that they could feel two hands touching them. These exclamations came, at times, from sitters who were several metres apart.

It appeared that Dr Barnett was also responsible for various lights that appeared and danced close to the cabinet for a short while.

A Wedding Blessing

Especially pleased to receive communications was Ken Saari who had flown over from the USA for the seminar and séance. Ken attended with his Newton Abbot fiancée Louise. This was a special occasion for them both since they had first met a year before when attending Stewart's last séance at the church. They were thrilled when near the end of the séance, the medium's main control, Walter Stinson, told them he would like to attend (in Spirit) their wedding in New York the following year. Unfortunately, because the séance went on for over three hours, the recording device had reached its capacity before Walter made his announcement. Ken and Louise said that, if it hadn't, they would have played that extract at their wedding. It was lovely to end an eventful day with a blessing from Spirit for their future life together. Ken told me later that the conversation he had held with Walter was '.... the most important thing that was ever said to me by anyone in my entire life'.

He had this to say about the materialised hand experiment;

'Walter invited both of us up to the table and allowed us to experience the materialisation of his hand. He banged it on the glass table three times and squeezed Louise's hand before disappearing into the darkness. Also, while we were at the table, it levitated off the floor and tilted in every direction just inches from us.'

End of an Era

It is the end of an era for Stewart Alexander. He has now ceased travelling long distances in this country and abroad in order to demonstrate publicly his physical mediumship and inspire audiences with tales of his wonderful experiences.

My sincere personal thanks go to Alf and June Winchester for the support they have given me in making these events possible; to Phil and Sheila Scott (principals of the Newton Abbot church) for their hard work and the use of their church. To the church workers who slaved away behind the scenes. To the Paignton church for hosting the trance demonstration and finally, to Stewart who tirelessly gave his time, energy and enthusiasm to make his short stay in South Devon so rewarding for all who attended the events.

I will close this account with words from Phil and Sheila Scott, president and secretary of the Newton Abbot SNU Spiritualist Church:

'Saturday 4th October will go down in the history of our church because it was Stewart Alexander's last demonstration of physical mediumship in this area. We were truly blessed. To say that the day was 'out of this world' would be an understatement. We heard from all of Stewart's regular Spirit team – White Feather, Walter Stinson, Freda Johnson, Christopher and Dr Barnett – and the atmosphere was electric.

In addition to all the wonders described by Lew, we also heard the voice of a small child calling out from the cabinet 'I want my Mummy'. We found his Mummy – she was one of the sitters and it was the anniversary of her boy's passing. Wonderful messages were given to sitters and the feeling of love in the room was palpable. The Spirit World is working so hard to prove that life goes on, and with Stewart as their instrument they are succeeding . . .

'Thank you' is never enough to say to him and his team, both seen and unseen. It was truly a day we will never forget.'

❖ ❖ ❖

In the following edited account, which first appeared on the *Psychic Times* internet site in November 2008, Louise Dobson (referred to in the *Psychic News* report under the subheading; 'Wedding Blessing') gives her own personal perspective of the séance she and her fiancé attended at the Newton Abbot church.

Spirit Communication at Devon Séance

Louise Dobson

I have sat to develop clairvoyance in a circle at the Newton Abbot Spiritualist Church in Devon for over two years, and felt blessed that I had the opportunity to sit with physical medium Stewart Alexander for what was likely to be his last public demonstration.

It was particularly poignant for me since the last time he demonstrated at the church, in November 2007, I met my soul mate, who had flown over from New York just to attend the séance. What a joy it was to be sitting there again with him, almost a year later.

Before entering the séance room, the sitters were addressed by Alf Winchester, one of Stewart's friends, who informed us of what was likely to happen, although we understood that there could be no guarantees. He then discussed with us the do's and don'ts of séance room protocol. We were given to understand that the Spirit people that manifest through Stewart use ectoplasm in order to materialise and speak, and that should it be exposed to light then it would shoot back into the medium's body at great speed potentially causing internal bleeding or even death. Of course it was of paramount importance to keep Stewart as safe as possible at all times. He explained to the new sitters that we would be sitting in complete darkness for an extended period of time and at that stage they were given the opportunity to leave if they felt unable to tolerate sitting under such conditions. Whilst a couple of new sitters acknowledged that they were somewhat apprehensive, the atmosphere in the room was full of eager anticipation and excitement. Alf then explained that Stewart's arms and legs would be bound firmly to his chair by means of plastic cable ties and these were checked by a volunteer just prior to the commencement of the séance. On his knees luminous strips were taped so that his location in the circle could be seen at all times. There was therefore no reason whatsoever to suspect any kind of fraud as there was nothing even remotely suspicious.

Evidential Demonstration

White Feather was the first to come through, a Native American Indian who noted how exceptionally good the energy was. When he withdrew, his place was taken by Christopher who is a charming young boy of about seven years of age.

His responsibility is to relax sitters. His high pitched, impish voice, and his cheeky laughter had us all laughing and this helped to raise the vibrations in the room even higher. He joked with several sitters but was instructed by his Spirit team, after only a few minutes, that he had to withdraw.

Next, a Canadian gentleman named Walter Stinson came through – he passed into the Spirit World in 1911. We were told that as a member of Stewart's Spirit team he would be responsible for all the physical phenomena that hopefully would take place during the course of the séance. He is a powerful character and is known to be rather flirtatious with the ladies. When one lady posed a question she was immediately invited to sit beside him on the medium's right side. Then, after addressing her question he performed for her the experiment of passing the medium's arm directly through the plastic strap that had secured it to the chair arm.

The red light was switched on so that everyone could see that their hands were interlocked in the air and that the strap had been left on the chair arm. His left arm was still firmly attached to the arm of the chair by the cable strap. The red light was switched off and the audible ectoplasmic rush was heard again. The lady then confirmed that the arm was back on the armrest, bound as before. The red light was again turned on so that all the sitters could confirm this for themselves. Throughout this experiment, which was under the direct control of Walter, the medium remained in trance. Walter then asked the lady to return to her seat and for all the sitters to place their hands on their laps with their palms uppermost.

The trumpets were placed between the feet of the medium and we were invited to sing in order to help raise the energy levels in the room. Soon, we could see two trumpets levitate and swiftly dance around the room at great speed never bumping into anything. They danced over the heads of the sitters. It should be noted that the ceiling was at least thirty feet high and that they flew up to it and then swiftly down again.

Dr Barnett, who speaks philosophically and is a member of Stewart's Spirit team, also came to address us as did Freda Johnson. It was she who reunited two sitters with their loved ones. This was very emotional for those concerned, as well as for everyone else in the room. One of the ladies sitting to the right of me was aware of her son who had passed over and was trying to get through. He was experiencing some difficulty and Freda suggested that they should speak again after the séance – in private.

And, in fact, when the séance ended everyone remained in their seats and the lady concerned was invited through to a small ante-room to sit alone with Stewart.

She returned obviously very emotional and confirmed that her son had indeed spoken to her.

Materialised Hand

Following Freda, Walter returned and again asked if any lady present would care to ask him a question? I spoke up and to my delight and surprise was invited to take a seat opposite Stewart at his little glass topped table. This was lit from underneath by a red bulb.

He then replied to my question which related to how best I might serve the world of Spirit and then went on to ask if I would like to view his materialised hand. The energy was palpable as I sat there and my legs started to shake uncontrollably. I was asked by Walter to place one hand on the table top and to describe to the other sitters exactly what I saw. As I gazed upon it I observed an undefined black shadow starting to form at one side of it and slowly it began to morph and develop slight projections. These began to elongate and to take on the appearance of fingers until eventually a fully formed claw-like hand (male by appearance) lay before me. This then appeared to crawl across the table and onto my hand and it proceeded to pat it three times. It felt warm to the touch and exactly as a normal human hand would look and feel.

I could even see the hairs on the back of it, and then it knocked firmly and loudly three times on the table top which was met by audible exclamations of amazement by my fellow sitters. Personally, I felt totally blessed to have experienced these amazing phenomena.

Walter spoke to me in his distinctive Canadian drawl and asked "Didn't you ever want to shake the hand of a man who had been dead for more than a hundred years now ma'am — hmm?" Everyone found this very amusing and I for one was buzzing from the whole experience. I kept asking myself how many people in the world have had an experience like that and I can confirm that it was not the hand of the medium. How lucky I felt!

He then invited another lady also to come and sit at his table and then my new found soul mate Ken 'my future betrothed' as Walter said, to come and sit next to him. However, although Ken and I had discussed getting married we had, at that time, made no formal plans or announcements. Therefore, that someone from the Spirit realms should acknowledge our intent rendered us totally speechless and I was overcome with emotion. And so, from out of all the sitters that night we found ourselves seated around the table with this amazing man from the Spirit World, waiting in anticipation for the next demonstration. Soon, we were invited to place our hands flat on the table top with our fingers spread out and with our thumbs touching. Our little fingers had to be in contact with those of our immediate neighbours. Then the table started to move, firmly pushed against my knees and then proceeded to levitate. We all sat there mystified, all of us aware that we couldn't possibly have lifted the table ourselves with both hands flat on it. After this Walter asked us all to return to our seats and Ken was addressed by him. 'Ken, you are not going to believe what is in store for you in the future!' He did not elaborate on this but filled us both with eager anticipation. He continued; 'When your big day arrives, and you KNOW what I mean by that, will I be invited to attend?' He was of course referring to our aspirations to get married in the future. After the séance, Ken and I contemplated how many past weddings there had been when someone from the world of Spirit had asked if they could attend. When the time is right, we will of course be inviting Walter, and we know 'FOR SURE' that he will be there in Spirit.

Eternity

What a totally amazing evening. One that was made so special because of the personal messages that Ken and I received and which the two of us will remember for eternity.

It was the third demonstration of physical mediumship that I had attended and my second involving ectoplasmic materializations. With absolute certainty I can state that never, at any time, did I suspect that any kind of fraud was taking place. For me, it confirmed what I have always known; beyond any doubt the soul and the etheric Spirit body are eternal and that we all survive the death of our physical body.

I take this opportunity to express my sincere thanks to Stewart Alexander for his hard work and tireless dedication over the years which has led to the development of his gift and its demonstration in public. In bringing the two worlds together he unwittingly made two people very happy who would otherwise not have met.'

❖ ❖ ❖

On the 20th November 2008 Ken (at that time the fiancé of Louise Dobson) posted on the 'Psychic Times' internet site, the following statement in reply to a reader's query regarding the appearance of Walter's claw-like materialised hand:

'I did not ask Walter that night why the hand appeared somewhat deformed and I assume that it was likely to have been in that state at the time that he transitioned into the Spirit World. During the entire séance (other than during the materialisation of the hand on the table) Stewart's hands were both firmly bound to the chair with very strong plastic cable ties that could only be removed with wire cutters, or a very sharp knife.

When the hand materialised, both Louise and the other lady at the table were holding the medium's hands. The Spirit team had dematerialised the cable ties so that the girls could hold his hands on the table throughout the experiment. Stewart was in trance during the matter-through-matter experiment and also the materialisation of the hand.'

❖ ❖ ❖

As I left Devon I did so with a sense of relief knowing that effectively my work as a public physical medium, demonstrating before large groups of strangers, was virtually at an end. My long journey back to Yorkshire was filled with thoughts of the places where I had been and the people that I had met over so many years and also of the kindness that had surrounded me at all times. On occasions I had marvelled at the work undertaken by my hosts to ensure a perfect blackout in rooms which presented many problems. Rooms with high ceilings and with large and many windows simply did not lend themselves to the total exclusion of light. Yet invariably this had always been accomplished. One could only admire the human spirit. Of course, it was predictable that rooms filled with a great many people would quickly overheat. Indeed, rarely did they have air conditioning or any form of fresh air ventilation and as a result the uncomfortable airless conditions were greatly exacerbated. Often, following a sitting, I had witnessed people leaving the séance room, looking as if they had spent time fully clothed in a sauna. The expression 'sweating for Spirit' jumps to mind. But such situations were of little consequence – to commune with the dead was everything.

And so, as I travelled back from Devon, I did so leaving behind me for ever a way of life which, although potentially an ever constant threat to my wellbeing, had nevertheless afforded me many unique adventures and spiritual experiences. Many lives had been changed, touched, and comforted by 'the great reality' and I felt both proud and singularly privileged. At the start of my journey I could never have foreseen or even suspected what lay before me – how could I have done?

Whether I have been a worthy servant of 'the great truth' will always be for others to judge but for myself I can rightly claim that out of the darkness has emerged untold joy.

That, surely, is what the journey has been about!

Chapter 18

Death - A Change of Location

I discuss the contentious topic of physical mediumship and some of its anomalies ~ I pay tribute to the people who have been a part of my journey. ~ My thoughts about survival of the human soul beyond death.

In late 1983, I found myself travelling to the Midlands on two separate occasions to sit with a medium who, according to the popular Spiritualist press, had a circle that was enjoying wonderful physical manifestations. These included the exceedingly rare phenomena of materialisation. Development had apparently been meteoric, and in a short period of time they had progressed from sitting in hope to obtaining outstanding communication with the Spirit World on a physical level.

My introduction to the circle had come through Alan Crossley, the man who a short time later would become my second mentor. As it was claimed from the Spirit World, that Helen Duncan was playing a principal role in the circle, and since Alan had known her well, he had at that time already sat with the circle on numerous occasions. He was quite satisfied that Mrs Duncan was communicating and materialising there and his confidence led to my own wish to attend a sitting. Never, in all my years of involvement in Spiritualism had I ever passed up the opportunity to witness for myself the physical phenomena of the séance room and frankly I could not wait to get there.

So, on that memorable day, I set off in eager anticipation. At that time my own physical mediumship was in its early stages of development and I rather hoped that it would benefit from exposure to this circle in the Midlands. The generally accepted theory is that such mediumship can be stimulated, or receive a 'kick start', when those with the potential to develop it sit with a well developed physical medium – the so called 'knock-on' effect.

Upon arrival at the home of the medium, I was greeted warmly and she and her husband proved to be attentive, friendly and generous hosts. I spent the afternoon listening to a most interesting account of the manner in which the circle had been formed and how development had rapidly burst upon them. In the evening I was taken to the home of their friends where the séances were held and again I was warmly welcomed. We sat in a circle configuration in easy chairs in a blacked-out room and the medium curled up in her chair in one corner. Soon she was in a trance and we were quickly joined by the Spirit World.

A little Spirit boy chatted away at various times and the deceased son of a well known scientist of his day spoke at some length with us. Luminous drum sticks beat upon a table top and the purported Helen Duncan took our hands and spoke in a broad Scottish accent. A virtuoso performance. After it was over I again enjoyed their warm hospitality as tea, sandwiches and cakes were brought out.

When finally I left to make the long drive home, I did so with the assurance that I could visit again. With a feeling that I had taken part in a wonderful spiritual adventure I could not wait to return. This had all been new to me. Floating trumpets and other phenomena of a physical kind had been manifesting in my own circle for some time but never had I personally witnessed such things. Always, when they occurred, I had, during those early days, been in a deep trance condition and personally I had observed nothing. Therefore what happened that night had been something of a revelation to me.

At last I had personally witnessed the kind of phenomena that I had, until then, only heard or read about – there was such a difference. The following day I wasted no time in arranging with the circle a return visit but because they had been inundated with requests from people wishing to attend their sittings I was faced with a long three months' wait.

The appointment was for myself and Mrs Kath Matthews who was keen to accompany me after hearing my excited report of all that I had experienced.

During that three month period Alan Crossley sat again on two further occasions with them and following each sitting he telephoned to tell me of wonderful new developments. Apparently, on the first occasion he had arrived early at the medium's house and she had been dressing in her bedroom. Alan had been sitting in the lounge with her husband when suddenly a toy rubber animal about twelve inches in height slowly began to walk up the wall towards the ceiling. Animation had ceased just before it got there whereupon it had fallen to the floor. On his next visit, he was, during the afternoon, sitting alone with the medium and they were in the middle of a conversation when suddenly she had fallen into a trance. Then the voice of Helen Duncan had started to speak from empty space near to the ceiling. Alan had watched the medium's lips closely but had detected absolutely no movement. Slowly the voice had started to descend until it merged with the medium at which point it began to issue directly from her lips.

Our own visit however was to present us with a most painful enigma which was to leave us both incredulous and stunned. We had spent the afternoon in conversation with the medium and her husband and only learnt over a sandwich, cakes and tea, that, for whatever reason, the séance was to be held at their home and Mrs Matthews and I were to be the only sitters apart from the medium's husband.

For the first part of the séance all had proceeded more or less as it had done during my first sitting three months earlier. We then came to a half-way point and her husband asked the Spirit people if he could be excused because he had an early start the following morning. Permission granted, he left the room to go to his bed and in closing the door total darkness was restored. The little Spirit boy then returned and wandered across the room to stand chatting before us. We could not see him but we could most certainly hear him. Then, suddenly he stopped and picking up a torch that had been on the mantelpiece at the start of the séance he said 'I am going to show you my legs' and with that he switched it on and pointed it towards where I judged his feet would be. This however failed entirely to illuminate anything because the light was entirely masked by several thicknesses of red cloth that covered the end of the torch. With straining eyes I told him that unfortunately we could see nothing. 'Just a minute,' he chirped, 'I will take some of this stuff off.'

As he did so then both Mrs Matthews and I very clearly saw the tiny bare legs of a little child and as we reported this to him so he became excited and he began to jump up and down. What we were looking at was not some kind of arrangement presented to appear as legs and feet. They were not, as was later suggested to us, arms and curled fingers posed as a facsimile. Beyond any reasonable doubt they were the highly animated legs and feet of a child. A feeling of euphoria swept over me, and, as I later learned, it did with Mrs Matthews. It was a most emotional moment. Then, the torch was switched off plunging us again into total darkness. But then the boy gleefully informed us that he wanted to show us his face. The torch came back on but once again the light failed to penetrate the red material. When informed of this he quickly removed a little of the covering but even then we were straining to see anything. Suddenly the remainder of the material fell away and we found ourselves staring in disbelief into the face of the medium who was holding the torch below her chin with the light shining upwards.

A quick fumble, the torch went out and the performance continued without a break. For the remainder of the séance neither Kath Matthews nor I said much.When it finally ended we had cakes and tea before eventually waving our goodbyes and driving away into the night.

As soon as we were out of sight of the waving medium, Kath asked, 'Did you see what I saw?'

Driving back home we discussed nothing else. In a split second we had gone from a state of spiritual euphoria to one of gut-wrenching incredulity.

For weeks following that event we were both bewildered by what we had undeniably seen. To attempt to rationalise the matter and find a simple explanation proved impossible and I agonised over it for many months as indeed I still do. However, neither then nor since have I ever doubted that on that night, in that blacked-out lounge, somewhere in the Midlands, I saw with my own eyes the tiny legs and feet of a small child when no earthly child had been present. My belief in that has remained unshakeable.

Sceptics of course, would argue, without the inconvenience of considering the reported positives of the mediumship that this entire matter was merely an example of a blind willingness to believe. If only it were quite that simple!

A Mediumistic Conundrum

Mediumship is not always a simple matter of black and white, of genuine or fraudulent. Occasionally, as psychic history records, it can be a mixture of both and that is particularly so in the arena of physical mediumship. But this I discuss in some detail in Part Two of the book. For now I merely record the episode because from it I learnt such a great deal. In 1992, when I took the decision to emerge from the home circle and demonstrate before the public, the memory of that incident was evoked and it served me well. To sit in public was a great responsibility and I recognised fully that to most sitters at such events I would be a stranger. It therefore was incumbent on me to do all that I could to remove any suspicion that consciously or unconsciously I might have been responsible for the production of pseudo-phenomena. For that reason, I elected to be restrained in my chair through ropes and cable ties and to have luminous tape attached to my knees.

There was also another reason. Alan Crossley firmly believed that whilst in a trance condition a physical medium is in a state of heightened sensitivity. In the highly charged atmosphere of the séance room the intense thoughts and desires of the sitters could influence the unconscious mind of the medium. According to Alan, he/she, in such a situation, would be highly vulnerable. Motivated by an uncontrollable subconscious compulsion to meet intense expectation within the public séance room they could unknowingly respond by producing bogus phenomena and, in that event, the Spirit World could do nothing. Lifting and waving a trumpet in the air or perhaps picking up a bell and ringing it and all under the cover of darkness.

That was Alan's theory, built, he maintained, upon personal experience. At one time he had sat with a circle where the medium invariably engaged in such action whenever he was not firmly controlled. But when he was securely held by his neighbours, the phenomena produced had been wonderful and far beyond anything that could have been produced by earthly human agency.

Again, we need only look back into history to the celebrated Italian medium Eusapia Palladino – (of whom more in Part Two, Chapter 2). It is sufficient here to say that she was extensively investigated by the research world a century ago and she would warn the investigators; 'watch me or I will cheat'. And the fact is that if they relaxed their control of her – if they released a hand or a foot – then indeed she would attempt to do so and was undoubtedly a master at evading all restraints. It seemed to be a compulsion over which she apparently had no conscious control. On the other hand, if she was totally restrained then the most wonderful phenomena, often at a distance, would occur in her presence.

Therefore, my own reasons for insisting that I must always be firmly secured in my chair at public séances were twofold, to satisfy the sitters and also to satisfy myself. Alan Crossley's theory may have had merit and I was not prepared to take any risks. Unfortunately, when some years ago, I made this point in a published article, a number of sceptics responded on the internet by forcefully insisting that such a view was unquestionably 'rubbish'. How truly marvellous it must be to have such knowledge of the subject that can allow such a confident public pronouncement.

The truth of course is that in matters of two-world communication (on any level) our understanding is extremely limited, possibly no greater than that which faced early man when he tried to comprehend the rising and the setting of the sun. Or indeed, our own difficulty in trying to understand life itself and the world and the universe in which we live. We start and we end from a position of considerable ignorance. That is a fact.

During my long journey of incidents and intimate experiences I have learnt many lessons and consider myself to have been most fortunate. Many genuine sincere people – believers and non-believers in survival – have crossed my path, from whom, as I said earlier, I have learnt a great deal. But more than that I have always tried to look beyond the surface of Spiritualism and its message and beyond its popular public image. For over forty years I have exhaustively researched all aspects of it and in the process I genuinely believe that truly my life has been enriched. Never have I taken anything at face value – always I have tried to apply objective logic not only in respect of mediumship in a general sense but more directly in respect of my own. I have tried to analyse it – I have tried to understand.

Never, when sitting with other physical mediums, have I left reasoning outside the séance room door and although I have always approached sittings as a Spiritualist, I have never abandoned common sense and critical analysis. Indeed, I have used the same approach that I have long advocated to people who have sat with me. Never should logic and reason be sacrificed. But then, I strongly maintain that the genuine and the fraudulent séance rooms are as different as black is from white. Five years ago I was invited to sit with a home circle which, I understood, was obtaining wonderful physical phenomena through a young man who apparently had developed his gift within a matter of months.

Direct voice and materialisation phenomena were apparently regular manifestations and I attended a meeting of the circle with high expectations. Sadly, within minutes of it starting I 'knew' that the manifestations were not merely dubious but fraudulent. Soon afterwards he commenced demonstrating in public but it would not be long before events proved my opinion correct. Unfortunately, such abhorrent practice holds Spiritualism up to ridicule and does nothing to enhance

214

the argument that physical mediumship is of considerable value to the Movement.

A Tribute.

Before closing Part One I would like to pay tribute to all the people whom I have met along the way and who helped me upon my journey in a variety of ways. My development as a physical medium, and the public work that I undertook, could not have been achieved had it not been through the single minded determination and support of all the individuals who made up the various home circles that I have sat in.

Even the ones that I classed as 'Bizarre' all played their part and taught me valuable lessons. The medium who channelled scientists, priests and Humphrey Bogart died several years ago as too did his wife.

Of my very first home circle, which was made up of family and neighbours, who sat with such patience without any discernible results, three of its six members have long since passed away.

The direct voice medium Leslie Flint, whom I visited in 1973 and 1974, went to the Spirit World in 1994, although he left behind him a wonderful legacy in the form of séance room recordings, copies of which are readily available today.

Jim and Ethel Hood (Chapter 2) with whom I sat briefly in 1976, until, allegedly, gout intervened, I have recently discovered also died some years ago. I have long since lost contact with Cynthia, who inadvertently trod on Jim's foot, and with whom, for a time, I continued to sit.

Mrs Kath Matthews, my first mentor, has been in a care home for the past few years due to her advanced years and sadly is no longer able to visit the present home circle due to her failing health.

Since the eventual ending of her special circle in which the pink pig appeared, I have, with the single exception of Ray Lister, lost contact with all the other members and today have no knowledge of their whereabouts. But for their help, I thank them.

Alan Crossley, my second mentor, passed away on Monday, 26th February 2001 and left behind him a wonderful legacy which we received in his oft repeated recollections – some of which were recorded in his three spiritual books. Today, his reputation as a Spiritualist who possessed considerable intimate knowledge of physical mediumship remains unblemished and those who knew him remember him with great affection. Because he was undoubtedly a creditable witness to the séance room wonders of the great mediums of the past with whom he had the good fortune to sit, I have taken a few of his rich memories and done my best to record them in this book. As a result I hope that they will now live on. He did not base his unshakeable belief in survival upon the written accounts of others but upon personal experience. He had been there, he had seen, and he 'knew'. The other members of the Project Circle are still on this side of life and to this day we are in contact with each other and share many wonderful and unforgettable memories.

My gratitude must also go to my friends Alf and June Winchester who, although geographically remote, (Norfolk) have supported my mediumship in a variety of ways for many years now. The many physical phenomena seminars that we have organised together would simply not have taken place without them. Their dedication to 'the great cause' simply cannot be overstated.

Of all the home circles with which I have been involved the most enduring has been my current one which has now been meeting every week for over twenty years. Here contact with the Spirit World, at its present level, was developed and the now long-standing Spirit team was largely established during this time. Although my name is widely known within the world of Spiritualism I record here my tribute to the individual members of the circle who have remained at my side over that long period. Without them, I doubt that there would have been a Stewart Alexander. Whatever has been achieved we have achieved together. When our séance room door closes then we know that once again we are to witness the removal of the barrier that exists between the two worlds and – although progress in development has so often been painfully slow – never once have we complained or lost trust in our spiritual contacts. Always we have known that their frustration at such times would equal our own. To us it was and has always been a privilege to simply sit in their presence knowing that the two worlds have, for a while, merged into one united whole. And our visitors from the other side have long been implicitly trusted without any reservations whatsoever. Of the individual members of the circle, all of whom are valued friends and who have shared 'the great adventure' I would like to single out for special mention Ray Lister and my sister Gaynor Singleton. Ray, as our circle leader, has accompanied me as a loyal and an ever dependable friend upon much of my journey. So often I have benefited from his wise council and my debt to him could never be repaid.

My sister Gaynor who had sat faithfully at my side down the years and who often accompanied me in my public work, tragically lost her earthly life in 2009. Her loss to her family, friends and the circle was incalculably painful and I personally lost not only a greatly loved sister but also a wonderful confidant and friend of fifty-six years. It was a marvellous tribute to her that our grief was shared by people from all over the world whose lives she had touched through her spiritual work, this past quarter of a century.

Man's Final Destiny.

Readers will hopefully appreciate that my personal journey, which commenced in 1968 has not yet reached its end.

Perhaps my conclusions regarding the most important question which has confronted mankind since first he appeared upon the earth will be of interest.

For much of my adult life I have contemplated man's eventual destiny and whether consciousness ends with death. I have wrestled with and seemingly been steered towards the conviction that it is merely the beginning – the doorway to a larger life the nature of which we cannot, in our world of limitations, hope to comprehend.

All of us, from the moment that we are born into this world, are heading in the same direction. There can be no escape from death. My views are based – as I hope that I have shown – not upon supposition, nor entirely upon second hand information, but rather upon long intimate experience both within and beyond my own séance room.

With all the force at my command I would insist that I have long been in a privileged position which has allowed me (and others) to momentarily peer beyond the curtain. Repeatedly the Spirit people have done their best to inform us – to give to us an understanding of their glorious world – that world that awaits us all. But, always, they have failed and one imagines that for them to succeed would be akin to any effort we may make to explain to a man without sight what colour is, or to explain to someone deaf since birth what the sound of rain or that of waves breaking upon a shore is like. But then we know from all that we have been told that the world of eternity far surpasses in every conceivable way that of our present one. To all those reading these words who know the pain of bereavement, as we all must do at various times during our earthly lives, I end Part One with the reassurance that truly life in all its magnificence continues beyond the grave.

Thank you for your company as, throughout these pages, I have trod, once again, that long ever twisting path of discovery which has been an extraordinary journey.

Many more accounts and reports could have been included but I deemed this unnecessary and chose only those which I felt were representative of the whole and which I hope have allowed readers an insight into my world of physical interaction with the dead.

A world of dark séance rooms in which all sacred human emotion was and still is laid bare. Rooms filled with laughter and with joy. Rooms in which inner peace and reassurance of survival beyond the grave was and still is experienced.

The world of the living and the world of the dead brought together as one for a precious few moments in time. And the message – always – death is merely a change of location.

And indeed it is.

Postscript to Part One
The Golden Thread

I confide how I faced the terrible tragedy of the death of my youngest sister in 2009 in a road accident. ~ The remarkable series of events that occurred within weeks which left no doubt as to their post-mortem source.

As I wrote in the previous chapter, my youngest sister Gaynor tragically lost her earthly life in February 2009. Her loss was excruciatingly painful not only to her family but also to her many friends all over the world. For me personally, the thought of continuing with my mediumship without her at my side was a matter which, at that time, was unthinkable.

The circle's immediate reaction perfectly matched my own and it was to be several weeks before we all gathered together – not to sit but simply to talk. That night proved extremely emotional for us all and particularly for Gaynor's youngest daughter Lindsey, who by then had been a member of the circle for nearly two years. But none of us was isolated in our grief and in so many ways it was an evening of just being together. The following week we gathered again at Ray and June's and did exactly the same – we talked. However, before we parted that night, I asked Lindsey if she would consider taking her mum's place in the circle sitting at my left side and without any hesitation she immediately agreed to do so.

The following week we sat as a circle – not in our first floor séance room – but in the lounge, and within moments I was entranced and dear Freda arrived to speak to the circle about Gaynor and about our loss. Understandably many tears were shed but out of that meeting between the two worlds came a realisation that was to result in a determination to continue. Perhaps for the first time all the members fully appreciated what our séances meant to so many people on both sides of life. Those who had in the past communicated with their deceased loved ones and those who would do so in the future. We all knew that we had a duty to continue to sit and we all felt that it would be exactly what Gaynor would want us to do.

At this point readers may understandably wonder how a medium actually faces bereavement and whether their knowledge of survival helps with the grieving process. Honesty is so important here and I would be less than truthful if I failed to record that immediately after the passing of my sister, my belief and my understanding of such matters failed entirely to lessen the acute pain which followed it. Yes of course I know only too well that life continues beyond death and yes of course I also know that the loved ones that we lose find themselves in a world which in every respect transcends our earthly one. None of that is in doubt but it is, of course, the physical loss that is so very difficult to bear. As Freda has so eloquently said very often in the past: 'When you lose a loved one to my world then it matters little what religious persuasion you may be. You can be a Buddhist, a Christian, or a Hindu or adhere to any other faith but when death strikes you will grieve. However, if you are a Spiritualist and you understand about the nature of life, then the day will arrive when your knowledge will be of such comfort and of such help.'

As I write these words I eagerly await that day.

We who had been so close to Gaynor knew that once she had recovered from the shock of transition and had acclimatised herself to her new surroundings, she would anxiously wish to send us a message.

With her knowledge of two-world communication, accumulated over so many years, her mind would turn upon the best way to reach us and what irrefutable evidence she could transmit in order to let us know that all was well. For reasons explained later, she would also know that this would have to be presented independently of our circle.

Of course we knew that as a result of acute emotional bereavement pain, most people at such times have a longing to believe that their loved ones have, in some way, survived death. They begin to look for signs from the deceased. As human beings we have difficulty contemplating the prospect that with death comes finality and so we cling to anything which might indicate otherwise in order that our pain may be eased. Although this is a normal process, we are, in our anxiety and vulnerability, in constant danger of 'making things fit'. Perhaps it is one of the few occasions in our life when discernment abandons us and in our yearning we are unconsciously prepared to grasp at anything which might help salve our pain. We may readily embrace anything which seems to suggest that our dead have signalled their presence and an unfettered mind can convert the most improbable and unconvincing event into one of certainty. If this helps us to accept and live with the loss of a loved one then that is fine, but in writing this I am highly conscious that I do not have such a luxury. In unequivocally stating that my sister communicated following her passing, I feel that readers, having read thus far, have a right to expect rather more than ambiguous accounts of events which may be considered the product of wishful thinking. Rather more in fact than loose supposition – rather more than conjecture. And so I now present the facts surrounding the remarkable events which commenced within days of her transition and continued over a period of several weeks. These left me, and others, in no doubt that she had done her best to signal from her new home that she was close and still very much a part of our lives. It is, however, for you, the reader, to decide how much veracity may be attached to what I am about to relate.

A few days following the shock of our loss, my wife was preparing a meal in the kitchen when suddenly she became aware that the digital radio had, of its own accord, changed station. From BBC Radio 4 it had inexplicably reset itself to Radio Absolute – a station that, up until then, we had never heard of. On that occasion, although quite mystifying, we simply accepted it and thought no more about it.

Two days later I was alone in the kitchen and listening to a drama production, again on Radio 4. At some point I was momentarily distracted and then as I listened again I quickly found myself somewhat puzzled. What I was listening to did not make sense in the context of the play. I wandered over to the radio and saw immediately that it had changed station – to Radio Absolute. Instantly it occurred to me that this switch to Radio Absolute from the original station had been a most intelligent choice if it were to be assumed that Gaynor had been attempting to signify her presence. Believing that she might have been responsible I thanked her.

Over the next few days it was to happen on several more occasions and additionally we began to experience even stranger happenings involving the digital wall mounted radio in our shower room.

On the first occasion that it happened my wife was taking a shower when suddenly she became aware of a strange noise in the background.

At the time she had thought that it must have been the extractor fan which, although never having done so before, had started to make odd noises. Not until she switched off the shower and stepped out did she realise that it was the radio and the sound was what is termed 'white noise'.

What made this quite extraordinary was firstly that all radio stations were preset and secondly that she had not switched the radio on prior to stepping into the shower.

In the weeks that followed this was to occur on several more occasions. The most remarkable happened one morning when my wife and I were both in the kitchen, which is on the ground floor.

Suddenly, we became aware of a loud noise from the floor above and could not think what it could possibly be. Upon reaching the shower room we discovered that once again the radio had switched itself on and the sound was again that of 'white noise'. Since there had been no one else in the house at the time, and therefore no one else could have been responsible, we duly thanked Gaynor for making the effort to alert us to her presence. We did the same a few days later when it again sprang into life early one morning when we were still in bed. There seemed to be no pattern regarding the time of day when these startling events would take place but sceptics may be interested to hear that they were to be short lived. Commencing within days of Gaynor's passing they continued to take place over a period of several weeks after which they suddenly stopped and would not recur until some eight months later. That was on the morning following the annual so-called 'Christmas Tree' séance that I have given each year at the York Spiritualist Church.

I was sitting in my study working on my book when suddenly, once again, the shower room radio burst into life with 'white noise'. Frankly, it startled me and my immediate thought was that the central heating boiler (located immediately outside my study) was responsible. As I left the room to investigate I quickly realised that it was not. What makes this particularly interesting is the fact that unbeknown to me at the time, my wife, before and during the séance the night before, had mentally asked Gaynor to make her presence known. Evidently, unable to do so, she sent her message the following day. Such occurrences, involving electrical interference and strange effects on radios, televisions, telephones and computers are fairly commonplace following a death and this is generally recognised by Spiritualists and some researchers. Being aware of this, and believing that Gaynor was responsible for the strange behaviour of our radios we have had no hesitation in letting her know that her efforts have not been in vain.

Extremely interesting as these events are they merely heralded the beginning of what I would soon come to recognise as irrefutable evidence of survival through a third party.

To share this with readers I must now introduce Dr Annette Childs, an American lady who, just days after Gaynor's passing, had, via the internet, purchased Part One of the Katie Halliwell trilogy of books describing my mediumship.

She had been an ardent student of afterlife studies for many years, yet despite her history of research into after death communications and mental mediumship, Katie Halliwell's book was to be her first introduction to physical mediumship. Clearly awed by what she read and wishing to learn more she subsequently e-mailed Ray Lister asking if she might be able to purchase the CD that complemented the book. Ray informed me that he had exchanged e-mails with the lady and I instinctively felt that I should make personal contact with her and did so by e-mail. An instant camaraderie was born. She quite openly expressed her shock at receiving an e-mail from me, when just a few days before this, she had never even heard of physical mediumship. Now, quite unexpectedly, she was finding herself involved in a very sincere and warm series of e-mails that quickly led to a genuine friendship between us. Soon I was to learn that she held a Ph.D. in psychology and had a private practice, working with the dying to assist them in the attainment of spiritual peace. She was also a bereavement counsellor and had researched and published important findings in respect of near death experiences. Apparently, since childhood she had possessed a mediumistic faculty although this evidently played a minor role in her professional life.

Additionally she was the author of two books[1] concerning matters of spiritual communication and both had won literary awards. Readers may be assured that in spite of our exchange of emails she knew nothing whatsoever about my personal life. However, sensing that our contact had not occurred through chance alone, I mentioned to her my sister's tragic passing and by return received wonderful words of comfort.

(1)' *Will You Dance?' (2002) The Wandering Feather Press*

'Halfway Across the River: Messages of Hope from the Other Side' (2007) The Wandering Feather Press

Looking back now, I believe that Gaynor orchestrated our connection for reasons which, although unsuspected at the time, would soon be revealed.

As I expressed earlier, despite my years of mediumship I had never fully understood the great gift that communication through a third party imparts to the bereft, until I walked in those shoes for myself. As Gaynor's brother I appreciated that anything that came through my mediumship would be of limited value for obvious reasons. Any apparent communication which proved evidential and which came via a stranger, and a stranger in America who knew virtually nothing of my own personal life, would be so important.

Although Dr Childs had certainly played down her mediumistic abilities, I felt compelled to ask her if she would try to link with Gaynor and to let me have any impressions that she might receive. Frankly, I must admit that the very suggestion now seems unreasonable, and yet at the time I felt driven to make the request although I did not know why.

However, it was a compulsion, and therefore I asked.

Her immediate response was one of compassion and humility. Yes, of course she would try, but she asked very earnestly that I hold out no great hope of success. Her thoughts at that time she subsequently and modestly expressed in the following words:

'I could hardly believe my situation! It was laughable. In a mere few weeks I had gone from virtually never having heard of physical mediumship to being in close and frequent contact with Stewart Alexander, for whom I was quickly gaining great respect. Here I was, a reluctant medium at best, being asked to provide any impressions that might be coming from his newly deceased sister. I was not sure whether to laugh or cry at my fortune... I was certainly nervous, thinking that any impressions that I might receive may prove disastrously wrong and yet I knew the great sadness in my new friend's grieving heart. An accurate evidential message could provide the type of healing for Stewart that he has provided for countless others through his work. These were my thoughts as I quieted my mind and asked to link with the immortal presence of Gaynor.

I simply asked that Stewart be afforded a bit of the same healing that he had delivered to so many through his physical mediumship. The impressions came in a flurry. So quickly that I was certain that they must be the result of my own mind playing tricks...

The strongest impression to come through was a full empathic vision of a young boy and girl with a pet snake. The boy was Stewart and the little one was Gaynor. As the children looked at this snake, there were deep feelings of fear and distaste.

The scene then quickly changed to one of two adults laughing quite heartily about this same subject. Gaynor was showing me in no uncertain terms that what had horrified them as children was great fodder for a belly laugh as adults.

Another very strong impression that I had was a beautiful scene of a rainbow stretching down to the sea, and there was a name being given that I could not pronounce. I typed it in my notes like this "The name of a town that starts with the letter 'L'. Its name is L____–by-the-Sea.

Next I clearly saw a bouquet of flowers with long green stalks and purple blooms.

In all there were six impressions, five of which proved relevant when I gave them to Stewart.'

❖   ❖   ❖

When Annette Childs e-mailed me the results of her attempt, I was astounded at the incident regarding the snake. As a child I had a pet snake that I was terrified of.

I kept it in an empty biscuit (cookie) tin with holes I had punched in its top. These allowed oxygen in and were also the means by which I kept the poor creature fed with maggots. The weeks passed – I never once lifted the lid and merely continued to keep it copiously well fed. And then one day my school teacher invited any pupil to bring into the classroom any unusual pets that they might have. And so, when I returned home, Gaynor and I took the biscuit tin lid off only to discover with horror that the maggots had made a meal of the snake.

It was a frightening and disturbing moment we shared... and when recollected on numerous occasions down the years, had caused great mirth between us. Remarkable!

Her second impression of a town called 'L---by-the-Sea' had no relevance for me, yet when I passed this information on to Gaynor's daughters I found that there was great meaning to this statement. There is a town in Cornwall called Looe which is on the coast and I was to learn that she had always told her husband and children that if she ever won the lottery it is where she would have chosen to live. Thus the image of a rainbow stretching out to sea from this town is quite appropriate to this notion.

The third piece of information transmitted involved a bouquet of flowers – a full description being given. On the day that Annette Childs emailed her impressions to me it was – here in England – Mother's Day. When I telephoned Lindsey to relay the information which again, had no meaning for me I described the flowers that Annette had written about. Amazingly she had just purchased a bouquet of flowers for her mum, and they perfectly matched the description given by Annette thereby proving, I believe, that my sister had been very aware of her daughter's gift to her.

Those pieces of information, contained in that one e-mail, together with three others of a more general nature, thus suggested to the family that Gaynor had indeed communicated through an American lady who at that time was virtually a stranger to us. Their evidential value simply cannot be dismissed or under-estimated.

Annette subsequently made the following remarks about these matters:

'I was humbled and amazed at the accuracy of the impressions. Gaynor's ability to reach me was solid and swift. I feel quite strongly that she most certainly had a hand in bringing Stewart and me together. When I ordered Katie Halliwell's book from Amazon.com the date was February 14th, just a few days after Gaynor's tragic passing. What moved me to find and order the book I cannot imagine but I can have no doubts that Gaynor was already weaving together a golden thread between Stewart and myself. When the book arrived I read it cover to cover in a few hours and could not believe that such a form of mediumship had eluded me for so many years. When I e-mailed the publisher, hoping that I could order the CD, there was no thought in my mind of ever being in contact with Stewart Alexander. Surely, it was at this point that he picked up the golden thread and followed it by contacting me.

I believe that both of us were following Gaynor's lead.'

❖   ❖   ❖

Since then I have received, from several mediums, further communications which purport to have come from Gaynor. Perhaps one of the most startling came from the celebrated Scottish medium Mary Armour. Without any embellishment whatsoever what follows is an account of what came to me through a mobile phone text message.

Every year my wife and I take a short holiday in the New Forest on the South Coast of England to visit relations. We have done so for almost forty years. Some weeks after Gaynor's untimely passing we were due to make our annual visit and since, whilst there we tend to walk a great deal, it is important that I should always take with me my walking boots.

A week prior to our visit, I removed them on the first floor of our house and left them on the floor of my study at the side of my desk. Throughout that week it often entered my head that I must not forget to pack them. On the morning of our departure, and moments prior to leaving home, I wandered into my study to collect a book that I wished to take with me and realized that my boots were still there. I picked them up together with the book, took them downstairs and placed them propped against the front door to ensure that I could not leave the house without them. As I turned and walked back towards the kitchen I heard a text come through on my mobile phone which was on one of the worktops. I picked it up, went into my inbox and this is precisely what I read: 'Gaynor says, don't forget your boots' – Mary.

What made this most extraordinarily evidential was that Mary Armour had absolutely no knowledge of the fact that my wife and I were about to take a holiday and no knowledge of the boots nor the fact that I was in danger of leaving without them.

Wonderful indeed.

Although the first part of this book has now reached its end the work of the Spirit has not. Looking back over the years I clearly see the 'golden thread' referred to by Annette, which has woven together the many elements of what for me has been – an extraordinary journey. One day my destination will be reached and when that day comes I shall be welcomed into eternity by the Spirit team, by my little Sis and by all my family, friends and associates who have preceded me there. With pride I shall not hesitate to say: 'I did my best.'

Part Two

Observations and Deductions

Chapter 1

Decline & Fall

An overview of early Spiritualism ~ Today's regrettable mediumistic standards ~ My thoughts on Spiritualism as a religion ~ A possible remedy to halt and reverse the Movement's undeniable recent decline ~ An Address by NAS President from 1998.

Prior to taking the decision to present this book in two parts – readers will be interested to know that I hesitated considerably. In Part One I have told the story of my deep involvement with the Spiritualist Movement throughout much of my adult life, and the way in which my mediumship gradually unfolded and the events and experiences (rich and otherwise) that I encountered along the way. Truly it has been a most remarkable and fascinating journey.

My indecision rested upon the possibility that Part Two of the book could, to some Spiritualists, psychical researchers and sceptics, make uncomfortable reading.

Disagreement and strong indignation would, I felt, almost certainly result because reality and falsehood surrounding the Spiritualist Movement today are largely intertwined. Indeed, there can be little reasonable doubt that Spiritualism, in a variety of ways, has existed over the past half century within a vacuum of self-imposed denial. But not to write Part Two would have been to deny myself this final opportunity to leave on record my carefully considered views. Readers should, however, understand that the opinions that I shall now present are based not upon a mere passing association with the subject but upon personal experience and long exhaustive research into the Movement's various aspects and facets. As a result I have gradually become familiar with its strengths and also its weaknesses. I have studied its history and I have sought to understand mediumship in its many forms and throughout I have done my utmost to weigh all in the balance of reason.

I am very familiar with the work of the great Spiritualist pioneers and mediums of the past and also those men and women from the worlds of psychical research and stage magic who have involved themselves with the Movement. I am no stranger to the controversy that has historically surrounded the entire subject and I recognise without hesitation how, in the mid nineteenth century it all began with such hope, vigour and intent. Since its birth, as I wrote in the Introduction to this book, it promised to replace materialism and prove conclusively that death was merely a passage into the next world. For over one hundred years people throughout the so-called civilised world were drawn to it believing that it was destined to replace orthodox religion and that eventually its message and its teachings would be established upon a scientific basis. Great men and women from the academic world succumbed to its dynamic appeal as too did a number of statesmen, men and women of letters, nobility, politicians, European royalty and people from all walks of life. Its converts became legion. For a time the Movement appeared to be firmly on course to achieve its aims, and yet, following the passing through Parliament of the Fraudulent Mediums Act [1] in 1951, it all started to go wrong. Instead of capitalising upon its hard fought victory for legalisation, it turned in upon itself and went into decline. The fighting spirit which saw its leadership, together with its rank and file, present a united front in the face of legal injustice slowly became a memory. The Movement's central message became fragmented, diluted and corrupted, with the result that gradually it lost direction.

Convictions and principles were watered down, manipulated, and compromised as a result of commercialism and egocentricity. A century of commitment, progress and promise gave way to pettiness and in so many ways, in losing sight of the broader picture, it sacrificed its soul. The infiltration of the orthodox Christian religion, which took root during Spiritualism's early days, and which has long been regarded by many as incompatible with the Movement, has these past few decades widely established itself. Some Spiritualists believe that it has done so to the detriment of the vital message.

Additionally, mediumship, the very bedrock of the Movement upon which it was established and built, and on which it rests or falls, has, in recent years, mainly transmuted into mediocrity. As a direct result, Spiritualism has paid a heavy price so that today it bears little comparison to what it once was, when the grave held no fear for its adherents who understood and accepted that under certain

(1) *The Fraudulent Mediums Act was itself repealed in 2008 and replaced by general consumer protection legislation.*

circumstances communication between the living and the dead was possible.

Sadly, the days when its leading mediums could command vast audiences at large demonstrations, because the evidence of survival they consistently presented was startling in its accuracy, have long gone. And, although not commonplace, back then there existed trance mediums who channelled philosophy and the so-called 'higher teachings' which left little doubt as to their spiritual source. Yet today, with precious few exceptions, there are few who are capable of doing either. Evidence of survival has largely given way to 'cold reading', counselling, fortune telling or a mixture of them all. Profound philosophical communications are now rarely transmitted and in their place alleged communications are generally poor and can only be described as confusing at best, and at worst an insult to intelligence. Indeed, so often I have regrettably found myself bewildered by what I have considered to be incoherent and mystifying nonsense delivered from the Spiritualist platform.

Prior to his passing a number of years ago, Alan Crossley, widely considered to be one of Spiritualism's most respected and creditable authorities, often expressed to me his own dismay in respect of this very matter. Indeed, I recall very clearly, during one of my frequent visits to his home, that he told me of an occasion when, some years earlier, he had attended a trance address at a local Spiritualist church. Apparently, the medium had been very well known, and for many months people had eagerly anticipated his visit.

On the night in question it had been standing room only and Alan, arriving early in order to secure a seat, had found himself sitting at the back of the hall to one side of two elderly ladies. The medium made his entrance, was introduced by the church President and quickly fell into a trance. Then, for sixty minutes, the alleged Spirit communicator had delivered his fathomless message, philosophy, or whatever it was. After the medium had apparently returned to consciousness and had left the room, Alan could not help overhearing the conversation that ensued between the two elderly ladies:

'Well – what did you think about that?' said one to the other, to which the other replied, 'Wasn't he clever? – I never understood a word of it.'

Alan doubted that any other person present that night would have understood it either – they had all sat through sixty minutes of unmitigated gobbledegook and the lady, he said, could have been speaking on behalf of the entire congregation.

An isolated incident? Sadly, no, and one is bound to wonder why the spiritual world would go to the bother of transmitting discourses which no one can understand. Without question, wonderful, sublime, and uplifting communications have been received in the past, are being received today, and hopefully will continue to be received in the future; that is not in doubt. When you hear true spiritual philosophy, and genuine higher teachings, then you know, just as you know when you hear a mishmash of facts and pseudo- facts – relevance and irrelevance.

The former lifts the spirit, inspires, enlightens, informs and nurtures the soul, whereas the latter leads only to confusion.

Regrettably, it is my firm belief that much today which purports to issue directly from a spiritual source in truth emanates directly from the medium's mind – subconscious or otherwise. As a result, Spiritualism, its credibility and rational standing are most certainly the poorer and that, I believe, is an inescapable fact.

Mediumship.

Mediums, in my view, are born – an abnormality of nature perhaps? Physical mediums are endowed with a richness of the extraordinary living energy, ectoplasm, and it is upon this that physical phenomena rest and depend. Under suitable conditions, and given the opportunity, the Spirit World will commence the long process which may eventually result in a suitable individual developing such mediumship. No amount of time, patience or sincerity will achieve this if the essential vital energy is absent. One could sit for ever in a dark room, under perfect conditions, and still fail to develop. These are the facts, as I believe them to be, in respect of this exceedingly rare form of mediumship.

Mental mediumship, although different in regard to its nature, its development and its presentation, nevertheless has various similarities. In my view the most important is sincerity of purpose and an overwhelming desire to be of service to mankind in both worlds but, as with the development of physical mediumship, great patience is required, together with the realisation that its unfoldment relies and depends totally upon the Spirit World. Of course, mental and physical mediumship simply cannot be developed to a marked degree should the potential not exist in the first place and yet each year, a considerable number of would-be mediums are engaged upon a quest to develop and attempt to do so through courses, seminars, individual tuition and even correspondence courses which promise to 'release the medium within'.

Prospective hopefuls and mediums at varying stages of development are encouraged to engage in them and today they are commonplace and the entire Movement now seems to me to be awash with them. No doubt mainly they are well meaning and full of good intentions and can, properly conducted, help in the development of those with genuine potential. I am equally certain that it is often a case, not of expert guidance, instruction and training, but of the blind leading the blind and sadly, in some cases, a simple matter of commercialism. No medium and no professed Spiritualist authority should ever presume to take precedence over the spiritual world or to present themselves as possessing infinite understanding of mediumship, its development and practice.

Unfortunately, so often that is the reality. With justification one wonders just how many would be mediums who follow such paths eventually end up demonstrating on the Spiritualist platform and, of those who do, how many truly attain a notable standard? I believe that the answer to that will speak for itself.

The truth is that irrespective of authoritative talk, claims and promises, only the Spirit World can develop a medium.

Having long since reached that conclusion, I must also state my belief that although it is rarely acknowledged, psychology plays a most important role in respect of all aspects of mediumship.

However, should an aspiring medium feel confidence in the teacher, and derive encouragement and constant constructive assurance from them, this would most certainly be a beneficial influence. Advice, support, encouragement and guidance can be sought from an accredited and highly responsible medium, but it must never be forgotten that this should not be to the exclusion of the Spirit World for it is only the Spirit people who are capable of unfolding an individual's latent ability. It is the Spirit World alone that is the ultimate authority. So the question that must be posed and answered is why today the Movement in general terms has such a poverty of high quality mediumship. To answer that we must surely begin by looking back into its early history for I believe that it is there that the answer lies.

During the second half of the nineteenth century and the first half of the twentieth, Home Circles in great numbers existed throughout America, Europe and England. It was a time when thousands of people sat in impassioned silence in an effort to develop the gifts of the Spirit and commune with the spiritual world. It was a time when Spiritualists listened intently to the inner voice of their own convictions, thus enabling the process of development to commence and expand in an atmosphere of harmonious aspiration. It was a time when wonderful mediums, both mental and physical, emerged from the obscurity of their circles to work publicly.

It has long been suspected, however, that many more chose to shun the public spotlight and stay within their circles to remain forever unknown to the outside world. For over a hundred years and prior to the advent and infiltration of commercialism into the Movement, mediumship was mainly developed behind closed doors. This removed any pressure of expectation and by sitting in stable and harmonious conditions the so-called 'gifts of the Spirit' occasionally emerged. Today, of course, home development circles still exist but in far smaller numbers. And, since we now live in an instant world, few people are prepared to dedicate themselves to years of patient sitting often with little to show for it. That is one of the Movement's tragedies.

Experts Here – Experts There – Experts almost Everywhere.

Whilst the general decline of mediumship can be said to be largely responsible for the sorry state of Spiritualism today, there are additional factors involved. In Part One of this book I explained that my introduction to the Movement came as a result of reading Arthur Findlay's remarkable book 'On the Edge of the Etheric'. It introduced me to a subject which previously I had regarded as nonsense. It sought to establish in plain easy-to-understand layman's language the scientific basis upon which Spiritualism rested. Dispassionately and carefully, Findlay addressed many vitally important questions, such as the mediumistic evidence for survival, the location of the Spirit World in relation to our own, the way in which mediumship functions, the nature of life upon the earth and man's experience at the moment of death and after. Much of what he imparted he had himself ascertained through attending many séances with the Glasgow trumpet medium, John Campbell Sloan.

By speaking directly and extensively to alleged Spirit communicators his many questions were answered and he was able to gain an insight into and an understanding of vital matters which had long been shrouded in mystery. Beyond question I found the book a veritable *tour de force* which intelligently and rationally dealt with the survival beyond death of the human soul.

Certainly, at the time of its first publication it was to receive extensive and excellent reviews never previously afforded to any other book which had dealt with the subject. For a while at least, cynics, critics and sceptics were effectively disarmed and silenced.

My own journey of discovery – all that I have done since first reading it, including the writing of this book, owes everything to that book. What Findlay wrote of seemed so straightforward – so reasonable, logical and easy to understand. No mysticism – nothing esoteric – nothing associated with the occult and nothing chimerical. As time went on, I was to realise that he had not been alone in his findings and in his common sense approach to Spiritualism – there were others.

Men and women of considerable intellect and academic and social standing had written in similar vein and these were the people who ignited my interest and continuously lit up my pathway of discovery. After a period of time, saturated by what I had read, I decided to visit the churches. Then, as I recorded in Part One, it all changed for me. Not always – but very often – such services as I attended were (and still are today) mainly conducted on religious lines with demonstrations of mediumship thrown in. Time and time again I would sit and listen to an address delivered by the visiting medium, or by a church official and invariably I would find myself lost and unable to comprehend and I would quickly become thoroughly uninterested. To me it was all so very baffling and a far cry from what Findlay and his like had written of. Repeatedly, I found myself marvelling at grossly misleading discourses which frankly left me both astonished and incredulous. Quite simply, so very often they had as much relevance to Spiritualism as palm reading. On other occasions I sat through addresses which, although no doubt delivered with great sincerity, were far more suited to the pulpit of the orthodox Christian religion. Following such services, I occasionally engaged fellow members of the congregation in conversation, and enquired whether they had understood the address which I had found so incomprehensible. Rarely did anyone admit to having done so, although many had earlier sat listening whilst nodding their approval and agreement. Those who were perhaps more honest (or perhaps less embarrassed) had just looked bored rigid.

In the many years that have since followed, nothing has changed. Indeed, if anything, the situation has decidedly worsened. Spiritualism, its message, its truths and its philosophy have gradually become submerged and suffocated by experts everywhere, many of whom freely dispense their questionable, false or perhaps misguided wisdom with authority and with seeming conviction. I cannot help but draw parallels with the early Christian church and what it subsequently became under the influence and manipulation of officialdom and its emerging priesthood. Simplicity gradually became complexity with its adherents constantly attempting to fathom the unfathomable.

For whatever reason organised Spiritualism has allowed itself to be diverted and corrupted by insignificance and by gradually widening its dynamic focus has additionally embraced and encompassed eastern philosophies and practices. All, no doubt, highly commendable in themselves, but of no relevance to Spiritualism.

Would mediums from the so-called 'golden age' of Spiritualism have known what a chakra was? I doubt it. Would they have understood what the God force or energy fields or Chi meant? Of course not. Yet, to my certain knowledge, such matters are now firmly rooted and embedded within the Movement.

Worse still, occasionally demonstrations of mediumship, addresses and workshops geared to 'release the medium within' etc. are often conducted by people who, it can only be assumed, are evidently in ignorance of their subject.

Indeed, in recent years it has been my misfortune to witness addresses delivered from the platform and the rostrum by young mediums or speakers who spoke 'at' as against 'to' their audience. From their lips fell the most condescending inappropriate platitudes, spoken with such self-assertive confidence. Yet they could not possibly have been in the Movement for any length of time. Such pontifical words neither informed nor uplifted. If anything they patronised. To use a modern day expression – if one can 'talk the talk' and do so persuasively whilst exuding confidence, and have the intention and desire, then it is possible that anyone could end up on the platform delivering their own particular brand of Spiritualism. Innumerable times I have found myself wondering if such people had actually understood their own words and the subject about which they had been speaking. Since they generally failed to pass on, in an unvarnished fashion, the message and teachings of Spiritualism it can only be concluded that they did not. Surely therefore, in common with the undeveloped mediums who happily demonstrate in public, such people perform a great disservice to the Movement.

Spiritualism & Religion.

For a great many years, an argument existed and raged, as to whether Spiritualism should be regarded as a religion. This was indeed a moot point, which provoked both comment and debate and which divided the Movement into two opposing camps – those who believed that it was and those who did not. However, the matter was seemingly settled in 1951 with the passing of the Fraudulent Mediums Act which, in effect, gave to the Movement religious and philosophical freedom and, as many believed, respectability.

Whilst it is not my intention here to elaborate to any great extent upon my own feelings regarding this important matter, I feel impelled to briefly comment.

Although the Act effectively legalised mediumship it came with a price, religious acquiescence. This, I firmly believe, led the Movement away from its true path and as a result the central message was weakened. Some early prominent and highly creditable pioneers of the Movement castigated the very idea that religion should play any part whatsoever in it and were absolutely opposed to its inclusion. Many of those championed the Movement and risked their professional and social standing to do so. They took the view that once its message had been accepted then a religious belief system would no longer be necessary. To steadfastly cling to earlier religious beliefs would be nonsensical, although no doubt something of a compromise by merging the two (Spiritualism and religion) would, for some, be a less radical change. They argued, that it was an immutable fact that survival beyond death owed nothing whatsoever to a religious belief system. To them, it was a fact of life and regardless of one's religion all life on this earth would survive the grave and the kind of life led here, together with a person's nature and character, would determine the condition and the dimension in which the individual found themselves in the next world.

My own views match those and I further believe that for the deceased who have held strong religious beliefs during their earthly life, the post-mortem experience may initially be influenced by their own convictions. That aside, it really matters nothing whether a person has been a Buddhist, a Christian, a Hindu, or has subscribed to any other faith because beyond death it will make absolutely no difference to our final destiny.

In my view this entire religious issue is yet a further example of a tragedy which has contributed to the sacrifice of the original message. However, should I be wrong, I know that I shall be in extremely good company. I will say no more than that.

Change and Progress

So far in this chapter I have concentrated solely upon the negative aspects of Spiritualism – its loss of direction and its decline as a once highly motivated, determined and largely unified Movement.

All but the blind would fail to recognise now that its golden years (generally considered to have been during and between the two World Wars) have long gone. A once proud Movement has largely collapsed and as a mere shadow of its former self it limps on whilst largely living on its past. As I stated earlier, commercialism now thrives and mediumship development courses – at a price – exist in abundance. Additionally, television now regularly broadcasts highly edited demonstrations of mediumship and such shows (for that is what they are) are presented as entertainment, any semblance of spirituality being stripped away to leave the viewer knowing nothing of true Spiritualism, its philosophy, teachings and the rich vein of history that runs through it. Such shallow productions neither inform nor advise and viewers remain in ignorance of the once great and vital Movement which for over one hundred years threatened to overturn established religion and rewrite the scientific text books.

Clearly such information has no place within such productions.

And so the question which now presents itself is whether Spiritualism can in the future find again its rightful path, rise from its own ashes and regain lost ground. If it can, then it must begin by recognising its current plight and if it can do that then it will have made a positive start. It then should reconsider and re-evaluate the point in history at which it all began to go wrong. It must identify the reasons and seek to rectify them and in so doing perhaps it could conceivably correct its course and move forward with regained positivity and commitment. Whilst I could wax lyrical about such matters, I shall refrain from doing so and instead restrict myself to principal comments and opinions which I firmly believe could help reverse Spiritualism's tragic tide of decline.

Firstly – the various factions and organisations within it should unite for the sake of the greater good.

Secondly – it should be clear-sighted and free from egotism and above all else it should begin once again to 'listen to the Spirit World' because by doing so anything is possible.

I firmly believe that therein lies the principal reason for its current plight. Forty years ago, or more, the Movement quite simply stopped listening. That situation must be addressed and corrected. When the messenger becomes more important than the message (the usual case where egotism exists) then the way will always be lost.

The whole matter of commercial mediumistic development must urgently be addressed. Yes, of course it is possible that success can be achieved through the various courses on offer. However, Spiritualists interested in development should rather be encouraged to sit in, or to form their own home circles. As previously stated – once, these were the very bedrock of the Spiritualist Movement, and it is from them – a whole new generation of such circles – that tomorrow's good mediums could well emerge. Since the development of true mediumship generally takes many years to reach fruition, positive progressive change in the Movement may be some years into the future but it is the only way – it is the future.

On the other hand if Spiritualism continues on its present course and fails to face and correct the stark reality of its appalling degeneration then in the not too distant future it will in its purest form most likely die away – a prospect far too painful to contemplate!

A Stirring address

In March 1998, Alf Winchester, as the President of the Noah's Ark Society, delivered a stirring address at the 150th Anniversary celebrations of Modern Spiritualism. Organised and conducted by the world's largest Spiritualist organisation, it had been held to pay tribute to the Movement's pioneers. In the hope of perhaps inspiring unity he took the opportunity to make a rousing emotional appeal to the audience of representatives from various Spiritualist organisations. As I read the transcript of the speech it occurred to me that it perfectly augmented and crystallised my own thoughts. Unfortunately, in 1998 it failed entirely to motivate or influence its listeners and, in fact, for some it proved controversial! With Alf's permission I reproduce the speech here in its entirety in the hope that it may, at last, fulfil its original intent.

Tribute to the Pioneers

Originally published in *The Noah's Ark Newsletter*, May 1998.

Alf Winchester

We are here to pay tribute to the pioneers of our Movement. I would therefore like you to consider whether we are doing justice to their legacy. Do you think that all is well in the Spiritualist Movement?

Are we attracting the young folk? Do you think we have the respect of the world at large? Fifty years ago the 100th anniversary celebrations were held in the Albert Hall. Spiritualism, then, had a higher profile, with many distinguished people promoting our cause. Fifty years ago articles on Spiritualism were common in quality newspapers. No quality newspapers now carry such articles. Why is this I wonder? Is it because our public image has changed? Are we seen as some sort of joke or a bunch of oddballs? Our image is not helped by TV chat shows which are orientated to making Spiritualists look foolish. They often deny time for eloquent Spiritualists to state their case, whilst tending to concentrate on the ones who are less able to put over their views and in particular on the cranky ones.

If our public image is not right, shouldn't we be doing something about it? Perhaps Spiritualism should form a Committee of suitably qualified Spiritualists to look into our public image and make suggestions as to how we can improve it. It may even be necessary to employ a firm of image consultants as the political parties do. I'm not suggesting we manufacture an illusion only that we must show the Spiritualist Movement in its true light. Let us make the Spiritualist Movement attractive to enquiring minds in the 21st Century.

Our predecessors fought for Spiritualism to be recognised in law as a religion. If we are a recognised religion, why is it then that we are often not allowed to express our views on television without the obligatory balanced view from parapsychologists and priests. If we are being treated unfairly or Spiritualism is portrayed on television in a derogatory manner what are we doing about it? As individuals we can bombard the broadcasting authorities with complaints. Better still if we, as a united Movement, can appeal to the broadcasting authorities, if their response is unfavourable, then perhaps we might consider taking legal action through the British and European Courts of Law. As long as Spiritualists, both individuals and organisations, sit back and do nothing, then the situation will never improve and could well deteriorate.

We read in *Psychic News* of instances where Spiritualist churches and mediums have been refused the use of premises. Why do we allow this to happen without making a big fuss? We could, for instance, send an avalanche of complaints to the person responsible and also to the press. If discrimination against Spiritualism can be proved and there is a good enough case, then legal proceedings could be instigated. Owners of premises will think twice about bowing to pressure from vicars and 'born again' Christians if they know that by doing so legal action might follow. Legal action is probably beyond the means of most individuals. The setting up of a legal fund and helpline would be a great asset.

I feel we need to return to the basics of Spiritualism. The Movement has been swamped with practices from other religions, other philosophies and cultures which are now being accepted as part of Spiritualism.

Some say standards of mediumship are declining. The Spiritualist Movement has, I'm afraid, its fair share of mediums of questionable standard. There seems to be an obsessive desire among Spiritualists to be trance mediums. These 'wannabes' include some who are good mental mediums but fail miserably as trance mediums. Many of them are deluded. I call it clair-delusion. It is one thing to deceive yourself, quite another to deceive others, particularly those in need of help.

All forms of mediumship have their place. None should be considered superior to the others but it is essential that, in whatever form, only the highest possible standard of mediumship is encouraged.

Spiritualists, both as individuals and organisations, are the regulators of the standard. If they do nothing then standards will continue to decline. Let us not be divided by our differences, but united in the certain knowledge that the soul survives death. Whether we like it or not the reality is that most of mankind is not ready to accept our message but, nevertheless, Spiritualism must put itself in a prominent position so that truth seekers can easily find it.

United, we can revitalise Spiritualism, and head held high, take our rightful place among religions. I'm not sure if we are in reality a religion; I think of us more as custodians of a universal truth. Let us build on past achievements and leave our successors a legacy that could benefit all mankind. We owe it to our predecessors and to our inspirers in the Spirit World.

I ask you to consider what I have said and if you feel it has some merit then please do something about it. Apathy, disharmony and egotism have killed off many a noble cause. Please don't allow Spiritualism to become a victim.

❖　❖　❖

Chapter 2

Fraudulent Mediumship & The Sceptics

I address the matter of alleged fraudulent physical mediums of the past and draw upon historic records to substantiate that not all was clear cut fraud ~ I analyse 'The Sceptic' and formulate answers to arguments which they have long made without challenge.

In this and subsequent chapters, I intend to examine such matters as past assumptions of mediumistic fraud predominantly as they relate to two of the Movement's most celebrated physical mediums. These engaged the Spiritualist and research worlds in bitter dispute as to the facts surrounding the allegations. At the time, and ever since, accusations and counter-accusations have been made between their supporters and their denigrators and now, eighty years later, the interminable arguments show little sign of abating. The events of those now far-off days continue to be analysed, dissected and liberally agonised over with neither side shifting from their positions. Spiritualists invariably ignore uncomfortable facts and many researchers seize upon them whilst disregarding those which fail to fit neatly into their own conclusions.

I shall return to this later but for now readers can be assured that throughout the history of the Movement, fraud and physical mediumship have always been linked and that so-called exposures were not unusual. Little-known mediums and ones of international repute (with very few exceptions) were, at some time during their careers, accused of devious practices. Few reputations were to remain intact and untainted. Occasionally accusations were justified, but conversely, with the benefit of hindsight, it can reasonably be argued that some may not have been so – a matter which I discuss in this and later chapters. Spiritualism, of course, has always recognised that genuine physical mediumship has existed in parallel with the fraudulent. However, with the exposures of false mediums who traded upon the emotions of the gullible and the bereaved, the Movement was to find itself repeatedly plunged into embarrassing controversy. Of course, it cannot be denied that one of the greatest weaknesses of the physical séance room has always been that generally manifestations are inhibited by the presence of any form or degree of light. Therefore, and quite understandably, such rooms have led many to suspect chicanery, although, irrespective of how it may appear, the total elimination of light is generally very necessary. In assuming that such conditions must invariably harbour fraud, one would be guilty of making a monumental error. As I pointed out in the first chapter of this book, one may as well argue that the darkroom was unnecessary for early photographic development. I went on to suggest that no informed person today would dispute the absolute fact that light is fatal to particular micro-organisms, nor that darkness is essential for the creation of life itself, in the germination of a seed or the development of an embryo in the womb.

Therefore it is hardly logical to dismiss and reject the darkened séance room, based upon mere suspicion and/or on ignorance of the facts.

As I stated earlier, physical manifestations rest and depend upon the presence of the living energy, ectoplasm, which is believed to be a protoplasmic substance extracted by the Spirit World directly from the medium through the ears, nose, mouth or solar plexus.

In its primary state it can be visible or it can be invisible. It can be tangible, it can be intangible, and it has often been reported as having the odour of ozone. When visible it can have the appearance of a vapour or a liquid and it may also take on the semblance of skin and hair and occasionally it will resemble butter muslin or cheesecloth. In the case of fraudulent productions, this is generally what it has proven to be.

However, whatever its nature, this exuded mysterious matter, when genuine, is a living substance which possesses an extraordinary capacity to quickly convert its molecular structure, one moment seemingly ethereal and the next transforming into a solid state which can be as substantial as steel. Physical phenomena of all kinds, from the movement of objects without physical contact, to the audible voices of the dead and visual solid manifestations owe their genesis to it.

Quite simply it is the very foundation of all séance room physical phenomena and although we understand little concerning it and of the precise way in which it operates, we do know that it is exceedingly light sensitive. The sudden introduction of light (natural or artificial) into the séance room, without prior permission of the Spirit World, can cause it rapidly to return to its source with a catastrophic effect upon the health of the medium. Such instances, involving a number of past physical mediums, are well documented by the Movement. Of course, these simplistic statements (some may judge audacious) I offer in my capacity as a medium and as a Spiritualist. Having done so, it is fitting to point out that the very existence of ectoplasm has long been questioned by many within the research world. That aside, it must be readily admitted that dark rooms unquestionably lend themselves to fraud and have occasionally harboured deceit and devious practice. It is possible that they still do. None of this is in any doubt and whenever, in the past, fraud was uncovered and exposed, the effect upon the Movement was understandably double-edged. On the one hand it was of importance to Spiritualism that it should be self policing and it endeavoured always to keep its own house in order. Fraudulent practice when discovered was rooted out and the Movement itself was probably responsible for exposing more fraud than were the researchers themselves. However on the other hand, accusations of common fraud were understandably embarrassing and uncomfortable, particularly when esteemed and highly respected mediums were involved who had previously been accredited by the Movement itself.

Although generally unknown today, the names Frank Herne, Mary Showers, Charles Williams, Charles Eldred, Albert Beare, John Scammell, Arthur Phillips, Charles Basham, Harold Barnett, Ronald Edwin Cockersell and William Roy are just a few of the many in this country who, for a time, were at the very pinnacle of their profession.

Eventually, one by one, they were exposed as charlatans who produced bogus physical phenomena by utilising, under cover of darkness (or within dimly lit rooms), all manner of subterfuge. Contrivances were employed, from expandable reaching rods (used to control séance trumpets) to cheesecloth, false beards and masks, to imitate materialised forms and ectoplasmic extrusions etc. These fraudulent mediums preyed upon the gullible, the credulous, and on the general unwillingness of some Spiritualists to face unpleasant facts and recognise fraud. Such was the situation in the past – such I suspect, may well be the situation today, and no doubt it will be in the future. When there is money to be made, and whilst there exists an overwhelming desire to believe, there will always be unscrupulous individuals only too happy to capitalise and deceive. This is not a matter for debate – it is not a matter for conjecture or dispute – it is a matter of absolute fact. The worlds of psychical research and Spiritualism have always been in agreement on that point.

However, that aside, it is important to point out that the late Maurice Barbanell, long time editor of *Psychic News*, and a man of vast knowledge in respect of all aspects of Spiritualism, maintained that where physical mediumship was concerned, it was an easy matter to cry fraud – anyone could do so. Indeed, many did, and invariably the accused were robbed of their credibility, after which they either sank into obscurity or, at best, were thereafter surrounded by grave suspicion. Dismissed by the world of psychical research, and occasionally by the Spiritualist Movement itself, such mediums, with their reputations destroyed, were generally consigned to the spurious and lamentable pages of Spiritualism's history. Of course, not all so-called exposures established fraud beyond reasonable doubt and in such cases one may wonder why – if a medium was wrongly accused – they invariably failed to present a coherent defence, or indeed in most cases, any defence at all? The truth is, of course, that in reality they may only have been guilty of an intellectual inability to defend themselves, and sadly this was to seal their fate.

Then, there exists a further possibility that may, in some cases, account for apparent fraud, and which I briefly alluded to in the final chapter of Part One; physical mediumship is seldom black or white, genuine or fraudulent. History tells us that confusingly, there are grey areas – a mixture of the two – fraudulent on some occasions whilst genuine on others. As previously stated, in the world of psychical research, this is classed as 'mixed mediumship' and although fraud in some cases would have been conscious and premeditated, in others it may have been unconscious. In the latter, is it perhaps conceivable that such mediums genuinely would not have understood their own apparent fraudulent actions?

And further – also as previously mentioned – could it be that in the presence of overt scepticism within the delicate sensitive atmosphere of the séance room (a breeding ground in which the thoughts of the sitters can become highly potent) a medium may unknowingly act upon such powerful thoughts and produce the fraudulent action that the sitter expects to find? If that is so, then rather ironically, the sitter would indirectly be responsible for helping to create the very fraud suspected. And the medium, having no knowledge of his actions, would – when later confronted – be genuinely mystified and unable to account for his actions. This would surely go a long way towards resolving an enigma which has baffled and confused serious students of physical mediumship for many years. Of course whilst such a proposition may, to some readers, be considered as a rather convenient excuse to explain away and excuse fraud, this should not be grounds for failing to acknowledge and propose it. Is it far-fetched and does it stretch credibility too far? Frankly I don't know – I merely present it and it is for you, the reader to decide, whether it has merit.

Of course, the hardened sceptic, always immovable from his cynical position of certainty, will casually dismiss it as unworthy of consideration.

But then such a fixed rigid stance is surely no more legitimate than that of the highly credulous Spiritualist. Whether then it is true or false, one thing is certain and that is that mediumship in general is profoundly complex and there can be no doubt that it embodies a compulsion to please and to produce results. That is particularly so in the physical séance room and, in the next chapter, I shall, as an illustration, examine the case of arguably the finest American trumpet medium in history – George Valiantine.

His fate in the 1930s was eventually sealed when he was apparently exposed in fraud by his principal benefactor and champion. It makes rather interesting reading.

Eusapia, Mixed Mediumship and the Sceptic

As an example of mixed mediumship and also of blinkered illogical scepticism, I briefly return to the case of the uneducated Neapolitan physical medium Eusapia Palladino. In the late nineteenth and early twentieth centuries she sat for a great many of the world's leading investigators. Always, she would warn them, that given the opportunity, she would cheat. Yet, when she was under perfect control, the most excellent physical phenomena would occur – often at a distance from where she sat. This included the movement of objects, the levitation of tables without any apparent physical contact, and other phenomena such as partial materialisations – hands etc. Conversely, she would invariably take the easy option to produce what was expected if control was broken and she was allowed to free a hand or a foot. For Eusapia, it seemed to be a psychological compulsion, and this often led to blatant trickery, with bitter recriminations and heated disputes between researchers and occasionally between them and the Spiritualists.

At that time, the SPR had a policy that any medium caught in fraud would never again be examined by them. As a result, and following a series of séances arranged by the Society in 1895 in Cambridge, during which Eusapia was repeatedly detected in brazen fraud, it published a damning report and effectively ruled that she would not be examined again. However, some years later (1908) and following repeated excellent reports from their European counterparts, the Society decided that it would make an exception and investigate her mediumship once again. Three of their most experienced and leading investigators, Everard Feilding, Hereward Carrington and W.W. Baggally (two of whom were well versed in stage magic) were commissioned and dispatched to Naples, where a series of sittings was held with the single intention of proving once and for all whether Eusapia was capable of producing genuine phenomena.

The venue for the sittings and the protocol and conditions for the experiments were arranged entirely by the investigators. Wholly successful, they led to one of the most thorough, meticulous and credible reports of an investigation into physical mediumship ever published. It appeared in the *Proceedings* of the Society in November 1909 under the title 'Report on a Series of Sittings with Eusapia Palladino' and seemingly left no loophole for sceptical counter-explanation and argument.

Undoubtedly, Eusapia, like others who were to come after her, was truly an enigma.

For over eighty years, that report stood as a most careful, comprehensive and detailed document that defied criticism. Eventually though, it was to be placed under the cold light of cynical analysis and scrutiny, although attempts to undermine it have, to my mind, failed entirely. Arguments advanced in order to avoid a paranormal explanation seem to me to suggest that no amount of carefully acquired evidence will convince those who quite simply refuse to believe. Indeed, readers familiar with the Naples report and with such critiques could conclude that they are an insult to the researchers involved, all of whom had impeccable reputations and were among the most careful, experienced and respected of their day. Is it therefore fair to say that just as there are Spiritualists who suffer from gullibility and an unwillingness to face reality, so there are cynics so locked into an irrational mind-set of scepticism, that they too lack impartial objectivity? Sir Arthur Conan Doyle, one of Spiritualism's great champions, when discussing scepticism as it related to the Movement, said: 'The man who believes nothing is just as foolish as the man who believes everything.' In the next two chapters, I shall have more to say about the ardent sceptic.

Having researched the matter for many years I have now concluded that the real motive which lay behind some claimed mediumistic fraud exposures was not what it appeared to be at the time. I have little doubt that some were made purely for purposes of elevating the profile of the accusers seeking to achieve enhanced status amongst their peers. Dishonesty exists throughout every conceivable stratum of society and the worlds of psychical research and of magic cannot be singled out for exemption.

The Sceptic

Scepticism, of course, takes many forms but I shall mention here just a few as they relate to Spiritualism.

Firstly – the most common are the sceptics who fail to familiarise themselves with the subject and whose opinions are based purely upon ignorance.

Secondly – there are those who may be referred to as the 'Informed Sceptics'. Having taken the trouble to enquire into the subject they find that the copious evidence in favour of the paranormal accumulated over the past 150 years by such august bodies as the SPR and by the Spiritualist Movement itself does not convince them.

Thirdly – there are the immovable 'Fixed View Sceptics' who lambast all aspects of the subject particularly on the internet. Not surprisingly, physical mediumship in particular has lent itself to their unreserved, derisory, pretentious comment and attack. Indeed, it would appear that such critics are uniquely informed, as in their world there can be no room for doubt as to their pronouncements. Logic, it seems, is invariably the first victim. Often outlandish and wholly misleading claims are made and facts are ignored or corrupted. Spiritualists and sympathetic researchers are all 'deluded' having 'lost their critical faculties'. All the manifestations of the séance room are nothing more than 'tomfoolery' and all who believe in them have been 'deceived'. How remarkable that these sceptics, in being so certain of their conclusions, have clearly arrived at the unquestionable truth. Opposing views are quite simply unworthy of consideration, even when based upon long careful investigation, knowledge and experience. In their eyes, every favourable report concerning mediumship is the product of a 'will to believe' thus resulting in the critical faculty being rendered inoperative and in the consequent abandonment of common sense. All mediums – physical or mental – are not merely dubious but unquestionably fakes, each using the same methods of deceit as the others. In their world genuine mediumship does not exist.

It does not appear to occur to them that some of the world's greatest minds have, over the past 150 years, been convinced by the evidence. To arrogantly dismiss that is surely to dismiss all informed human testimony. But then, in the world of the 'Fixed View Sceptic' there is alas no room for a serious and careful consideration of fact. Such a prospect would complicate the entire matter. In many ways they are akin to the gullible 'Bless-you-friend' Spiritualist who is incapable of separating normal from supernormal occurrences.

In their world every creak of a floor board or expansion of a hot water pipe – every noise from an unidentified source – every feeling of coldness or every flickering light is credited to the Spirit World for which it is liberally thanked. Indeed, many times in both the séance room and the churches, I have observed the absurd and the ridiculous running in parallel with the rational.

And I have often thought that it was little wonder that Spiritualism as a Movement is surrounded by scepticism. In many respects the 'Bless-you-friend' Spiritualist and the 'Fixed View Sceptic' have a great deal in common.

The 'Professional Media Sceptic' appears as an obligatory fixture whenever programmes concerning the paranormal are broadcast on radio and television. Such authoritative figures apparently provide a 'balance of views' with the notion that they possess open minds that are 'willing to be convinced'. Unfortunately, perhaps in order to safeguard their media careers, the reverse is true. Successful mental mediumship (such as clairvoyance and clairaudience) when under investigation, is invariably attributed to 'cold reading'. This is where a psychic or a medium is said to employ a practised technique that involves reading and quickly analysing a sitter's body language as they respond to the purported messages given. Although it is generally acknowledged that a sitter will unconsciously give out signals that can be read by a purported psychic to ascertain whether guesses are in the correct direction, such a practice cannot account for mental mediumship at its best.

Of course, most genuine mediums placed within a cold insensitive studio environment knowing that they are under sceptical observation (irrespective of assurances to the contrary) will not perform well. The fact is that they are not unfeeling frigid machines – their mediumship functions as a result of extreme sensitivity. On that basis alone positive results will always be highly unlikely although should they occur, then the 'Professional Sceptic' would almost certainly dismiss them as the result of chance or of 'cold reading'.

In the past physical mediumship has fared no better. On several occasions television studios have recreated the dark séance room with the claim that by means of the infra-red camera all secrets would be revealed. Viewers have been allowed to see how physical phenomena are produced by fraudulent means under the cover of impenetrable darkness and although such productions may appear to be convincingly damning they bear no relation to the Spiritualist séance room. For example the professional sceptic, whilst acting as the medium, may not be fully controlled and is therefore perfectly free to move around the room as he wishes and/or to use devices secreted about his person to create bogus phenomena. In the event that he is secured to his seat, then an unseen and unsuspected accomplice will be present to create the phenomena whilst the unwitting sitter looks on. It can therefore be seen that the whole production is carefully stage managed and whilst no doubt entertaining to the viewer such a demonstration is highly misleading. The reality of a genuine séance is that the medium is fully restrained and secured to a chair with hands often firmly held by neighbours. Additionally, before entering the séance room the medium is thoroughly searched to ensure that no contrivance has been secreted about his/her person which could later be used to produce fraudulent phenomena. The séance room door will also be locked prior to the commencement of the séance and no accomplice can then be relied upon to enter and help out with the proceedings. And the phenomena which manifest bear no relation to those shown on the television screen. Here the words 'chalk and cheese' spring to mind. The indisputable facts are that no magician - no sceptic, professional or otherwise, has ever been able to create and present phenomena similar to those of the genuine physical medium whilst sitting under exactly the same or even similar conditions.

Finally we must consider the 'Scientific Sceptics' who, having made their names in other branches of science, believe that this qualifies them to pronounce about paranormal phenomena without having bothered to learn anything about them. Such people may even think that they have a duty to the public to cleanse the world of ridiculous superstition. The late Dr Walter Franklin Prince, one time highly respected research officer of the American Society for Psychical Research and President of the English SPR (1931-32) once said that, 'by crossing the boundary of their knowledge such people lose proper judgement and balance[2]. It is not surprising then that such people can become so fixated and dependent upon their own scientific discipline and system of understanding that they are prepared to believe anything rather than accept the evidence for psychical phenomena. To accept that would perhaps threaten the very foundation and fabric of their established science.

Scepticism is indeed a complex multi-faceted affair.

Into The Unknown!

As human beings we strive always to rationalise, simplify and absorb new facts at a level equal to our ability to understand. If we apply common sense to Spiritualistic matters and consider in a broad sense the mechanics of mediumship and the séance room in the light of our existing knowledge, confusion should be rare. And yet, it cannot be denied that often we encounter aspects of both which confuse, mystify and transcend our understanding. To illustrate that point, I have chosen throughout this chapter to highlight in brief a selection of seemingly inexplicable matters as they relate to mediumship.

Readers should understand that I have not sought to offer rigid solutions in respect of 'mixed mediumship' but to present my carefully considered views as they relate to it.

However, within Spiritualism and in respect of mediumship in general, there are seemingly many anomalies which defy comprehension. But then surely this is hardly surprising given the nature of the entire subject. Always we should remind ourselves that mankind is in abject ignorance about many things. A layman may consider that the ever extending frontiers of science have led to an extensive understanding of the world and of the universe in which we live. It may, for example, also be assumed that we now possess an insight into consciousness itself. The fact is that we do not and in so many areas we remain in ignorance despite centuries of distinguished human intellect, acumen and endeavour. Why then should we imagine that questions of life and death and of communication between the two states (on any level) should be matters which hold no secrets? And why should we assume – as many Spiritualists tend to do – that death bestows upon man absolute knowledge and understanding of everything? If Spiritualism is correct and truly we are in contact with a Spirit World and its

(2) The Enchanted Boundary (1930)

denizens, then why should it be assumed that they are infinitely wiser than ourselves in all matters? Has the mystery of all things been discovered in the afterlife and have the secrets of life itself been uncovered? I would suggest that, just as we in our world are in ignorance of so much, so they in theirs understand little more. Confidently we are only able to assert that, in a spiritual sense, the next world state far surpasses anything that we can presently imagine or that we can experience in our own.

Chapter 3

George Valiantine

One of the most celebrated 'trumpet mediums' in history George Valiantine fell from grace in the 1930s, accused of blatant fraud ~ I revisit the case and suggest he may have been too hastily dismissed and give reasons why.

1924 saw the publication of a book entitled Towards the Stars'[1] by the Irish playwright, author and businessman Herbert Dennis Bradley (1878-1934), in which he cogently and dramatically told of his introduction to Spiritualism, and more directly, to trumpet mediumship.

His account commences in the year 1923 when, for the first time, he visited America on business and was invited to a séance by Joseph De Wyckoff, a wealthy and influential American barrister, who was deeply involved in Spiritualism. Bradley described him as intellectual, clever, critical and shrewd.

The invitation had been accepted on the basis that the experience 'could prove amusing'.

And so, on the 16th June 1923 he arrived at his friend's country residence and was introduced to the medium George Valiantine, whom he judged to be an ordinary provincial American. Following dinner Bradley had taken his place with four other guests on chairs that had been arranged in a circle in a room that had been blacked out and in the centre of which stood two aluminium trumpets.

The medium had been made to wear luminous bands around each wrist so that any movement on his part would instantly have been detected.

According to Dennis Bradley the whole affair had struck him as somewhat idiotic and he had wondered at intelligent people engaging upon such an infantile form of amusement.

(1) *'Towards the Stars' – 1924. (London.T.Werner Laurie Ltd)*

He went on to inform his readers that 'it was a dull business,' and to while away the time, with nothing happening, they had broken into song and the sound, according to Bradley, had been rotten. Twenty minutes passed and in boredom, he had started to think about the good books he could have been reading and the good Cognac he could have been drinking. In his own words, 'this was my mental attitude; half interested in an amused way, then irritated, then contemptuous'.

Then, suddenly, he had sensed another being in the room and the gentle voice of a woman had broken the silence.

I quote now from'Towards the Stars' and although the actual text has been condensed for the sake of brevity, it remains true in all essential details.

I was called by my name twice and the voice sounded about three feet away on my right and it was full of emotion.

I maintained my ordinary calm, critical and observant self and was not in the slightest degree affected or disturbed.

In an ordinary tone I answered 'Yes'. My Christian name was repeated twice and there was an emotional break in the voice as if the possessor of it were overjoyed at being able to greet a friend after a long journey.

The Voice – 'Oh I love you! I love you!'

The words were charged with electrifying beauty and great tenderness. I have heard the same phrase spoken in ordinary life by some of the world's greatest actresses, but never have I heard it expressed with more tender feeling.

My mind travelled back, searching the past to recall the memory of one who might have loved me. I could find no clue.

H.D.B. – 'Will you please tell me who you are – your name?'

The Voice – 'Annie.'

Then I understood all but with scepticism I asked for the full name.

The Voice –' I am Annie, your sister.'

Then we talked – not in whispers but in clear audible tones and what we said to each other were things of wondrous joy. Every word was heard by the others present but none I am sure, knew anything of my family affairs and could not have known that I had a sister who had died ten years previously. When on earth she and I had a peculiar sympathy with each other: a mental understanding not unusual between brother and sister. This understanding between us is inexpressible. Her voice on earth was soft and beautifully modulated, and her elocution was distinguished. In conversation she was a purist in her choice of words. I have never met a woman who spoke in the same odd way.

When she addressed me after ten years of silence, she used sayings in her own characteristic manner.

Every syllable was perfectly enunciated and every peculiarity of intonation was reproduced. She was overjoyed that she had found a means of speaking to me.

We talked so much and in so intimate a strain that presently we both felt that it was not courteous to those present to occupy so much of their time listening to such personal conversation.

Before she went I asked her if she would come again and she said that she would. Thus I experienced the most staggering event of my life.'

Readers will no doubt agree that this extract from the first of Bradley's three books about Spiritualism is most poignant and will be interested to hear that the event, so carefully recorded, marked the beginning of his patronage of George Valiantine. Indeed his support and influence was to quickly catapult the medium to fame and fortune. Acclaimed by the Spiritualists and well known to the psychical research world his celebrity standing as a remarkable medium was, however, to be short-lived. With the publication of the final book, 'And After'[2], in 1931 Valiantine was largely discredited and his career was to end in farce surrounded by suspicion and doubt. Quickly, he was to disappear into ignoble obscurity save for the arguments, speculation, theories and supposition that ever since have been endless.

Yet, no one single person, informed, objective and unprejudiced, has been able to unlock the truth surrounding Valiantine and those events of so long ago. To Spiritualists of the day he was one of the most remarkable of mediums.

Allegations that he was a charlatan were largely ignored – duplicity was unthinkable. To many researchers, whose arguments centred upon the allegations of chicanery that periodically surfaced throughout his

(2) 'And After' – 1931. (London. T. Werner Laurie Ltd)

career, he was partly or wholly fraudulent. Uncomfortable positive elements of the mediumship that inconveniently favoured the supernormal were and still are largely brushed aside on the presumption that fraud in one direction must apply in all. So what then is the truth, and can any light now be shed to illuminate one of the most puzzling mediumistic mysteries in history?

The Glory Years

Although the medium had been well known in Spiritualistic circles in America for some years, he was relatively unknown in this country until Dennis Bradley hosted his first visit in early 1924. This was to result in the publication of his book 'Towards the Stars' later that year, and 'The Wisdom of the Gods'[3] the following year. According to Bradley, Valiantine had not discovered his mediumship until he was forty-three – seven years prior to his first visit to this country. Apparently it had developed rapidly from audible rapping sounds to the eventual attainment of trumpet voices.

Discovered by the barrister Joseph De Wyckoff, who did much to bring him to the attention of the American public, and who introduced him to Bradley, he was to become for a while the most celebrated trumpet medium in the world.

Although reports concerning his séances in Europe, America and England were generally positive and somewhat dramatic, there were occasions when allegations of fraud were made against him. One of those was to come from De Wyckoff, the man who from the start had been so instrumental in launching and supporting his public career.

Whilst suspecting fraud he was not however entirely convinced of it, and his first and later accusations were somewhat tempered by his insistence that in spite of the occasional deceit, unquestionably Valiantine did possess marked mediumistic powers.

However, in the years to come, Dennis Bradley, who never minced his words, invariably and robustly defended the medium against all and every accusation. A self-opinionated and arrogant man, he believed that he possessed powers of cold objective reasoning and he claimed to understand people and their characters. There can be no doubt that from the moment it became public knowledge that he was championing and promoting George Valiantine, his reputation was on the line. Therefore,

(3) *The Wisdom of the Gods* – 1925 (London. T. Werner Laurie Ltd)

it is not difficult to imagine that to him any insinuation of fraud would have been unthinkable. When, in December 1923, De Wyckoff informed him by telegraph cable that he had discovered Valiantine in undeniable conscious fraud, Bradley had been both shocked and bewildered. As a member of the English SPR and its American equivalent, De Wyckoff was known to Bradley as a fair, scrupulous and careful investigator who simply abhorred deceit. The matter had to be taken seriously.

Dennis Bradley recorded in his book 'Towards the Stars' that neither De Wyckoff nor God himself could shake his personal conviction that for thirty-five minutes he had talked with the discarnate but living spirit of his sister on family matters which had been unknown to anyone but themselves. It had been her voice, her personality and her spirit and soul. Later that month De Wyckoff and his wife arrived in England and met with Bradley to discuss the events which had led to the accusation.

Apparently it took the form of handwriting covering several sheets of paper which the medium had shown to him claiming that they had been written directly by the spirits. Later De Wyckoff was to discover that the handwriting matched that of Valiantine and this had been confirmed as such by a handwriting expert. The medium however had strenuously and emphatically denied any wrongdoing and said that he had never acted fraudulently in his life. Whatever the truth was, the meeting between the two men was to end with the American entertaining doubts that he had, after all, caught the medium out.

Shortly afterwards De Wyckoff was to send Valiantine a letter to that effect whereupon their good relationship was restored. This in turn led to George Valiantine being invited by Bradley to England, where he arrived on 1st February 1924, returning home to America just over a month later. During his visit he stayed as a guest in the home of his English sponsor where he gave several séances. Additionally he was to sit for the British College of Psychic Science (a Spiritualist organisation based in London) and also, on one occasion, for the august Society for Psychical Research. All arrangements were made by Bradley.

During that visit, and those that followed, many notable people of the day were to experience for themselves Valiantine's seances. These included such luminaries as Sir Arthur Conan Doyle, P.G. Wodehouse, Dame Clara Butt, Ivor Novello, and Somerset Maugham. Newspaper editors, journalists, well-known writers, musicians, actors, and several from the world of politics and medicine sat at least once and some on several occasions. According to the records, as detailed in the three books, many were convinced that they had heard genuine Spirit voices emanating through the trumpets.

Indeed some were quite certain that they had held sustained conversations with their own living dead. Just as impressive were claims that many of the trumpet voices had spoken in various languages including Spanish, Portuguese, Italian, Sicilian, French, Russian, Japanese, German, idiomatic Welsh, Arabic, and Archaic Chinese.

Yet, according to Dennis Bradley, the medium was an uneducated man who spoke only English. He insisted: '...had he merely posed as illiterate – then, in truth, he would have been one of the most cultured scholars in the world.'

There can be little doubt that his séances in England, in Europe, and of course, back home in America, were often impressive. And it was to be at one held in his own country that one of the most extraordinary communications in paranormal history was to occur. From that day to this the event has confounded the critics who, typically, have either ignored it or attempted to explain it away with unconvincing arguments. In brief, a voice was heard to speak in Archaic Chinese claiming to belong to the Chinese philosopher Confucius.

Present, on that occasion, by invitation of noted New York Judge and lawyer W.M. Cannon, was one Dr Neville Whymant, a noted authority on Chinese history, philosophy and ancient literature. A one-time lecturer in Chinese at Oxford University he spoke thirty languages including many dialects. The invitation had been made because oriental voices had started to 'come through' at the séances which none of the sitters could understand. Dr Whymant therefore participated purely in his capacity as an oriental linguist.

It is interesting to note that his later reports made it quite clear that at the séances which he attended various languages had indeed manifested and that some had been spoken at length. He also stated that on occasions communications had been so intimate that he had felt like an eavesdropper although luckily the darkness had covered his blushes. However, it was to be one particular séance that had truly astounded him – in his own words:

'... out of the darkness was heard a weird, crackling, broken little sound, which at once carried my mind straight back to China. It was the sound of a flute, rather poorly played, such as can be heard in the streets of the Celestial Land but nowhere else.'

There then followed an audible voice which conveyed an eastern form of Confucius – a title as opposed to a name. This was to be the beginning of one of the most ostensibly remarkable trumpet direct voice communications in the entire history of Spiritualism.

Bradley, writing of it in his third and final book, 'And After', stated that Whymant had asked the ostensible Confucius various questions and that on each occasion had come back the correct answer (in Archaic Chinese). Intrigued, he had then posed a question, the answer to which had defeated and baffled scholars for centuries and he explained to readers that: '...amongst the most famous writings of the illustrious philosopher was a certain passage which appears to be incorrectly written, as its meaning is obscure.'

Whymant had decided to seek information as to the correct interpretation of this piece of writing, believing that it did not represent the true words of Confucius – that in the course of editing by subsequent writers its meaning had become distorted and lost. He thereupon asked the Confucius voice, 'There is among your writings a passage wrongly written; should it not read thus?' and he tells the reader:

'At this point I began to quote as far as I knew, that is to say, to about the end of the first line. At once the words were taken out of my mouth, and the whole passage was recited in Chinese, exactly as it is recorded in the standard works of reference. After a pause of about fifteen seconds, the passage was again repeated, this time with certain alterations which gave it a new meaning. 'Thus read,' said the voice, 'does not its meaning become plain?'

Of this extraordinary occurrence Dr Whymant maintained that:

'If we assume fraud and postulate the concealed presence of some Chinese scholar, passing himself off to the sitters as Confucius, it must have been someone almost superhumanly expert'.

Apparently, at that time there had been only six scholars in the world whose knowledge and command of the Archaic Chinese used would have been able to impress him and none of them had been in America at the time.

Clearly, the mediumship of George Valiantine was not merely a matter of trumpets sailing around in darkened rooms – it was rather more than that. Often, deeply impressed sitters, having attended a séance, maintained that it had been the most wonderful experience of their lives with many claiming that it had been the voices which spoke through trumpets that had so deeply convinced them. Indeed, many bore witness to having held intimate conversations with spirits that they firmly believed to have been their deceased loved ones. But of course, critics today cling to the recorded accusations of fraud, which from time to time were levelled against the medium – inexplicable phenomena being ignored or passed over. For example, I have yet to hear a convincing explanation to account in normal terms for the apparent supernormality of Valiantine's 'daylight sittings'. These would be held in broad daylight and voices would issue from the small end of the trumpet which would be held by him to the ear of the recipient. Usually these would be one-to-one sittings, with only the medium and sitter present, but where there were witnesses (and some included noted experienced SPR investigators), those with a clear view of the medium's mouth, claimed not to have discerned any movement of his lips. One such experience was reported to Bradley by a surgeon, Admiral Nimmo, who had two private sittings with Valiantine in full daylight. He maintained that the communicating voice had come distinctly from within the trumpet and that it had displayed intelligence and had volunteered evidential information. Since the surgeon had been extremely impressed with his sitting, he had arranged for a second one, taking with him an associate doctor. Again, voices from within the trumpet had been heard to issue from its small end. Yet throughout the sitting both doctors had kept Valiantine's face under acute observation and both had failed to detect any movement whatsoever.

Throughout his career George Valiantine was many times tested and attested by intelligent careful observers. One particularly impressive series held in 1931 – the year in which the medium visited England for the final time – was held shortly after Dennis Bradley himself accused the medium of fraud. Arranged by a Dr Vivian – a well known researcher of the day – they were attended by two of her medical colleagues. Bradley described them as extremely intelligent and claimed that they had taken an impersonal and critical view of the séances. Whilst some had apparently been rather poor, a few had proven to be excellent. Dr Vivian and the two other doctors had later described to Bradley, in some detail, one particular séance at which sixteen voices had spoken. And according to them, whilst two voices had been speaking simultaneously, the medium's own voice was heard drawing the attention of the sitters to this extraordinary occurrence. Of course, that phenomenal incident would not have surprised Bradley, since he himself had occasionally experienced exactly the same and had described the phenomenon in his book, 'And After'. This is what he wrote:

'Dr Barnett (Spirit voice) spoke with each of us. The conversation with Valiantine was rapid and natural, the questions and answers overlapping. When Valiantine was addressing the voice he spoke in distinctly respectful and somewhat subservient tones, such as 'Doctor, can you tell me why so and so and so and so' and the overlapping voice of Dr Barnett replied to him. The overlapping of these two voices was noticeable and dramatic. The only analogy I can give to describe the effect is that attained in certain productions of the Theatre Guild of New York, when the producer has, by careful rehearsing, trained the actors to talk through each other's voices, that is, to be explicit, to rehearse them in such a way in quickness of dialogue that the last three words of a sentence spoken by one character are anticipatingly (sic) replied to by the first three words of the sentence delivered by the second character; therefore at least three words of the two voices overlap and are delivered simultaneously.'

On another occasion described by Bradley, three individual voices had spoken with fluency all at the same time, two from high up in the room and the remaining one from the centre of the floor. Readers will appreciate therefore, that unless we are to assume the presence of an accomplice (or more than one!) to explain away these apparent extraordinary phenomena, then the inexplicable must be considered as the only explanation left to us!

Critics of course will gravitate to the accomplice theory or they will, in accordance with long established tradition, simply ignore the matter.

That aside, it must be acknowledged that although the evidence supports the paranormality of at least some of the Valiantine phenomena, his principal supporters (Bradley and De Wyckoff) were eventually to conclude that he had, from time to time, resorted to chicanery.

The Finger Print Farce

In direct contrast to the first two books in which Valiantine was hailed as the most exceptional trumpet medium in the world, Dennis Bradley in his final book made it very clear that the medium had, on occasions, undoubtedly resorted to fraud.

At séances held in 1931 in Bradley's home, it had been discovered that fingerprints, made upon smoked paper in the séance room, supposedly by the Spirits, were in fact of the medium's own right big toe or elbow joint. Dennis Bradley consulted Scotland Yard with the prints and they conclusively confirmed his suspicions. When challenged, Valiantine, according to Bradley, had broken down and claimed not to understand how such a thing could have happened.

When given the opportunity to exonerate himself partly from blame by admitting partial obsession or unconscious fraud, and again, when offered a loophole in the form of mixed mediumship (i.e. partly genuine – partly fraudulent) he refused to take it. Instead he steadfastly maintained that he had no explanation. Faced with irrefutable evidence, and Bradley's assertion that the 'Guides' must have been complicit, the argument had, apparently, disturbed Valiantine.

In Dennis Bradley's own words:

'He would not accept it, and said, in a strangely genuine tone,

'I will never say a word against them.' I argued with him that on the proven facts and logical deductions, so far as I was concerned, it had to be one of two things. Either he was genuine and his 'Guides' were occasionally fraudulent, or his 'Guides' were genuine and he was occasionally fraudulent.

I put it in this way to lead him on, but it had no effect. I gave him the choice of confessing his own guilt and defending Spirit phenomena, or maintaining his innocence and condemning such phenomena as malicious and evil. But the logic of this made no impression. He never wavered in his denial of personal guilt.'

Clearly, neither did he waver in his defence of the 'guides'.

Of course, the sceptics of the day and those that have since followed, have readily seized upon these revelations whilst conveniently forgetting all the previously presented evidence in favour of the mediumship. Having clearly been exposed by his principal sponsor in this country, people understandably began to wonder about all aspects of his phenomena, and to entertain thoughts that fraud in one specific direction must surely indicate fraud in all.

All that had gone before would quickly be surrounded by grave suspicion, and predictably, many people (just as today) thought in terms of black and white. All was genuine or all was fraudulent – there could be no middle ground and the sceptics and the Spiritualists predictably exercised selective memories and assumed their immovable positions.

In that respect, in the years that have since passed, nothing has changed.

A few days after the confrontation, the abashed medium left the home of his sponsor to fulfil additional commitments. The first of these was for a man merely identified by Bradley as a Mr X, but clearly, since he owned a country estate, he was a person of substance and standing. Indeed, we are told that during a previous visit to this country, Valiantine had undertaken a series of sittings for Mr X spread over a one month period and was paid £1500, plus generous expenses. A fortune in those days!

His second commitment, as stated earlier, was to give a series of twelve seances for the researcher Dr Vivian. In common with Mr X she had been informed by Bradley of the damning exposure but she held to the view that a great many genuine mediums had, in the past, been discovered from time to time in spasmodic phases of fraud.

Both series of sittings therefore went ahead.

Once again during the seances for Mr X Valiantine seemingly resorted to fraud. A fingerprint obtained on smoked paper was, on subsequent examination, found to be that of the middle finger of his left hand. With that discovery Mr X was faced with the difficult (I would say impossible!) task of attempting to reconcile apparently deliberate fraud with the extraordinary communications of a personal nature which he had himself previously experienced. And, of course, the entire matter appeared to contradict basic common sense. Prior to those sittings the medium, as we know, was already under grave suspicion regarding the nature of his séance room fingerprints. It therefore seems inexplicable that he should have attempted to perpetrate the self-same fraud upon his host.

Taken at face value, it surely bordered on insanity! What then are we to make of such an irrational act? Perhaps, as Bradley himself suggested – it may have been a matter of 'mixed mediumship' – a psychological compulsion to please. Whether such fraud was conscious (premeditated) or unconscious will doubtlessly remain a mystery for ever.

What we can safely say, however, is that ever since, many well-informed and other less well informed writers have offered their own views on the strange case of George Valiantine. One of the most measured, learned, erudite and sober accounts was to be published in

June 1932 in the *Proceedings* of the SPR under the title 'The History of George Valiantine'.

Written by Mrs W.H. Salter, a highly respected, credible and vastly experienced SPR council member, it presents a detailed analysis of the physical and mental aspects of the mediumship.

Whether it is fair and unbiased is open to serious question and in my view it illustrates that appraisals and findings are often based upon the author's predetermined agenda. Of course, in a subject which is beset with complex difficulties and for which we have few answers, it rather comes down to personal interpretation of the known facts and the side of the fence that one occupies, conclusions often being based on inherent and ingrained belief patterns.

Mrs Salter's derogatory analysis I believe illustrates this view perfectly, although in her approach to physical mediumship she by no means stands alone – innumerable critics before and since have trodden the same path.

Her evaluation of all aspects of his mediumship and her judgement concerning the alleged séance room phenomena clearly display her bias in favour of their 'normal production'.

Supposition and speculation are evident throughout and her readers are steered to arrive at her own conclusions that the phenomena were either highly dubious or fraudulent. I list below a selection of statements taken directly from her article which I then follow with my own comments.

I begin with an extraordinary event that occurred at a séance held in Bradley's home in 1924 when a servant unwittingly switched on an external light which illuminated the séance room sufficiently for sitters to see each other.

A trumpet had been seen to be hovering with no discernable means of support and it had immediately fallen to the floor. Unfairly, some may judge, Mrs Salter suggested that 'as the light came on it is obvious that there may have been some support which the sitters did not have time to see'.

This to me seems an extraordinary suggestion.

I rather imagine that with the sudden introduction of light all the sitters would have observed instantly 'the support', had it existed.

Bradley himself, who was present on that occasion, makes it clear that the medium had been distressed and that he complained of stomach pains and a few minutes later when a sitter proposed switching on the séance room light, a Spirit guide had asked him not to do so. A sitter who then went to Valiantine's aid discovered that he was enveloped in a whitish film which he described as a slimy, frothy bladder. Pressing a finger into it he reported that it could not be pierced. We are also told that Valiantine's face and hands had been icy cold and that following the séance he was put to bed to recover. A doctor had to be summoned the following day. On the medium's stomach, a black bruise had been discovered, which Bradley assumed must have resulted from the ectoplasm returning in haste at the sudden introduction of light.

However, Mrs Salter insisted that without additional evidence, the incident would remain unexplained. She then went on to suggest that in view of the medium's 'frequent recourse to trickery' at the moment that the inconvenient illumination entered the room, he was probably trying to deceive the sitters. The whitish film, she suggested, may have been an illusion and she queried the frothy bladder!

She wondered what sitters might have seen had not the Spirit control objected to the séance room light being switched on.

Surely, no comment is required – readers may form their own view.

Mrs Salter wrote repeatedly of alleged direct trumpet voices in the darkness, whispering odd words which were usually indistinguishable. In her words:

> 'I think it is likely that an important part is played here by suggestion, helped out by the distortion and indistinctness of utterance ...'

She also suggested that Valiantine may have learned prior to his sittings a little about the people who were to participate and may later have used the information to feed back to them at the séances. As there is not a shred of documented evidence to support that view, it must be regarded as supposition. Her suggestion entirely ignored the sitters who claimed to have held sustained conversations with the voices of people they had known in life. She deals with this by complaining about the lack of written records concerning them. However, most of the people who attended the séances were not scientific researchers but ordinary people who would not have considered preparing outline or detailed accounts on the basis that later they might have been required and subjected to scrutiny.

266

Of the languages said to manifest at the séances, Mrs Salter insisted:

'For this remarkable linguistic range there appears at first sight to be a wealth of testimony, but on closer inspection this wealth dwindles to a few poor farthings, and these, I suspect, are brass.'

She then proceeded to analyse a sample of those alleged utterances and to question the integrity of sitters although, by her own admission, she had no reason to doubt a favourable report that appeared in an Italian spiritual magazine.

This told of how trumpet voices had spoken conversational Italian at a Valiantine séance. She answered this by suggesting that it would have been easy in the darkness for any one of the sitters to have acted the part of a supposed communicator.

It was further suggested that the medium might have had knowledge of other languages, sufficient to whisper an odd word here and there and then leave the rest to the imagination of the sitters.

Is it unreasonable to suppose that such a dismissive proposition was advanced merely to dismiss entirely any suggestion that the phenomena might have been genuine?

Clearly, that had to be avoided at all costs and without any evidence whatsoever to support her claims she indulges in 'what might have been'.

One incident that Mrs Salter described involved a Mr Caradoc Evans, who had held a conversation in Welsh with his alleged father. A statement (presumably by Mr Evans – evidently made after the event) is given but she then goes on to ask:

'But is it accurate? As the sittings take place in complete darkness, one assumes, in the absence of any statement to the contrary, that no notes were made at the time.'

What, one may ask, is the value of any human testimony?

Complain when no records are kept and then question their validity when they are!

Mrs Salter admitted that the Confucius reports were *prima facie;* the most remarkable example of communication in a foreign language. But then she pointed out that this whole affair rested upon the opinion of just one man – Dr Neville Whymant. She stated: – and because this is an important point, I quote verbatim –

'Without in any way impugning Dr Whymant's good faith, one may question whether he has made sufficient allowance for the liability of the ear to be deceived when straining to catch the indistinct whispers of which these trumpet communications mainly consist.

My own impression that suggestibility may have played a considerable part in the conclusions to which Dr Whymant has come, is strengthened by the observations made by Lord Charles Hope in the Phoenix sittings.'[4]

She went on to speculate whether the medium could have produced a 'passable imitation of Chinese, including perhaps a few actual words of the language' pointing out that America was full of Chinamen and that this would therefore not have been surprising.

Much of similar vein was to follow.

However, despite Mrs Salter's suggestions about indistinct whispered voices in the dark, and her obvious attempt to play down and dismiss all direct trumpet voices – in whatever language – readers must bear in mind that Dr Neville Whymant was, at the time, one of only six scholars in the world capable of speaking Archaic Chinese. In addition he spoke over thirty other languages. Surely, it is fair to conclude that this alone strongly suggests that he was a man of rare intelligence and ability and we must assume that he risked both his reputation and his academic standing when he vouched for, and placed on record that 'voices of many languages' had manifested at those séances. Yes – an odd, indistinct whispered word in the dark could indeed lead to the imagination being triggered – of that there can be no doubt. But, if the witnesses are to be believed, then occasionally, long two-way conversations took place and then what are we to make of the Confucius communication?

The unalterable fact is that Dr Whymant firmly believed that an entire passage had been recited from the famous writings of Confucius. It had clarified aspects of a text which had remained obscure and which had puzzled scholars for centuries. Are we seriously to believe that the voice merely muttered a few indistinct words in the dark and that Whymant's imagination had done the rest?

Surely this must be regarded as nonsense?

Readers familiar with Mrs Salter's published appraisal of the

(4) *Lord Charles Hope was a Council Member of the SPR and Phoenix was a reputed Trumpet medium from Glasgow.*

mediumship may with some justification claim that my analysis is far from complete and that I have merely scratched its surface. Whilst that is quite true I can only answer by pointing out that I have tried to present a very small selection representative of the original material in order to give the reader a flavour of the whole.

To illustrate that, throughout her critique, she repeatedly assumed, presumed, and speculated. Sadly in matters of such gravity many Spiritualists and many investigators have long been unable to detach and conduct themselves in an impartial fashion. My contention in the case of Valiantine is that neither the fingerprint episode nor the occasional fraud allegations should be allowed to detract from the fact that beyond reasonable doubt he appears to have developed and demonstrated a form of mediumship which was and is still exceedingly rare.

If we can attach any importance to human testimony then that conclusion would seem to me to be inescapable. That said, it must be admitted that the events which led to his fall from grace cannot be doubted and nor can his guilt be defended. But these must be viewed in the light of the many positive elements to his mediumship. The counterfeit fingerprints may drive us to the inescapable conclusion of blatant fraud but this should not be the basis upon which the mediumship is cursorily dismissed in its entirety. As I have repeatedly said – when examining any case, all the facts must be considered, and the temptation to be selective and manipulative with them must be avoided. It is so important. Mrs Salter evidently was unable to do that and ended her analysis with the following statement which I quote in its entirety. She wrote thus:

Will students of psychical research never learn that we have no right, scientifically speaking, to claim a supernormal origin for an occurrence until we have established the improbability of any normal origin?

Although I have no argument with that, I would suggest that the Spiritualist may have worded it thus:

Will students of psychical research never learn that they have no right, scientifically and/or morally speaking, to be selective with evidence and/or to advance any explanation inappropriate and/or speculative, or to ignore, twist or distort facts that are in favour of a paranormal explanation, should they fail to meet with predetermined conclusions of a normal origin?

And Finally.

Beyond doubt this potted biography and analysis of such an enigmatic medium falls short in many areas. But then I hope that I have made out a *prima facia* case for concluding that when confronted with the damning evidence against him, George Valiantine may have been telling the truth when he insisted that he simply could not understand it.

Having said that I must add that my single intention throughout has not been to try to exonerate him but to simply point out that in matters of the séance room two plus two does not always equal four. There is such a great deal that we simply do not understand and I shall refer to this again later. For now I merely repeat that Valiantine, like every other medium, should be judged not upon isolated incidents (no matter how seemingly damning) but in the light of the entirety of his work. That said, there can be little doubt that the mystery surrounding his mediumship will, in common with that of Eusapia Palladino and others, last forever.

Herbert Dennis Bradley was himself a quite complex character who often heaped vitriol upon anyone who held a different opinion about the Valiantine mediumship from his own. But that aside he was also fearlessly honest. The entire affair was comprehensively detailed in his final book despite the fact that he must have realised the inevitable backlash that was bound to arise from many quarters. Perhaps, therefore, it is only fair and fitting that the final comment about the enigmatic George Valiantine should belong to him.

I therefore quote directly from his last book, 'And After', the final chapter of which, appropriately, he called, 'The Last Chapter'.

This is what he had to say:

'The rise and fall of Valiantine presents an intriguing psychological study.

The records of his phenomenal mediumship prove that at the time he was at the height of his powers, he could be accounted as the most remarkable physical medium in history. Later, when his mentality developed a materialistic outlook, decay set in. His reason for attempting these imprint frauds will remain incomprehensible. He was receiving no money from me, and for him to imagine that in the presence of imprint experts he could commit palpable fraud and escape detection was a sign of sheer lunacy. With the actual personal imprints of famous men (deceased) in our possession only a madman would offer his big toe for comparison. Yet, Valiantine, despite his illiteracy, is by no means a stupid man... From my observations of him, from the first moment of his last and final visit, it was apparent that he had developed a form of megalomania. Flattery, adulation and the gifts of large sums of money had led him to imagine himself a man of super importance. Since developing professional mediumship Valiantine became unquestionably the highest paid living medium. ...Considering the marvellous accumulation of subjective phenomena – i.e. incontrovertible mental evidence given in the 'direct voice' on matters completely outside his knowledge – it remains an enigma that he should have attempted such palpable and stupid objective fraud. No man in his right senses would destroy a brilliant reputation by imbecile and meaningless acts, with the distinct possibility – even probability – of a ruinous discovery.

The fact of Valiantine's fraudulently produced toe prints cannot negate or explain the fact that, under the mediumship of this imperfectly educated and semi-illiterate American provincial, archaic Chinese was spoken by the voice of 'K'ung-fu-T'zu' on several occasions, during which this voice discussed abstruse problems in Chinese literature. Here then is an example of the heights and the depths.'

And with that, I leave George Valiantine and move on to the medium who was once known to much of the world as 'Margery the Medium'. To believers she was 'The Eighth Wonder of the World' but to her denigrators she was the perpetrator of the greatest psychic fraud in history.

Chapter 4

The Remarkable Mrs Crandon

I examine the case of Mrs Crandon ('Margery'), the most controversial physical medium in history and the subject of never-ending scrutiny and controversy ~ Radio, television, endless books and articles have sought to offer 'the truth' surrounding her ~ I present facts of the case which have been conveniently forgotten.

On 1ˢᵗ November 1941, at a hospital in Boston, Massachusetts, several years after the death of her husband, a woman lay in a coma, dying. She was suffering from cirrhosis of the liver as a result of alcohol abuse. At her bedside, hoping that she would regain consciousness, was Nandor Fodor, one of the world's foremost psychical researchers.

At around midday his patience was finally rewarded – she opened her eyes and stared at him. Quickly he leaned over and whispered 'Mina – this is your final opportunity to tell the truth. Was your mediumship genuine?' The lady thought for a while and then, with a smile upon her face, she whispered back: 'Why don't you guess – in fact, you will all be guessing for the rest of your lives.' Then she slipped back into oblivion and at 3.30 that afternoon she died.

So ended the earthly life of Mina Crandon who, for over a decade, was known to the world as Margery[1] and was internationally celebrated by a great many psychical researchers and by Spiritualists throughout the world. Regarded as 'The Jewel in the Crown of American Spiritualism' and also as 'The Eighth Wonder of the World', she was, for several years, generally considered to possess a unique mediumship. Her notoriety and fame undoubtedly reflected upon her academic husband Le Roi Goddard Crandon, A.M., M.D., F.A.C.S. Connected to Harvard University he was a respected surgeon and a pillar of Boston

---

(1) *The name given to the medium by the researcher J. Malcolm Bird during the first academic investigation of the mediumship in order to protect the identity of the Crandons. Thereafter, and throughout the remainder of her career she was always referred to as Margery.*

society and was said to have been both sober and somewhat dour. However, it is believed that once his wife's mediumship had started to reveal itself and to become known as one of the most notable of the day, the doctor began to entertain thoughts that his name and that of his wife could, one day, be linked with the greatest revelation of all time – that man survives death.

From the early 1920s and into the 30s, their address – 10, Lime Street, Beacon Hill, Boston (America) would become to the Spiritualists and researchers of the day the most well known in the world. Scientists, journalists, clergymen, magicians, researchers, men and women of letters, and Spiritualists all attended her séances. Academic committees were formed and undertook long investigations in an attempt to quantify and qualify her mediumship. In the eighty years that have since passed the case has been analysed, dissected and fiercely argued over. Yet despite all the evidence for and against – the accusations, the bitterness, claims and counterclaims – supporters and critics have generally failed to shift an inch from their positions. To many she was quite simply an incomparable medium who withstood with pleasant resignation and goodwill the many attacks made upon her honesty – a kind of sacrificial lamb on the altar of psychical research.

To others she was enigmatic, and her case was one of psychological complexity whereby the genuine and the fraudulent were so intertwined that it has always been impossible to decide with any degree of certainty where one began and the other ended.

To yet others the case exemplified how a clever attractive woman could use her feminine attributes to dupe even the most intelligent of men.

Whatever the truth was, the level of disagreement at the time was so intense that eventually the American Society for Psychical Research was virtually split from top to bottom between her supporters and denigrators and was almost destroyed. Ever since, the world of academic psychical research has unanimously bestowed upon the Crandons the fate of ignominy, believing that together they perpetrated the greatest séance room fraud in history.

In 1927, a journalist from the *Boston Herald* writing to the American Society for Psychical Research commented:

'It is profoundly and sardonically humorous...It has mystery, veiled motivations, true tragedy, howling farce, and a pervading aura straight from 'Alice in Wonderland'. Almost everyone who becomes involved shoots off at tangents; respected clergymen, and savants suddenly become voluble liars; there are meaningless statements apropos of nothing; logic and normality take extended holidays.'[2]

And in 1934, Dr Walter Franklin Prince, one of the most important and influential investigators of the day said:

'The Margery mediumship will in time come to be considered the most ingenious, persistent and fantastic complex of fraud in the history of psychical research'.[3]

On the other hand, Eric Dingwall, foreign research officer of the English SPR said, when he investigated the mediumship on behalf of the Society that he found Mina to be:

'... a highly intelligent and charming young woman, exceedingly good-natured and possessed of a fund of humour and courage which makes her an ideal subject for investigation'.

Her husband he judged to be:

'a hard working and skilful surgeon with an extensive knowledge of many social questions and problems. The phenomena, if fraudulent – and there was little, if any, direct evidence in support of such a supposition – must have been as a result of collusion between the two of them'.

The only reason that he could think of for this was that a hoax designed to discredit Spiritualism might have appealed to Crandon's fervent rationalism.[4]

However, although there were widely differing views, the fact is that Margery for some years literally dominated American psychical research and captured the imagination of a great many people, many of whom believed in her. Others, and there were many, chose to balance themselves on the well worn fence of indecision. Dr Hereward Carrington, distinguished researcher and author of many books on psychical research, who sat with some of the most notable mediums of the early twentieth century said of her:

'It certainly is one of the most baffling and extraordinary cases

(2) 'Margery', 1973, Thomas Tietze. (Harper & Row)
(3) 'Margery', 1973, Thomas Tietze. (Harper & Row)
(4) 'Science and Parascience', 1984, Brian Inglis (Hodder and Stoughton)

in history. This is true no matter how we choose to regard it'.

He went on to say:

' ...Despite the difficulties involved in arriving at any just estimate of this case, and despite the uncertainty of many of the phenomena and the complicated social, ethical, personal, physical and psychological factors involved, a number of seemingly genuine, supernormal manifestations yet remain, which are of the profoundest interest to psychical, as well as ethicosociological (sic) science'.

Perhaps that statement ought to reflect the position of most interested parties but alas, it does not. Verdicts so often have been reached following appraisals of previously published material which themselves were based not upon accuracy and objectivity but upon a failure by the authors to deal in reality. Few, it would seem, were able to concentrate and carefully consider both the negative and positive aspects of the mediumship.

If its defenders and critics have one thing in common it is that so often both have invariably failed to entertain uncomfortable facts which flew in the face of their own views.

As in the case of George Valiantine, many reviewers have been guilty of selecting evidence to support their predetermined conclusions.

However, that aside, there can be no doubt that towards the end of her career as a medium, Margery was considered by many to have been wholly fraudulent. Indeed, since her death, that belief has been converted to an established fact, and as such, is generally accepted and seldom questioned.

Even amongst her supporters many have concluded that she was a genuine medium who, for whatever reason, possibly resorted to fraud from time to time. In this, and in the final chapter, I would like to re-examine in brief, facts of the case which have, with the passage of time, largely been neglected and often conveniently forgotten by her many critics.

Forty Years of 'Margery'

Mina Crandon – Margery, was a veritable paragon in the world of Spiritualism who possessed, according to her supporters, both mental and physical mediumship to an extraordinary degree. Throughout her versatile mediumistic life and up to the present day, acres of newsprint and other voluminous published material has appeared about the many controversies that constantly surrounded and raged around her. She and her husband, by turns, have been toasted, celebrated, lambasted, berated and castigated. In short 'Margery' has literally been done to death. However, Dr Crandon, in sharing the limelight with his wife, steadfastly and unwaveringly supported her throughout and seemingly believed that one day, through her mediumship, it would be proven that the Spirit World was forever knocking on the door of our own. As a result of his determination to realise that dream, she was, over a period of several years, to face with fortitude all manner of indignities at the hands of the researchers with whom she continually co-operated.

My personal fascination with the mediumship extends back over forty years during which time I have studied it in some detail. Readers familiar with the case will know that Walter Stinson, her deceased brother, was the principal communicator and orchestrator of all the reputed manifestations within her séance room. When therefore, in 1992, he showed up at my own home circle, and quickly established himself as an important addition to our Spirit team, my interest understandably increased considerably. With confusion, speculation, truth, half truth and untruth long surrounding Margery, here surely, was an opportunity to learn the facts and the truth from the horse's-mouth.

An eye witness account of the events surrounding his sister's mediumship which, for so long, had been bathed in mystery – an elucidation which might answer the critics. However, from the start, rather regrettably, Walter made it crystal clear that he had no intention of wasting time and effort discussing such matters. They belonged to the past and nothing could be achieved by dwelling upon them. Should he have chosen to do so then the only possible outcome would undoubtedly have been further dispute and controversy. Indeed, whenever circle guests have tried to speak to him about the Crandons' circle, always he has replied, 'Ask Stewart – he knows more about it than I myself do.'

Since the day of his arrival he has insisted that his sole intention in working with and through our circle has been to refine and further develop communication on a physical level. Evidently, he is determined to do all in his power to help prove beyond question that life continues beyond the grave. Occasionally, he has also insisted that at some time in the future he will vindicate his sister from the injustice and slander that has long been attached to her name. He has told us on more than one occasion that 'back then' he gladly co-operated with science because he was persuaded that it was right to do so. It was expected of him and at that time he shared his brother-in-law's optimism that the mediumship could be established on a scientific basis. Yet, in the final analysis, nothing was to be proved and nothing was to be achieved.

The decision to proceed down that path led only to incessant dispute between the supporters and critics of the Margery mediumship. This time, Walter, armed with the benefit of hindsight, fully intends to do things 'his way'.

My own position in respect of Margery I formulated long before Walter's arrival at our circle. By studying, over many years, all the known facts, I finally came to believe that the systematic destruction of her credibility by critics had been a cynically grave injustice. At the risk of inciting protest from the research world, I would suggest that throughout, the many detractors of her mediumship have largely dealt in conjecture and supposition.

Additionally, and invariably, the known facts of the case have, as previously stated, often been economically selected, and in the process have been transformed and corrupted to that of pseudo-fact. To prove their case her critics have largely concentrated upon phenomena which, from the documented records, lend themselves to a normal explanation. Those which defy such an interpretation have repeatedly been skated over or simply ignored altogether. Factual errors, cynical statements and claims made by earlier writers and commentators have so often been picked up and repeated by later critics thus establishing a conclusion based upon the corruption of reality.

As a result, today, one of Spiritualism's most remarkable mediums is mainly remembered for all the wrong reasons. In order to address this, I present not a lengthy review and detailed examination of the mediumship, but a brief overview of now largely forgotten facts.

These may afford the reader a more balanced insight into the extraordinary séance room world of the Crandons.

Tests and Yet More Tests

It may reasonably be argued that from its early days it was Le Roi Goddard Crandon who influenced his wife to accept that in order to authenticate her mediumship it had to be examined by the world of science. As a result mechanical and electronic contrivances were devised and taken to the Lime Street séance room by visiting researchers and by academic committees set up to examine the mediumship. Throughout the 1920s and early 30s several were to be presented to Walter for the purposes of establishing whether the alleged paranormal phenomena were genuine or spurious.

One such invention involved a bell that was mounted inside a specially constructed wooden or glass-sided box. This could only be made to sound by the operation of electrical contacts that had been effectively sealed within it. And yet, in compliance with the instructions of researchers, Walter would cause the bell to ring once, twice, or three times and often while an investigator carried the so-called 'bell box' around the séance room in his hands.

Another device named the 'Sisyphus' involved a celluloid ball which, in red light, and before the eyes of the observers, would be made by Walter to defy gravity as it rolled up an inclined channel. This would be mounted within a box with net curtain sides so that normal access, under the gaze of the researchers, was not merely unlikely but would have been impossible. Another involved the use of finely balanced chemical scales with equalised pans. A small weight would be placed in one of the pans which should have made it drop, whereas Walter caused it to rise so that the empty pan descended to the base of the apparatus. Of course, sceptics may reasonably wonder whether the researchers' precautions to isolate their clever devices from interference could have been circumvented by the Crandons. The answer to that must be that no evidence exists to suggest that it was a possibility and any suggestion otherwise could only be speculative. A study of the original documents (and there are many) would confirm this although readers may be interested to read the so-called Tillyard Report in the next chapter since it may help substantiate this argument.

However, of all the devices and contrivances one of the most elaborate had Margery seated within a glass-sided cabinet (similar to a telephone box) with her hands protruding through holes at either side. These were secured in place by means of looped piano wire anchored outside the cabinet and for good measure her hands would be held by the investigators stationed one at each side so that she could not draw them within. Around her neck would be a dog collar to which a strap would be fastened; the other end of which would be secured to a turnbuckle bolted to the floor behind her seat. Her feet would be anchored to the floor with wire encircling her ankles.

This elaborate control was to ensure that any physical phenomena that manifested within the cabinet could not possibly have been as a result of trickery of any kind. Under such barbaric and stringent control, Walter still succeeded in causing phenomena to manifest.

And finally, in yet another experiment, an ingenious device (a so-called voice-cut-out machine) was used conclusively to confirm that the so-called Walter voice was genuinely independent of the medium and did not emanate from her. Once again Walter was successful. Investigators and committees came and went. Tests and more tests were demanded. Occasionally, accusations were made against the mediumship and throughout the inevitable fierce controversy that followed Dr Crandon defended his wife by insisting that the arguments advanced were either preposterous or based upon falsehood.

The escapologist Harry Houdini was a case in point. He was appointed to the *Scientific American* enquiry in 1924 which held a long investigation into the mediumship. As a member of the distinguished academic investigative committee he was to sit with Margery on just five occasions – other members were to sit many more times. Soon after, he rushed into print with a small booklet containing diagrams said to reveal the methods by which, he claimed, she had created her fraudulent phenomena. At that time Harry Houdini was well known for his exposure of dubious mediums and it is perhaps reasonable to suspect that from the start he was determined to expose the celebrated Margery.

The public would have expected the great Houdini, to 'see through it all' and he was not about to disappoint. As the noted researcher Brian Inglis pointed out: 'By the time Houdini arrived to investigate Margery he had by his own admission already compromised himself, as he had told the publisher of the *Scientific American*, 'I will forfeit a thousand dollars if I do not detect her in trickery.' Theoretically this left it open to him to admit that she did not resort to trickery. But in practice he had burnt his boats; he had been on a lecture tour of the United States as advance publicity for his book, and during it he had vehemently denounced Spiritualism as the cause of distress, madness and suicide.

He could not, at this stage, have backed down. A mutual friend in fact showed Conan Doyle a letter in which Houdini made it clear that his simple intention was to expose the Crandons.[5]

Not surprisingly, his booklet was to demonstrate his own mindset of both egocentricity and incredulity. His detailed explanations ignored the conditions of control under which Margery had sat. Like many who were to come after him, he misled by turning fantasy into reality. As Paul Tabori, the noted journalist and psychic researcher said: 'Houdini's knowledge of wriggling out of strait jackets and handcuffs was as great

(5) *'Science and Parascience' – 1984 (Hodder and Stoughton)*

as his ignorance of psychics, and his mind was made up before he started'.[6]

The great magician exemplified what was to recur many times in the future with critics freely engaging in wild speculation and making claims without bothering to justify them.

Surely one would always wish to learn upon what grounds and upon what information past reviews have been based. One is often left with the inescapable impression that denigrators of the Margery mediumship often failed to appreciate what constituted proper evidence, the importance of which cannot be overstated.

She Was There.

Some years ago I was, for a period of time, in correspondence with Mrs Marion Nester[7] – an elderly daughter of Dr and Mrs Mark Richardson who were friends of the Crandons, and regular sitters at the Lime Street séances. Both were loyal supporters of the mediumship throughout its duration and Dr Richardson was responsible for inventing and creating the ingenious 'voice-cut-out' machine that was to establish the direct voices as being quite independent of Margery. To be in communication with Mrs Nester was, for me, a great privilege, since it afforded me the opportunity to hear directly from someone who had been personally intimate with the mediumship. Therefore, anything that she could tell me I considered to be of great value. Information from her was a direct link with those events of long ago and unlike most commentators her opinions were not based upon those gleaned from earlier writers. She once told me that she and her sisters had grown up with the mediumship and that they had witnessed all manner of physical phenomena which today we can only read about. They had been there and watched, in good red light, as the ball had been made by Walter to roll up the inclined plane of the 'Sisyphus'. They had been there and had heard the bell as it sounded within the sealed box, remote and out of reach of Margery. They had heard Walter's voice as it spoke through a microphone which had been mounted within a locked soundproof box. They had observed phenomena which, according to our understanding, should not have occurred, but they did. Mrs Nester also told me that the single topic of conversation around her parent's dining table had been

---

(6) *'Companions of the Unseen' – 1968 (H.A.Humphrey Ltd – London)*

(7) *From 1967 until her retirement in 1983 Marion Nester was a member of the ASPR staff – Director of Education and the editor of its Newsletter.*

the latest controversy to erupt around the Crandons. Investigators had come and gone and although most would accept as genuine the séance room phenomena that they had just witnessed, and had even signed affidavits in their favour, by the following day they had had afterthoughts and demanded more tests. Apparently, her father referred to them as 'those bloody-minded researchers' and found this repetitive situation difficult to bear. One researcher, when challenged to explain how one particular phenomenon could have been fraudulently produced, could only reply: 'Some little device probably'. Thereafter, 'some little device probably' had become a catchphrase amongst Margery's supporters. However, as Mrs Nester pointed out: 'He (her father) did not then have the benefit of modern insight into what the researcher Brian Inglis called 'retro-cognitive dissonance' and the researcher D. Scott Rogo referred to as 'the morning after syndrome'.

Today, it is recognised that people block from memory events which their belief system cannot accept. 'But,' said Mrs Nester, 'my father could only put it down to sheer cussedness.'

In April 1985 she finally committed her recollections to print in an article entitled 'The Margery Mediumship – I Was There' published in the American *Fate Magazine*.

What made it of such profound interest was that she was one of the last surviving witnesses of the Lime Street séances. Therefore, she had written from a position of personal intimate experience and was able to tell what it had been like attending them. Describing the personality of Walter, Mina's brother and spirit control, she wrote:

'He spoke from a point in space by direct voice, in that he did not use the medium's vocal cords. He talked throughout every séance, chatting with the sitters, taking a full part in what was going on. I can still almost hear his voice. He came through as a real person. We never thought of him as a purported communicator. He was simply Walter, our friend and advisor, an integral, functional part of the circle. We couldn't see him, but he was certainly right there in the room. He almost bristled with forceful personality. There was nothing spooky about Walter Stinson.'

Although Mrs Nester's article included many other important points one of the most salient I found was a quotation from the outstanding Irish medium Eileen Garrett, founder of the Parapsychology Foundation in America, who apparently once said that: 'Margery's best friends were her worst enemies'.

Marion Nester explained that 'they' were so eager to go further that they had held sittings night after night. In one month alone (July 1925) there had been 29 séances, the point being that since physical mediumship is known to impose a strain on the medium, Margery's constitution must have been under enormous pressure. To be strapped and held immobile with thick surgeon's tape[8] in extremely hot rooms (prior to air conditioning) Mrs Nester felt must have been terribly uncomfortable for Margery but pointed out that she had usually been pleasant and obliging.

More Inconvenient Facts!

From the beginning of the mediumship in the early 1920s until Margery's untimely death in November 1941, many persistent and inexplicable séance room phenomena were to manifest. In addition to those already mentioned one of the most astonishing, of which there is a photographic record, occurred on November 13th 1931 in the locked, searched and sealed Lime Street séance room. Those present were the medium, a photographer and a researcher. The event was subsequently reported in the *Proceedings* of the American Society for Psychical Research and I quote:

> 'We are showing as an example of teleplasmic (ectoplasmic) development, a well-formed arm and hand enlarged from a section of a flashlight photograph taken at Lime Street. In fact, it is so well formed that some critics claim that it belongs to a living person'.
>
> '...This hand, of which we have just spoken, was materialised under the most rigid conditions of control'.[9]

The photograph shows the researcher holding the medium's hands in his whilst she is in full view in front of her cabinet. A male arm and hand, clearly visible, protrudes through the cabinet curtains and is seen to be holding a small stool at a height of approximately 1.5 metres which, we are told, it had just picked up from the floor. It seems clear therefore that if we are not prepared to accept the word of the researcher and the photographer only one other explanation remains. The hand belonged to a third man, standing out of sight behind the curtains. In that case, both men were lying although, if we are to believe that, then we must wonder as to the motive. The confirmed sceptic, of course, would

---

(8) *For purposes of the Test Séances, Margery's arms and ankles would be bound to her chair by means of thick surgeon's tape thereby rendering her immobile.*

(9) *Proceedings ASPR. 1926-1927. Volume 3. 'The Margery Mediumship'. (1933)*

take the only escape route remaining and suggest that there must have been a romantic connection between Margery and the researcher and Margery and the photographer. Both men would have known of each other's clandestine relationship with her and would have been complicit in a conspiracy to 'cover up' what they knew to be fraud. Readers may find that to be an unlikely proposition!

A further extraordinary phenomenon which up to the present day has defied any normal explanation, involved the interlocking of wooden rings[10] both made from different kinds of wood. Experimenters, prior to the commencement of a séance, would place both rings on a table in front of Margery only to discover, at the end of it, that Walter had interlinked them.

Sometimes the linkage would be done during a séance and made available for close examination. Then, moments later, they would separate again. And although this may appear inconceivable to the casual reader it is a well-documented phenomenon which occurred on quite a number of occasions.

Unfortunately, in all cases, their linkage did not survive for long. After a period of weeks (or months at best) a crack would appear in one of them thereby destroying for all time enduring evidence of their paranormality.

It seems that their molecular structure was unstable and this led to Hannen Swaffer, the well-known Fleet Street journalist and Spiritualist, advancing the theory that some kind of 'law of frustration' was in action to deny us any permanent physical proof.

These then are some of the many positive elements of the mediumship, although, understandably, it could be argued that by ignoring the negative I have been as guilty as the critics. I have done what I have repeatedly accused them of doing – I have tried to authenticate and establish a conclusion by carefully selecting evidence. But, if I have done so, I hope, at least, that I have shown that Margery may well have been dismissed too readily. However, in the final chapter I shall attempt to present a balance by introducing readers to the matter of the alleged spirit fingerprints. These were to cast serious doubt on all the Lime Street phenomena and, in the eyes of many, were to strip away, perhaps for ever, every vestige of confidence in the mediumship.

---

(10) *Some years ago, within my own circle, Walter resumed the experiment involving the interlinking of rings, this time using looped plastic cable ties.*

Chapter 5

The Final Denouncement

Continuing the case of Mrs Crandon ~ more forgotten facts and an appraisal of the 'false finger print affair, ~ I suggest that history may have dismissed her too readily ~ My attempt at a balanced and fair defence. ~ A new perspective and insight into that which has puzzled both critics and supporters for many years ~ Final word from 'one who was there'.

Although fraud was occasionally suspected at the Lime Street séances it would not be until 9th March 1932 that a serious and damning allegation would be made. For then it was discovered by the leading researcher E.E. Dudley, that some of the alleged Spirit fingerprints made at séances over a period of several years and claimed by Walter to belong to him, were, in fact, identical to those of Margery's dentist[1] who at the time was very much alive. Understandably, this was a major revelation – a death blow which would lead to the downfall of the mediumship, from which it was never to recover. Everything that had gone before – the carefully controlled experiments conducted over all the previous years – would, in the end, amount to nothing. In the eyes of the research world Margery's credibility was gone, and that, despite Dr Crandon's strenuous attempts to provide a convincing explanation to counter the crushing revelation. As was rightly pointed out at the time, many people had been convicted and executed as a result of far less fingerprint evidence and therefore the doctor's attempts to rehabilitate the mediumship proved futile. Suspect surreptitious fingerprints, as in the case of George Valiantine, proved to be her undoing and the affair would effectively mark the end of serious research at Lime Street. With it the dreams of Dr Crandon to establish scientifically his wife's mediumship would never be realised and although an assumption of

---

(1) *The Crandons' dentist had suggested the use of a dental compound known as 'Kerr Wax' in order for the print impressions to be made. Submersion in a dish of hot water placed on a table in front of Margery rendered it malleable. Once a 'paranormal' print had been made it was secured by then submerging the compound in a dish of cold water. The dentist was however exonerated from any complicity in the affair.*

blatant fraud seems inescapable, I would urge great caution. For if the prints were the product of fraud, then how are we to equate this with the phenomenal aspect of the mediumship for which there exists a plethora of evidence? This was meticulously gained and documented over a period of several years and the careful impartial reader must surely bear this in mind.

Yet critics, without troubling themselves with such an inconvenience, mainly chose to ignore or skate over this entirely and have done so ever since. A more equitable critic, when considering the affair, may wish to know the conditions of control which pertained at the time of their production. Indeed, that same question was posed on 11th November 1976 during a lecture presented at an SPR meeting by the eminent long-serving council member and now Vice President of the Society, Mary Rose Barrington. To answer it we must begin by acknowledging that Dr Crandon was generally in attendance at his wife's séances. Therefore, if the prints had been fraudulently produced, the assumption would be that he may have been complicit in their creation. However, the fact is that occasionally, they were obtained at so-called 'solus sittings', when the medium had sat alone with a single researcher and since readers may agree that this is a crucial issue, I shall now briefly detail one such case.

In 1928 Dr Robin J. Tillyard, M.A., Sc.D., F.R.S., one-time Chief Entomologist to the Commonwealth of Australia, on route from New Zealand to England, stopped off in Boston to sit with Margery.

So impressed was he by what he witnessed that upon arrival in England he arranged a meeting with the world renowned physicist Sir Oliver Lodge who himself was deeply involved in psychical research. As a result of that meeting Lodge was to write to Dr Crandon as follows:

Dear Dr Crandon,

I hear from Tillyard that he is returning to New Zealand via America. He is, I believe, writing about his experiences with 'Margery' in 'Nature'. If his article is admitted, it will be an important step towards challenging the attention of the scientific world. He has an idea that it would diminish the opportunities for accusations if he were allowed a solitary sitting with 'Margery' in a room arranged by himself, of course with your approval; and thinks that if he got results under those conditions the sceptics would be reduced to accuse him of collusion – which, considering his position as a scientific man, would be absurd. I know that he is impressed with 'Margery' and you may have confidence that he would treat her fairly.

... It is not a privilege that I would recommend you to grant to too many people, though if it were feasible I would value it myself. I trust that she keeps in good health and that neither of you has been bothered with any recent controversies.

Yours sincerely,

Oliver Lodge.

Dr Crandon responded favourably to the letter and agreed to Lodge's request. The Tillyard solus séance took place on 10th August 1928.

In July 1931, the letter, together with an account of the sitting and the conditions in which it was held were published in the Journal of the British College of Psychic Science.[2]

Although extensive and detailed I intend only to mention here sufficient information to enable readers to learn of the severity of control imposed upon the medium prior to and during the seance and also the relevant and principal phenomena reported.

The venue selected by Tillyard belonged to an eye specialist whom he identified merely as a Dr X. Providing suitable rooms at his place of business, on the day of the séance the one to be used for the experiment had been 'shut up' hours earlier and no one had been allowed to enter. Knowing the importance of the sitting Dr Tillyard sought the help of E.E. Dudley who was an officer of the American Society for Psychical Research. It would be his responsibility to take charge of the séance equipment including the ingenious 'voice-cut-out' machine[3] installed to prove that Walter's voice was absolutely independent of Margery. Additionally he had sole possession of her séance clothes which he was to thoroughly search and establish that nothing was hidden within. He also prepared the special wax in which it was hoped Walter would leave his fingerprints. The Crandons were driven to Dr X's rooms and upon arrival Margery was taken by a nurse into a backroom, disrobed, searched thoroughly including her mouth, teeth and hair and then dressed in her séance garments. Later, the nurse provided a written

(2) 'Psychic Science: The Quarterly Transactions of the British College of Psychic Science.' (July, 1931)

(3) See footnote 3&4 on the following page.

statement confirming all details of the search etc. Dr X then thoroughly searched Tillyard so that critics could not later allege collusion should the séance prove successful. Dudley and Tillyard then entered the séance room and arranged a small wooden table immediately in front of the wooden chair in which the medium would be seated. A second chair was placed to the side of Margery's chair for Tillyard.

The two dishes that would be used in the fingerprint experiment[4] were then placed on the table by the researchers and Dudley set up the 'voice-cut-out' machine on an additional table.

Both tables and chairs were then closely examined and it was confirmed that they contained no drawers or hollows which could have been used for purposes of concealment. The nurse then brought Margery into the room and reported a negative search of her person and then she withdrew from the room together with Dudley leaving Tillyard and the medium alone. The door was then closed and locked. Margery was secured in her chair by means of surgeon's tape around her bare wrists and around her ankles effectively binding her to the seat. A thick blue pencil mark was then drawn across the bandages and continued on to the skin so that it was impossible for her to remove either hands or feet from them without the pencil lines later showing that she had done so.

Outside the room were Dr Crandon, Dr X, the nurse and E.E. Dudley and inside, the severely restrained medium with Robin Tillyard holding her hands for good measure.

Later, Dr Tillyard was to record that after the lights had been extinguished he had noticed that shafts of light were entering the room despite the drawn-down blinds. Efforts to rectify the situation were unsuccessful with the result that it was never really dark and throughout the séance he was able to see various objects dimly. This, of course, is an important point. There would have been no way that Margery could have known with certainty just how much the doctor could actually see. One may therefore judge that under such circumstances, it would have been most unwise for her to attempt to act fraudulently without risking possible exposure. Tillyard's report then went on to record that Walter had greeted him quickly in the direct voice and had spoken throughout the séance in a clear loud animated fashion. He was to issue instructions

---

(3) & (4) *Readers who would like to learn details about the voice-cut-out machine and about the method of securing séance finger prints in wax should consult original documents of which there are a great many.*

regarding the two dishes – one containing hot water in which the wax was to be placed in order to soften it. And in the other there had been cold water, into which the wax would be transferred in order to set the impression. This entire procedure, as always, would be conducted by Walter and the doctor listened whilst the water was disturbed and splashed, with Walter joking at one point that it was so hot that he had just scalded his hand. Although there is a great deal more that could be included about that section of the séance it is only necessary for me to inform readers that fingerprints were successfully obtained. Later with the 'voice-cut-out' machine activated and with the medium awake and participating, Walter had said to the doctor 'Well, here I am, what do you want me to say?' Tillyard, taken aback, had replied, 'Say anything that you like, Walter' and he had done so with apparent ease. At the conclusion of the séance, which lasted forty minutes, the red light had been turned up and the door unlocked and the others returned. It was then discovered that there had been no change to the blue pencil marks but that the binding tape could only be removed with difficulty as the hot weather had caused the glue to melt so that it had adhered tightly to Margery's skin.

The researcher concluded his report with mention of the fact that upon returning with the Crandons to 10 Lime Street, the Victrola[5] that stood on the first floor landing had started to play before any of them had got beyond the entrance hall. Apparently, although always kept locked, it had been a frequent occurrence, unnerving visitors. Walter always gleefully claimed that he was responsible.

The following day, Robin Tillyard wrote to Sir Oliver Lodge[6] as follows:

My Dear Lodge,

The Tillyard solus séance took place last night, between 9 and 10pm, in muggy weather, not suitable for good séance work, with a thunderstorm brewing which broke shortly after our return home. It was by far the most wonderful séance I have ever attended, and as far as I am concerned now I should not worry if I never had another sitting in my life.

Dr Crandon made no conditions and placed Margery unreservedly in my hands.

(5) *An early type of gramophone.*

(6) *'Psychic Science: The Quarterly Transactions of the British College of Psychic Science.' (July, 1931)*

I think the arrangements which we made were scientifically severe and at the same time put on record the most marvellous result in the whole history of psychical research. I am sending you my full report of this séance ... I will attach to the published account Dr X's statement as to his searching of myself and Miss Y (the nurse) and her statement about her two searchings of Margery ...

It seems to me quite impossible to find a single flaw in this wonderful result. Whether science, under its present limitations, can ever hope to offer any explanation, philosophical or otherwise, of these extraordinary phenomena, I very much doubt myself. But my object is to record scientifically that they do occur, that they are part of the phenomena of nature...

This séance is, for me, the culminating point of all my psychical research... For you, my very dear friend, who has never seen anything like this, I can only ask that you and your whole family will accept my statement as absolute truth...

As for Margery and her husband, not one man in ten thousand could have handed over his wife as trustingly to a comparative stranger as Dr Crandon did last night, and not one woman in ten thousand could have faced such a situation bravely, as Margery did. The privilege granted me by them I shall always hold to be one of the greatest events of my life, and they are now bound closely to me by spiritual bonds which can never be broken, and which, I am fully persuaded, will last over into that wonderful life of which death is only the entrance gate ...

Your affectionate friend

(Signed) Robin Tillyard.

P.S. I must not omit paying tribute to Walter – the finest 'ghost' I know.

In the light of the wording of that letter I think it is very clear that the séance had made a profound impression upon him and left absolutely no doubt in his mind that:

a) precautions to eliminate the possibility of deception had been absolute.

b) the physical phenomena witnessed at the séance had been genuine.

Of course, it could be claimed that there can be no place for human emotion in what was supposed to be a scientific test. However, I believe that in writing to Oliver Lodge in the way that he did, he clearly displayed that the event had shaken and touched him deeply.

An Enigmatic Riddle.

Readers, at this stage, may find themselves somewhat confused.

In effect we now have seemingly flawless séance room conditions of control which, we may conclude, go a long way towards authenticating the paranormality of the fingerprints. This, however, has to be balanced against the fact that some, as previously stated, were later found to be identical to those of a man who, at the time, was still very much alive, indeed those of Margery's own dentist, who had originally suggested the use of Kerr wax in order to secure paranormal prints.

Such an anomaly has to be one of the most baffling ever to arise within the history of organised Spiritualism and psychical research.

It is a riddle; an enigma which has now raged unabated for almost eighty years and which I doubt will ever truly be solved.

In short, it has, over the years since her death, been transformed into a kind of soap opera. 'Margery the Medium' is destined to play for ever without reaching a reliable conclusion. Indeed, its lasting intrigue is such that in September 1998, the BBC broadcast on Radio 4 a drama production entitled 'The Witch on Beacon Hill'. Typically, it proved to be hugely speculative. Highly dramatised it told of the supposed events surrounding the meeting of Margery and Harry Houdini and of their subsequent interaction. Regrettably, in common with many other accounts of the mediumship, it owed nothing to accuracy and everything to fantasy.

And in recent times, although she herself never knew them, a female descendant of the Crandons has, much to the delight of the critics, entered the fray by adding her own negative perspective.

Meanwhile, researchers continue from time to time to offer their own slant on what has now largely deteriorated into a nonsense. But that aside, there seems no explanation to counter the proposition that the prints were simply the product of fraud, critics long theorising that a three-dimensional artificial die (a thumbstall) may have been used. When pressed into soft wax, in the manner of a rubber stamp, this would have created the print impressions. One wonders, of course, how difficult it would have been to create such a die? If however, we are to accept this explanation then it rather begs the question why (assuming Dr Crandon himself created it) he did not choose to reproduce the prints of someone totally unconnected with his wife's mediumship? By doing so he would have neatly avoided any future possibility that the actual identity of the unsuspecting donor would ever have been discovered. One would imagine that it would not have been too difficult for an inventive devious mind to secure such prints which later could have been copied to create the putative 'Walter die'.

In 1994, at a meeting of our home circle, Walter himself was invited to comment on the affair in the hope that he could throw light on the matter. It was an opportunity for him to answer the critics and finally bring to an end the speculation and the allegations that had existed for so long. If he could do so then perhaps the dark stain attached to his sister's mediumship would finally be removed. That was my hope but at that time I did not appreciate that there simply were no easy answers that would, at a stroke, sweep the mystery away. Although, as always, reluctant to discuss the past, on that one occasion he did not turn away from doing so but spoke to the circle with passion and with evident candour. He began by warning us that 'anything' that he chose to say would inevitably lead only to further controversy. He had no doubt that it would, for example, be doubted that he was who he claimed to be. Also, he would be speaking according to his own recollections and anything that he said would inevitably be minutely examined. Any discrepancy from the historic records would then be picked up by supporters and critics and vigorously argued over and disputed. Therefore, the situation would not be resolved at all but further complicated. The controversy would simply grow and as a result the home circle would inevitably feel the effects. This would grossly interfere with its further development and he reminded us that he had learnt from the Lime Street days and had no intention of repeating his past mistakes. All of this I believe to be incontestably true and for all those reasons I hesitated considerably before taking the decision to reveal the following.

Firstly, he insisted that originally the fingerprints had been genuine but that later there was a die which was created by his brother-in-law as a 'fail safe', to be used at crucial tests, on the occasions that the doctor was present and not controlled. And if it became clear to him that there was insufficient psychic energy to allow paranormal prints to be made. Although no doubt the truth, this admission by Walter was somewhat pointless. The prints, bogus or genuine, were identical and a duplicate to those of a living man. But, having made the statement, he went on to steadfastly maintain that his sister had known nothing about the die.

Of course, it would be a simple matter to conclude that such a lamentable act by the doctor was inexcusable. But then, he was evidently no paragon of virtue and like us all he had his weaknesses. We were told that over a period of years, having unsuccessfully tried to establish the mediumship scientifically he finally felt justified in creating the die – it was to be a kind of insurance policy, the end result would justify the means? However, it would be an action that later he would come to regret, but then, as the old saying goes: 'the road to hell is paved with good intentions'. Under the sustained stress and unrelenting pressure that was so often present at so-called 'test sittings' perhaps we can understand and not condemn.

When, that night, we asked Walter if he had known at the time of this occasional deception and therefore been complicit, he replied that he had done so. If that is true, and he insisted that it was, one may wonder how a spiritual guide could possibly fail to object to such fraudulent actions.

Readers may regard such a prospect as unthinkable but we are dealing here with a complex matter involving human nature and basic human weakness.

Of course it may be asked, why, if the doctor had forged the later prints, Walter had simply chosen not to expose him. Should he have let the proverbial cat out of the bag?

Well – perhaps he should have done so, but then, can any of us say with certainty that if we had been confronted with such a situation, we would have acted differently?

In truth would we have chosen to reveal the sham or would we too have covered it up by choosing to turn a blind eye? This is a moot point.

What we can say, based upon Walter's admission, is that in the end he committed an error of judgement no doubt justified within his own mind based upon feelings of loyalty, compassion, and misplaced kindness. The implications of an exposure may have been too dreadful to contemplate. Whatever the explanation, the fact, according to him, is that for a long time all involved believed that the fingerprints were genuine and mainly they were.

All these years later he is still unable to account for the fact that beyond any reasonable doubt those he knew to be paranormal were eventually found to be identical to those of his sister's dentist. It is as much a mystery to him today as it was then.

However, we can only wonder at Dr Crandon's dishonesty and speculate.

Was it a simple matter of fierce ambition that would not allow for a single failure? We shall never know. And if we were to place the worst possible interpretation upon those prints – if we were to agree with the sceptics and conclude that they were all the product of fraud, then what remains would still be an unanswerable mystery. How then would we account for the phenomena which persisted for several years as outlined earlier in this and in the previous chapter? To ignore it – to make light of it – to sweep it under the carpet – to argue and infer that since fraud was established in one direction it probably accounted for all – would surely be an insult to fairness and to reason!

Omnipotent or Human?

Since the birth of modern Spiritualism, it has generally been assumed by Spiritualists that spiritual guides, workers and helpers from the next world are saintly and therefore incapable of error. The prospect that they could perform an incongruous act would be unthinkable and communication from them is invariably seen to be sacrosanct.

The truth however is somewhat different. It should be recognised that to communicate with the Spirit World is to commune with human beings and not with omnipotent ones.

My own current intimate knowledge of, and contact with Walter Stinson, and my long evaluation of all relevant facts, have led me to the firm conviction that neither his sister nor her many supporters truly fully understood the apparent damning evidence which was, at the time, levelled against the authenticity of the fingerprints. If the question is asked whether we understand rather more than the fundamentals of mediumship, I would, without hesitation, reply that we do not. Only arrogance would suggest otherwise.

Many years of personal involvement in the Movement of Spiritualism, both inside and outside the séance room, have convinced me that the only difference between ourselves and those who have passed through the gates of death is that they are a little further upon the path of life and therefore their perspective in all things is a little broader. As Walter has so often said 'We are still very much a part of the human race.' As such they proffer their opinions and 'the truth' as they see it – expressed according to their knowledge gained from their surroundings – their reality.

They are not all knowing – they have their own limitations.

With few exceptions they are not highly evolved or advanced souls but merely people much like ourselves but who are in the next stage of life. Because of that they can see a 'bigger picture' but that is all. And – the matter of the fingerprints – why Walter's and those of the dentist were proven to be (beyond reasonable doubt) 'one and the same' – I doubt that we shall ever know.

Perhaps the solution after all is really quite simple. In common with ourselves, the Spirit World may have no more idea how to account for the enigma than we ourselves do. With our present limited knowledge of the world in which we live perhaps we cannot, as yet, hope for one. It is a sobering thought!

The Last Word

Throughout this and the previous chapter I have tried to show that the unique Mina (Margery) Crandon deserves better than posterity has ungraciously conferred upon her. Readers may, of course, consider that throughout I have tried to defend the indefensible and/or that I have tried to make out a case for the justification of fraud. Some may believe that my defence was inevitable since the legitimacy of my own mediumship largely rests upon the Walter personality as he manifests today. The eternal sceptic will believe all of these things and regard my arguments as nonsense. If that is so then I would feel a sense of disappointment, although I would hope that at the very least unbiased readers may concede that I have 'tried to think outside the box of limitation' and that I have sought to introduce arguments which deserve serious consideration?

If that is so then I can ask for nothing more.

And so, I am happy to conclude this, the last chapter of my book, by giving the final word to Marian Nester. My justification for doing so rests upon the fact that she was there. For that reason and upon that basis her conclusions about those events of long ago deserve to be heard. This then is her message to all who have pondered, speculated, pontificated, debated, argued and wondered about 'Margery the Medium':

Originally published in *Fate Magazine (USA)*

From 'The Margery Mediumship – I was There.'

Marion Nester

Nowadays as I look back at the Margery mediumship, it is my opinion that the case did in fact produce many valid psychic phenomena, especially psychokinesis. This considered assessment is based not only on my early experiences but on my many years of professional contact at the American Society for Psychical Research and elsewhere, with contemporary thinking and modern research on mediumship and the survival question.

As I read the voluminous on-the-spot records (the minutes of hundreds of Margery's séances from 1923 to 1937) it seems clear that impressive fraud-proof experiments were being carried out by knowledgeable, honest people. For example; the paranormal linkage of the wooden rings was spectacular and was never explained away. Some powerful force was at work.

Quarrels and turmoil certainly bedevilled Margery's mediumship. I think perhaps that they were inevitable given the wide differences in personality, approach and even fundamental belief systems amongst the many strong minded individuals who took part in the investigations. But, I feel strongly that the quarrels must not blot out the achievements. Margery should not be summarily dismissed as often seems to happen nowadays.

There is plenty in the records to show how much the case had to offer and how important Margery is in the history of psychic research.

❖   ❖   ❖

Postscript to Part Two

Some Final Thoughts

My final comments in respect of the contents of the book and my final words to the reader.

As I wrote the last word of the final chapter of this book I reflected on the fact that I had just finished a project that had taken over two years to complete. All that I had written about had gradually taken shape over a much longer period. The events, the adventures, the experiences, frustrations, disappointments and successes all went towards making it possible. Two years in the writing but over forty years in the making. That is the reality.

I thought back to the time when I had first conceived the idea and what my intention had been.

It was, I felt, my final opportunity to convey and to leave on record a faithful account of my journey through Spiritualism and to explain how death has accompanied me through most of my adult life. To readers, who perhaps picked up this book in ignorance of Spiritualism, that statement, had I made it at the beginning of the book, may have appeared incomprehensible, bizarre and depressing. However, as I hope that I have shown, my journey has, in fact, been quite the reverse. I have lived with the 'great reality' and I have witnessed repeatedly how, given the opportunity, the dead can interact with our world. In certain respects this book may be considered unique, since to my knowledge, since the birth of the Spiritualist Movement, only one other physical medium has written in similar vein. He was the celebrated Victorian, Daniel Dunglas Home whose autobiography 'Incidents in my Life' was first published in 1863 and his honest review of Spiritualism, 'Lights and Shadows of Spiritualism' in 1877. Whilst I do not suggest that my mediumship has any similarity to his, or that it is in any way comparable, I do say, that in common with him, I feel very strongly about the subject of which I have written. Spiritualism was very important to him and his mediumship was simply an uninvited aspect of his nature. Spiritualism is also important to me but I differ in respect of mediumship since, in direct contrast to him, I actually invited it in. Where we do converge is in agreement of the fact that he recognised, over a century earlier, the corruption that even then existed within the Movement. I see the same today.

Having said that, I knew, as I wrote the book, whilst some readers would accept it in its entirety, in the spirit in which it was written, others would not. Although possibly accepting the chronicle of my development as a medium, I knew that some would object, disapprove and reject a number of my observations and the opinions that I have expressed about the current state of the Movement. On the other hand, I also knew there would be a great many sceptics who would disapprove of the book in its entirety and find my arguments unconvincing. So, although I have done my best to ensure accuracy, where I have written about historic matters, I anticipate that these will be subjected to both reasonable and unreasonable scrutiny.

If an error or errors were to be discovered, then it is likely that the entire legitimacy of the book would be in doubt. Therefore, to my critics, I would simply say that given the nature of the subject, disagreement is predictable and unavoidable. However, I hope that many readers will accept that everything I have written – every observation included and every opinion expressed – has been infused by 'truth' as I sincerely believe it to be.

In respect of my own mediumship, I have never refused to allow accredited researchers into my séance room as observers. Nevertheless I am aware that there are many interested individuals and organizations who have long questioned why I have always refused to allow it to be scientifically tested.

The notion being that in refusing to cooperate with the researchers and have my mediumship microscopically investigated, I may have something to hide!

Such advocates insist that by committing to such tests, conducted, they would argue, by sympathetic investigators I would perform a great service to the Movement. Indeed, to the whole of mankind. I am further assured that such an investigation would make use of non invasive perfectly safe technology. Therefore, at a stroke my mediumship would be authenticated (or otherwise).

That is the theory. Unfortunately, the reality would be entirely different.

Without wishing to offend anyone, I would suggest that such a view, whilst no doubt perfectly sincere, is based largely upon either a false premise or innocent ignorance.

In Chapter 5 I touched upon the use of infra-red equipment within the séance room and I outlined my reasons for resisting it. I also expressed my thoughts about the scientific examination of physical mediumship. Although it would be pointless to repeat those arguments, I must emphasise once again, that any investigation, in my carefully considered opinion, would ultimately lead nowhere. To clarify that, I once again refer to historic fact, which, if ignored, would be an act of foolishness. This tells us that virtually every known physical medium in history co-operated at some time during their careers with organised psychical research, always with the assurance that investigations would be fair, open minded and sympathetic. Yet almost without exception they ended the same way. Exposure, in some cases justified, and allegations of fraud or suspected fraud.

In cases where the mediumship appeared to be genuine, tests were usually considered inconclusive. But that is only a part of it. Researchers not involved in the investigations were seldom prepared to accept positive findings. Habitually they looked for the loopholes which they suspected had allowed the medium concerned to produce, by normal means, bogus phenomena. This then led to a demand for further tests with mediums being constantly in a 'no-win' situation.

Of course it may be considered that a favourable report, from a researcher with impeccable credentials, would be greeted with both respect and approbation. Unfortunately, history shows us that this was not so. Invariably, such reports were questioned and doubted and in some documented cases incited ridicule. Never was anything conclusively proved. The past 150 years of psychical research are littered with examples involving some of the most celebrated Spiritualist mediums in history.

From Eusapia Palladino to Eva 'C' and from Margery to Helen Duncan they all co-operated with 'sympathetic' researchers and all met with the same fate. For their pains they were forever to be surrounded by suspicion and doubt.

I have often wondered how their mediumship might have developed had they chosen to sit exclusively within circles composed of harmonious Spiritualists. Free from the pressure to perform and away from the cold clinical atmosphere that accompanied such investigations, we can only speculate as to the phenomena that might have developed. Unfortunately, this we shall never know.

Of course it may be argued that modern technology, which was unavailable to the researchers of yesteryear, would prove to be a panacea today. Whilst it may appear to be that way – whilst it may appear to be a 'fix all' – sadly it would not be. It would be a mistake to believe otherwise. At worst it would set in motion – doubt – fierce dispute and controversy and it would not prove the reality of survival and communication.

At best, it would be seen that paranormal action was a reality but it would doubtlessly be explained away as an abnormal physiological function possessed by and unconsciously directed by the medium.

Then, the established orthodox church would, just as it resisted the birth of modern science, become involved. Positive results would threaten the very fabric of its belief structure. It has always opposed Spiritualism, believing that in some way it is demonic. Meanwhile, the mediumship and the circle would suffer in every conceivable way.

My position in respect of my own mediumship is that I have never, nor will I ever seek notoriety nor any form of enhanced status through it or because of it.

All I wish – all that I have ever wished – is to play my part in encouraging and inspiring others to form their own circles to sit for the development of mediumship – mental or physical. Additionally to allow people to witness for themselves the reality of the séance room and to derive from that the reassurance of survival. Always, my vision to achieve both has been single minded. If that has led to missed opportunities to help establish the reality of a life beyond this corporeal veil, then truly I am sorry. Every man must chart his own course through life. Mine was chosen by heeding my inner voice and in deference to the influence of the 'shining ones'.

I have now said all that I wish, or indeed, all that I intend to say about my life as a physical medium. In the end it will be you the reader, and ultimately posterity, that will judge me.

My hope is that this book will be accepted by all who read it as an honest document which has told in unvarnished fashion the story of 'An Extraordinary Journey'.

My Warm Regards
Stewart Alexander

Breinigsville, PA USA
26 January 2011
254158BV00005B/42/P